31 Days to Effective, Fervent Prayer

Eric Copple

Copyright © 2018 by Eric Copple

Table of Contents

Acknowledgments

The original seed for this study was planted by a very dear Christian brother with whom I enjoyed some wonderful fellowship several years ago. When I knew him, Scott F. was a prayer warrior of the first order. It thrilled my spirit to watch him light up and become extremely animated when he discussed God's Word or anything related to practical Christian living. That man loved Jesus, and it showed.

In numerous extended conversations that Scott and I had, we discussed a mutual observation that was of pressing concern to both of us. We noticed that many of our brothers needed to be goaded toward more active, more fervent, and certainly more *biblical* prayer. Scott had penned a very brief study on prayer at one time, and asked if I might be able to elaborate what he had written into a much larger and more detailed examination of the subject. In all candor, what resulted from the ensuing months of labor bore *little* resemblance to the work from which I began. But since I solicited feedback from Scott and a handful of mature Christians during the writing process, Scott and I both felt good about the final product. We then submitted the completed study to our pastor, to obtain his approval before distributing it to other members of his congregation.

The study was generally well received. Perhaps 20 or so men used it to varying extents. In hindsight, however, I realized that I had not sufficiently taken into account the relatively low level of reading comprehension that many prisoners have. The oversight was particularly inexcusable in my case because I worked as a tutor in a voluntary education program for about two years. Some of the Christian men in our little congregation who wanted to become more ardent prayer warriors had difficulty comprehending what I wrote: too many long sentences and ten-dollar words, and too much complicated punctuation. For a few of the brothers, the frustration that this confusion caused compelled them to abandon the study altogether. I was humbled by the discovery of my failure to reach these believers with language they could understand, and held these lessons in my heart.

After working to complete my college degrees, I sensed the Lord prompting me to dedicate more time to writing. I was always committed to using the time that God entrusted to me as productively as possible. But writing, I recognized, could function as a means of serving Him within the limitations imposed upon me. Through the agency of my Christian mother, He led me to the idea of beginning my serious involvement with writing by expanding the study on prayer into book form. I knew as soon as I heard the suggestion that it was of the Lord. It was one of those wonderful occasions that arise sometimes in our lives as believers when the Spirit within us affirms unmistakably, "This is from Me."

Recognizing that I have a tendency to write for—shall I say—a more learned audience, I have tried in this book to simplify the language to some extent. I have made a conscious effort to avoid overly sophisticated vocabulary. At the same time, I intended the book to be made available to (Christian) readers in general, not just the small subset that resides in prison. I figured that most believers who might be inclined to explore this study would probably have the reading comprehension needed to understand it. I hope that I have achieved a reasonable balance.

Brother Scott, as he was known, was too humble to be concerned about receiving recognition for his service to the Lord. But it is unlikely that I would have written this book without the initial seed that he sowed. As an added bonus, if acknowledging him here leads anyone to speak to him about the subject, then that person will be better for it. Scott was (and is) a beloved brother, and I look forward to seeing him again in Christ's Kingdom.

I also need to acknowledge a tremendous debt of gratitude to my selfless mother, Robin, and my stepfather, Louis. When I completed the writing of the book, I typed a manuscript—on the typewriter that she purchased for me—and sent it to them. All of the subsequent work involved in bringing this book into existence was their doing; necessary, given my circumstances, but no less appreciated.

Dedication

This book is dedicated with utmost gratitude to my mom, Robin.
An obedient Christian for more than forty years,
she has been the most consistent Christian influence on me.
Throughout my life, she has demonstrated *agape* love, grace,
and faith persevering through adversity.

Important Notes

1. The footnotes are definitions either quoted directly or adapted from those recorded in *Chambers Etymological English Dictionary* (C) or the *Oxford American Dictionary* (O). Some definitions are an alloy of both sources (CO). They are provided in the hope that they might help to make the book a bit more accessible to a wider range of readers, some of whom may not be familiar with all of these words. My intention is certainly not to insult anyone's intelligence. Instead, my aim is to avoid repeating the mistake that I made with the original prayer study.

2. For the same reason of accessibility noted above, abbreviations have been avoided throughout the book: i.e., e.g., cf., ff., v., vv., p., and pp. These terms were deliberately omitted in the hope of avoiding unnecessary confusion for some readers. Moreover, the names of books of the Bible are always written out in full.

3. This book heavily stresses spiritual warfare and the role of prayer as a weapon on the spiritual battlefield. For anyone interested in reading more about "the whole armor of God" that Paul mentioned in Ephesians 6, I heartily recommend *The Christian in Complete Armour*, by William Gurnall. It is kept in print by The Banner of Truth Trust. Although it is several centuries old, I have never encountered an exposition of that subject that is anywhere near as good. The Lord used Mr. Gurnall to pen a true jewel of Christian literature.

4. All Scripture quotations in this book are taken from the New King James Version of the Holy Bible. Copyright©1982 by Thomas Nelson, Inc. Used by permission. All rights reserved.

**"The effective, fervent prayer
of a righteous man avails much."
James 5:16**

Author's Notes

Time Constraints

This book was originally conceived as a relatively close examination of the biblical teaching on the subject of prayer. The study would be completed over a period of 31 days. And the scope of the investigation would be sufficiently comprehensive to develop "effective, fervent prayer" in a dedicated Christian reader. Both the format and the content were elaborated with those objectives in view.

As the book was nearing publication, however, my editor called my attention to an important consideration. The issue that she identified was one that had occurred to me while writing the book. Receiving her confirmation, I knew that the concern needed to be addressed, which is the purpose of this note.

Each of the articles supplied in the study contains a lot of information. Simply reading them, meditating on the points conveyed, and looking up the scripture references could be a tall order, even for an avid reader. Doing this day after day for 31 days might be expecting too much. And these demands on your time do not include the critical step of **incorporating** the instruction provided into your prayer life. I state confidently that you will only develop "effective, fervent prayer" to the extent that you implement what you read in these pages.

The 31-day structure of this book is not binding. It is offered as an aid to facilitate study, and is not meant as a burdensome yoke. If you believe that you would benefit from additional time with a particular day's material, then please take it. Understanding, internalizing, and enacting what you read are much more important than completing the *31 Days* in 31 days. Several articles are relatively long; day 9, for example, on "The Model Prayer." It would not be unreasonable for some readers to spend two or three days pondering them. Ultimately, you decide how much time you require for each "day."

Group Applications

My editor has participated in numerous small-group studies during more than four decades of walking with the Lord. She suggested that I prepare a version of this book that is specially tailored for use by small groups. As God provides me with ability and opportunity, I am resolved to craft such an edition. (The Holy Spirit reminds me of Proverbs 16:9 in this regard: "A man's heart plans his way, But the LORD directs his steps." See also James 4:13-15.)

A small-group edition would likely include questions at the end of each day's article. These would be designed to stimulate deeper meditation and to prompt group discussion. The expanded version would also incorporate multiple detailed indexes at the back to enable group members to refer to specific parts of the book with ease. And since many small groups meet once per week, the 31 *days* of this book would translate easily to 31 *weeks*—or something along those lines.

My ardent hope and prayer is that this book will benefit you in your individual studies. If it does, then please pray effectively and fervently for me as I undertake the labor of preparing a small-group edition. Composing anything of substance in prison is quite challenging. And writing that faithfully communicates the transforming truth of God's Word is only possible as the Lord enables. In this, as in all things,

> "To God our Savior,
> Who alone is wise,
> Be glory and majesty,
> Dominion and power,
> Both now and forever.
> Amen" (Jude 25).
> E.M.C.

To contact the author, please use this email address:
effectiveferventprayer@outlook.com

Prologue

"'Do not fear, for those who are with us are more than those who are with them.' And Elisha prayed, and said, 'Lord, I pray, open his eyes that he may see.' Then the Lord opened the eyes of the young man, and he saw. And behold, the mountain was full of horses and chariots of fire all around Elisha" (2 Kings 6:16-17).

God blessed Elisha with the capacity to see with his physical eyes the heavenly hosts that blanketed the mountainside. To strengthen his companion (probably Gehazi), the prophet asked God to provide the younger man with the spiritual sight that would enable him to perceive the angelic army for himself.

Elisha understood and embraced what his life entailed as a prophet of the Lord. He also recognized the tremendous, cosmic conflict that has continued uninterrupted since the moment of Lucifer's fall from grace.

The War in the Spiritual Realm

On both sides of the invisible, spiritual battlefield are massive armies of incredibly powerful warriors. We know them by the grossly inadequate categories of "angels" and "demons." The term "angels" does not begin to capture how awesome and mighty these beings are, nor how terrifying they can be. Similarly, "demons" are, in reality, vastly more horrible than anything the imaginations of filmmakers could produce. Although most people do not think of the matter this way, God demonstrates His mercy toward us by concealing these beings and their warfare from the world. If everyone could observe at all times what happens in the spiritual realm, human society and the interactions on which it depends would be impossible. All but the most stout-hearted (and probably them, too) would be too paralyzed with terror to do anything. Most of us would beg desperately to be unmade rather than continue such a frightening existence.

Elisha was appointed to a mode of service that very few people share. Throughout human history, only a small number of God's servants have been called to be prophets. At times, according to His wisdom, God has gifted some of His people with the capacity to peer through the veil that separates the material world from the spiritual. Presumably, such ability was supplied to Elisha because it would benefit him somehow in his particular avenue of service to the Lord. In the context of the passage in 2 Kings, it certainly seems reasonable to suppose that the vision of a huge, angelic army carpeting the mountainside would be profoundly reassuring to the prophet.

Most of us will never behold more than fleeting glimpses of what resides beyond the veil; at least, not while we inhabit our mortal bodies. Some things remain concealed from us on this side of eternity.

> "Eye has not seen, nor ear heard,
> Nor have entered into the heart of man
> The things which God has prepared for those
>   who love Him" (1 Corinthians 2:9).

Only as it suits His purposes does God permit the majority of us a peek at those realities that are normally hidden. And yet, though we may not observe these things with our physical eyes, the Lord has not left us wholly ignorant of what is happening.

The Only Two Sides

Knowing that a continuous, spiritual war is underway all around us, all the time, what, if anything, are we supposed to do about it? Why not just carry on with our lives, trying to "do good," and let the angels and demons have at each other? There are two problems with this position. The first is that, whether we realize it or not, neutrality has never been an option. There are only two sides in the great controversy between heaven and hell, between good and evil, with no middle or neutral ground. Every person is enlisted on one side or the other. "Do you not know that friendship with the world is enmity with God? Whoever therefore wants to be a friend of the world makes himself an enemy of God" (James 4:4).

Some believers might be very uncomfortable with the notion that they are involved in unending spiritual war. Perhaps even more unsettling is the realization that, before we were saved, we *all* fought for the other side. The Bible establishes this point very clearly. Jesus Himself proclaimed, "He who is not with Me is against Me, and he who does not gather with Me scatters abroad" (Matthew 12:30). Every person who is enlisted—because of the inherited sin-nature—in the ranks of hell's infantry *must* become a genuine Christian in order to switch sides. To put it another way, the route from Satan's side of the battlefield to God's goes through Christ. "But without faith it is impossible to please Him, for he who comes to God must believe that He is, and that He is a rewarder of those who diligently seek Him" (Hebrews 11:6). "Impossible" does not mean "very difficult" or "highly improbable." It means that there is absolutely no way for a person to please God without faith.

Once that person does surrender to the Lord and trust Christ for salvation, however, several additional transformations occur. Formerly an enemy of God, the believer is adopted into God's own family, becoming a son or a daughter of the Almighty (1 John 3:1-2). That child of God is also "sealed with the Holy Spirit of promise, who is the guarantee of our inheritance until the redemption of the purchased possession, to the praise of His glory" (Ephesians 1:13-14). The "filthy rags" that function as a uniform for Satan's foot soldiers are removed and destroyed, replaced with the brilliant white robes of Christ's righteousness in which all of His troops are clothed (Isaiah 64:6; Revelation 7:9). As a consequence of these profound realities, the Christian changes allegiance and is then deployed to the spiritual battlefield to join in combat against the hosts of wickedness. There the "Commander of the Lord's army," Jesus, directs the assault on heaven's adversaries (Joshua 5:15). He determines in His infinite wisdom both the strategy and the tactics that will be used. But before discussing how to do battle, one earlier point needs to be addressed.

The Immortals—Angels and Demons

The second reason that we are not able to leave the fighting to the angels and demons is that they are not mortal beings. They can assume material forms and can possess or indwell humans and animals (with some limitations). But they have no physical bodies of their own that could be harmed or killed in order to achieve victory in combat. The spiritual hosts warring against each other are not fighting for possession of territory or for any geopolitical reasons—the motives for most human wars. Instead, they are contending for influence in and control over the affairs of human beings, both as individuals and in their societies. At the risk of oversimplifying the object of this intense warfare, demons fight to drag as many people as possible into the torments of hell. Angels, on the other hand, labor at all times with two goals in mind: to bring glory and honor to Almighty God the Creator, who is worthy to be praised; and to direct as many souls as they can to the Lord Jesus Christ, the only Savior. By extension from these two aims, angels provide a tremendous amount of aid to humans, believers and unbelievers alike.

The Human Place in Everything

In addition to *participating* on both sides of the spiritual conflict, humans constitute the center of engagement. They alone of all God's creations were made "in His own image" (Genesis 1:27). That being the case, they occupy a special place and have a distinctive role to fulfill in God's plan for His Creation. One of their responsibilities, the Bible attests, is to fight in collaboration with the angelic hosts in opposition to the demonic. Or, to put it another way, a duty to contribute to this spiritual warfare—to "do our bit," as the British say— inheres in the very fact that we are human.

Before we became Christians, that obligation was easily satisfied. As a result of our common sin-nature, aiding the forces of evil came *naturally* to us, a point that Paul the Apostle discussed in Romans 7: "For I delight in the law of God according to the inward man. But I see another law in my members, warring against the law of my mind, and bringing me into captivity to the law of sin which is in my members" (verses 22-23). Addressing the same tendency toward

13

sin, the Apostle Peter challenged, "Beloved, I beg you as sojourners and pilgrims, abstain from fleshly lusts which war against the soul" (1 Peter 2:11). These men understood from abundant personal experience that the Christian life is not a game or a dance or a feast; it is war. Christians are at war.

The Certainty of Victory

Recognizing that our earthly lives involve perpetual warfare does not mean that we have to plod through them with our shoulders slumped, looking forlorn and defeated. We need not despair, thinking that there is just too much evil in the world for our small contributions to make any meaningful difference.

In truth, if victory in this controversy depended upon human capabilities, then all hope would be lost. Thankfully, the same truth applies to all Christians today that Elisha shared with his servant: "...those who are with us are more than those who are with them" (2 Kings 6:16). When the prophet spoke of "more," he intended something far beyond strictly numerical superiority. He meant that the angels surrounding both of them were greater than their enemies in both number *and* power.

When we venture into the fray of spiritual combat, we may also rest assured that our allies in the conflict are "more than those who are with" our adversaries. Or, for greater encouragement and resolve, we can apply to ourselves the words that the Spirit of the Lord delivered through Jahaziel: "Do not be afraid nor dismayed because of this great multitude, for the battle is not yours, but God's" (2 Chronicles 20:15). Furthermore, we can repeat Paul's challenge: "What then shall we say to these things? If God is for us, who can be against us? ...Yet in all these things we are more than conquerors through Him who loved us" (Romans 8:31, 37). Fighting in a terrible, cosmic controversy that includes all of humanity, legions of angels, and hordes of demons, with Almighty God on our side, victory is certain.

The Spiritual Means of Spiritual Warfare

Let us acknowledge that there is a spiritual war boiling all around us, mostly unseen but altogether real. Let us further recognize that all human beings participate in this combat on one of only two sides. They may not be *aware* of their involvement, or they might wish to have none, but they are present on the battlefield nevertheless. Lastly, let us accept and even embrace the fact that we, as Christians, are instructed by our commander to engage actively in the struggle against the forces of evil. In the light of these sobering truths, how, we are right to ask, do we contend with something that we cannot see? How can we expect to prevail "against principalities, against powers, against the rulers of the darkness of this age, against spiritual hosts of wickedness in the heavenly places" (Ephesians 6:12)?

Paul answered these questions definitively in a passage from 2 Corinthians that is well known to many students of the Bible:

> "For though we walk in the flesh, we do not war according to the flesh. For the weapons of our warfare are not carnal but mighty in God for pulling down strongholds, casting down arguments and every high thing that exalts itself against the knowledge of God, bringing every thought into captivity to the obedience of Christ..." (10:3-5).

Because our adversaries are spiritual beings, our defenses and our weapons must be spiritual as well.

Defensively, we will be well-protected when we don "the whole armor of God" (Ephesians 6:11,13). With the various pieces of this armor in place, we will "be able to stand against the wiles of the devil" (verse 11). Withstanding an enemy onslaught is a necessary part of any effective battle strategy, and stout defenses are commonly just as important to victory as a capable offensive component. Our enemy will not stand by idly while we pull down his strongholds and decimate the vanguard[1] of his forces. On the contrary, his counterattack will be both swift and fierce. For that reason, our defensive structures must be in place *before* we venture into combat. "Therefore take up the whole armor of God, that you may be able to withstand in the evil day, and having done all, to stand" (verse 13). But weathering enemy assaults will not in itself achieve victory. We must also attack. And yet, to assail a spiritual foe, we need spiritual weapons.

Paul was a seasoned veteran of intensive, spiritual warfare, so it is not surprising that he understood extremely well what is required to achieve victory on the battlefield. In his description of "the whole armor of God" in Ephesians 6, he listed the necessary elements in order. First he detailed five pieces of armor (four on the body plus a shield), all defensive instruments designed to protect the soldier from serious injury. He then included the first *offensive* weapon, "the sword of the Spirit, which is the word of God" (verse 17). This sword is an exceptionally effective implement when skillfully wielded, "piercing even to the division of soul and spirit, and of joints and marrow, and is a discerner of the thoughts and intents of the heart" (Hebrews 4:12). (To read an example of this sword employed by the Master Swordsman, review the account of Satan tempting Jesus in Matthew 4:1-11).

At the end of his discussion of "the whole armor of God," Paul mentioned what is arguably the Christian's most powerful device for destroying enemy fortifications and inflicting injury on opposition forces: **prayer**. Arrayed in God's armor, gripping "the shield of faith" with one hand and brandishing "the sword of the Spirit" with the other, we should be "praying always with all

---

[1] vanguard (O): the foremost part of an army or fleet advancing or ready to do

prayer and supplication in the Spirit, being watchful to this end with all perseverance and supplication for all the saints" (Ephesians 6:16,17,18).

Prayer is the most potent weapon in the believer's arsenal. And unlike physical instruments of war, prayer cannot be exhausted, nor can the enemy defend against it.

The Spiritual Battlefield

To gain a better appreciation of the importance of prayer as a weapon in spiritual warfare, imagine a battlefield from before the age of gunpowder. Two massive armies appraise each other from across an intervening expanse of deserted territory, pockmarked with craters and the crumbled ruins of war. Commanders on both sides have arranged their forces into groups and formations of varying sizes and configurations, according to the strategy and the tactics that have been determined for the engagement. On one side stands a Man, obviously the Commander, arrayed in brilliant white robes with a shimmering golden sash draped across His chest. He emits a penetrating light of a silvery-white tone, stark but beautiful, apparently generated within Himself. Somehow this glow illuminates the whole of His side of the battlefield, unhindered by any obstacle or distance, and reflects from the white linens, breastplates, helmets, and swords of His soldiers.

On the Man's face is fixed an expression of perfect serenity, of total confidence, though His eyes blaze like fire as He scans the scene before Him. Surrounding Him, and blanketing the ground to the edge of sight, are innumerable flaming horses and chariots of fire. It is unclear if these horses and chariots are actually *made* of fire or are simply burning without being consumed. Piloting these vehicles are luminous beings, in appearance similar to men but much larger, and seemingly formed from light. Other fighters of similar kind stand ready in numerous places, some at the controls of assorted instruments of war.

At the opposite side of the field, the enemy's forces are shrouded in shadow. A venomous green mist rises slowly from the deep shade where the foot soldiers must be assembled, unseen but felt. Across the empty expanse, a faint whisper of a breeze carries the pungent stench of rotting flesh and the sickening odor of decay. Little can be seen of the forms of the enemy troops, but their malevolence[2] and a sense of seething evil are palpable[3]. The air almost tingles from the intensity of their hatred for the army of light confronting them.

Wherever battle is joined, enemy darts sing through the air and deflect from countless shields of faith—some crafted of a hard wood similar to oak, others of steel, and some of a strange material, strong as adamant (a type of diamond

[2] malevolence (O): an attitude of wishing harm to others; ill will
[3] palpable (C): readily perceived by any of the senses

or other gem material). Savage blows from ugly, crudely-formed weapons are turned easily by helmets of salvation or ping harmlessly on breastplates of righteousness. Furtive[4] daggers emerge unnoticed from the obscurity of moving shadows, black as jet, but their blades are bent and blunted by the impenetrable belts of truth worn by all soldiers of light. These fleet-footed fighters dash about the field, expertly shod with the preparation of the gospel of peace. Meanwhile, gleaming swords beyond numbering cleave the air with a flash, inflicting grievous damage on the evil adversaries, often severing their gnarled limbs at the joints.

Here and there an extraordinary spectacle can be witnessed among the ranks of the soldiers of righteousness. Sometimes individually, sometimes in groups, they drop to their knees in the midst of battle, raise their hands toward the heavens, and mouth words that seem to infuse their opponents with a blend of terror and renewed malice. Immediately afterward, the sky fills from the direction of the rearguard with a barrage of streaking projectiles like comets, more numerous than locusts in a plague. These incendiary missiles rain devastation on the enemy, landing all around the kneeling figures but never touching them.

As soon as the last of these has found its mark, a deep rumble like thunder rolls over the field and the earth vibrates, followed closely by great companies of flaming horses and blazing chariots sweeping forward and surrounding the soldiers on their knees. Some of these fighters are simply helped to their feet and given a drink of what looks to be pure water, but which evidently charges the soldiers with redoubled life and intensity. These warriors return to the fight, often accompanied by the luminous beings piloting the chariots. Some of the other kneeling figures are brought up into the cockpits of the chariots and whisked speedily to the rear of the army's lines, either for a respite from battle or to confer with their Commander about a change of orders.

The Correlation to Modern Warfare

This imaginative dramatization is not intended to be a precise description of what actually occurs in spiritual warfare, though numerous symbols are used which will be immediately recognizable for many students of the Bible. Rather, the brief narrative is meant to illustrate the **power** of prayer as the premier weapon in the Christian's arsenal. When a believer is actively engaged in combat with spiritual adversaries, prayer is like signaling to the Artillery Corps to discharge a massive salvo[5] of projectiles on enemy positions—to "fire for effect." Or, to place the simile in more modern circumstances, prayer is like a platoon that is pinned down by a machine-gun battery calling in air-strikes. Once the "fast-movers" have softened the enemy emplacements with rockets

---

[4] furtive (O): sly, stealthy
[5] salvo (O): firing of a number of guns simultaneously

and bombs, the platoon can move in and secure the area until reinforcements arrive. Whatever combat imagery is used to communicate what happens when Christian soldiers pray, it should be clearly understood that prayer is an extremely powerful and effective instrument of spiritual war.

The Servant of the Lord

The life of Joshua provides an excellent example of prayer in action on a battlefield; in this case, a *real* battlefield. Joshua was skilled in every aspect of combat as it was known to his people in that era. He was a consummate warrior, yet he was called "the servant of the LORD" (Joshua 24:29). He even met personally with the "Commander of the army of the LORD":

> "And it came to pass, when Joshua was by Jericho, that he lifted his eyes and looked, and behold, a Man stood opposite him with His sword drawn in His hand. And Joshua went to Him and said to Him, 'Are You for us or for our adversaries?'
>
> So He said, 'No, but as Commander of the army of the LORD I have now come.'
>
> And Joshua fell on his face to the earth and worshiped, and said to Him, 'What does my Lord say to His servant?'
>
> Then the Commander of the LORD's army said to Joshua, 'Take your sandal off your foot, for the place where you stand is holy.' And Joshua did so" (5:13-15).

As a skilled and experienced soldier, Joshua fought tenaciously and often victoriously. And yet, despite his military successes and the position of high authority that he occupied, he was a humble man and a devoted servant of God. He spent considerable time in prayer, understanding that the true battles were not his but the Lord's (recall Jahaziel). Submitting to the sovereignty of God, Joshua engaged in some of his fiercest combat through prayer.

Consider one occasion, when five kings of the Amorites formed an alliance to make war against Israel (Joshua 10). After the Lord delivered their adversaries into Israel's hands, Joshua and his men pursued them, seeking revenge:

> "Then Joshua spoke to the LORD in the day when the LORD delivered up the Amorites before the children of Israel, and he said in the sight of Israel:
>   'Sun, stand still over Gibeon;
>   And Moon, in the Valley of Aijalon.'
>   So the sun stood still,
>   And the moon stopped,

Till the people had revenge upon their enemies" (verses 12-13).

Presumably, the miracle that God produced in this instance, in response to His servant's petition, involved the whole planet! And the physics of this scene are mindblowing! The Earth's rotation on its axis and its revolution around the sun both stopped "for about a whole day" (verse 13). Despite this radical disruption in the planet's normal motion, none of the complex and interrelated systems that are impacted by these movements were destabilized. Tides; air masses and weather systems; gas distribution; moderation of global temperature; the carbon cycle; magnetic fields; the functions of innumerable plant and animal species: all were suspended without harm so that God's people could continue the assault on their enemies. Such are the lengths to which the Lord will go to aid His people when they are in need. And such is the power of prayer when rightly used in accordance with God's will.

The Way to Wage War Wisely

Among its many jewels and nuggets and pearls of wisdom, the Book of Proverbs contains the following gem:

> "Plans are established by counsel;
> By wise counsel wage war" (20:18).

Any military commander would agree that it is both foolish and rash to conduct a war without any of the following elements:

1. We must understand our foe—to the extent possible—as well as our own limitations.
2. We must develop a carefully deliberated strategy or plan based on that information.
3. We must deploy to greatest effect all weapons and defensive measures that are both available *and* appropriate.

"Wise counsel" includes a sober appraisal of our adversary's advantages, capabilities, and weaknesses, as well as our own. It also involves seeking a variety of informed opinions concerning how best to confront the enemy, in terms of both strategy and tactics. And finally, it entails weighing and enacting decisions regarding efficient use of all offensive weaponry and defensive implements that both can *and* should be used to achieve victory.

Prayer is arguably the most devastating instrument in the Christian's arsenal for engaging in spiritual warfare. Through prayer we enter into the presence of the God of the universe, the One True God, our loving Father whose power and wisdom extend infinitely beyond our imaginations (Hebrews 4:16). By prayer we can elicit help from innumerable companies of angels, who delight to aid God's children in His service (Psalm 103:20-21; Matthew 26:53). Through prayer, Satan's strongholds can be torn down like the walls of Jericho, his grip on people's minds loosed and his influence in their lives restrained, and his minions barred from working their evil in human affairs.

Prayer is exquisitely powerful. But it must be understood that the potency of prayer in no way derives from the person praying. Nor does it stem from anything intrinsic in the act itself. In other words, prayer is not powerful because of *who* is praying, nor because of *how* that person prays. The sole power of prayer resides in the One *to whom* people pray. And since for Christians that One is the Lord Almighty, whose power is infinite, two additional truths follow:

1. The omnipotence of God—the fact that He is all-powerful—means that there are no inherent limitations to prayer's power. Prayer is simply an avenue or a means of communication between Christians and God. Through it they have the ability and the privilege of asking Him to exercise *His* power in a specific way.

2. The Lord decides whom He will and will not hear, whose requests He will and will not provide, and exactly how He will fulfill those petitions that He determines to grant. Because He is absolutely sovereign, the liberty of action is always His.

Some people will recognize how powerful prayer is and try to call out to God, but that does not mean they will be heard:

"One who turns away his ear from hearing the law,
Even his prayer is an abomination" (Proverbs 28:9; compare Psalm 66:18).

The Lord knows those who are genuinely His. He sees the heart of every person and is never misled by outward appearances that might deceive other people (1 Samuel 16:7; Jeremiah 17:10; Hebrews 4:13). *Only* those who are legitimately saved can expect to have their prayers answered. Only they can hope to experience the awesome power of prayer, as the Lord Eternal works mightily in and through their lives.

The Three Roads of an Enlisted Christian

A furious spiritual war rages incessantly all around you. If you **profess** to have surrendered your life to Jesus Christ and received Him into your heart as your Lord and Savior; if you believe you have been regenerated and sealed with the Holy Spirit, then in reality you have **only three options**...

1. You can choose to remain a spectator to the ongoing battle (which is not to suggest that you will be unaffected by it). If you select this course,

you will be *like* the "wicked and lazy servant" who hid his master's talent in the ground and did nothing with it. Ultimately, that disappointing coward was "cast into outer darkness" ("The Parable of the Talents," Matthew 25:14-30). For a professing Christian, being 'cast…into outer darkness' is definitive proof that the person was not truly saved.

2.   You may half-heartedly feign to fight with no commitment or zeal. In following this path, you will become neither cold nor hot. And just like the lukewarm church of Revelation 3, you might find yourself vomited out of the Lord's mouth. (In this context, refer to Romans 12:9-21, particularly verse 11.)

3.   You can fight alongside the angels of the army of the Lord and your brothers and sisters in God's family. You can put on "the whole armor of God," pick up "the shield of faith" and grip "the sword of the Spirit." And you can march forward with the hosts of the army of light to visit devastation on the evil hordes that lust for your misery.

From one Christian soldier to another, heed the counsel that Joshua proclaimed to the nation of Israel: "Now therefore, fear the LORD, serve Him in sincerity and in truth…. And… choose for yourselves this day whom you will serve…. But as for me and my house, we will serve the LORD" (Joshua 24:14, 15).

The Intent of the Book

If you resolve with Joshua to follow the third course, to serve God by participating actively in battle against our spiritual foes, then a vibrant and flourishing prayer life is absolutely essential. Granted, the percentage of believers who march this rugged road always has been relatively low. But the triumphs and trials of these dedicated soldiers are shared by "so great a cloud of witnesses" that the effects of their disciplined and selfless labors can be quite far-reaching (Hebrews 12:1—consider reading all of Hebrews 12 for the light that it sheds on this subject).

This prolonged study of Christian prayer was composed with a very specific intent held constantly in mind. We hope to assist and encourage any Christian who uses this resource to pray more fervently, more diligently, more biblically. The whole work was written with abundant and earnest prayer and an extremely close examination of Scripture. We probed the profound riches of God's Word, searching always for the gems of truth that the Lord, "the author and finisher of our faith," provided to be communicated to our brothers and sisters in Christ (Hebrews 12:2).

We feel compelled to emphasize that we were (and are) utterly devoted to glorifying the majestic name of our Lord. To the extent that this book honors Him by aiding His people, we count it a singular success. And extending from our total commitment to putting Him first, we strove at every stage to place our Father's will ahead of everything else, following the example of our Savior. Ultimately, when the final product was completed and submitted for possible use by other Christians, we hoped to ensure that the glory of God and His only would be magnified and exalted. *Soli Deo Gloria*!

The Structure of the Study

Our conception of the content of this book is that it would be most profitably digested when consumed in 31 portions, one each day for 31 days. Hence the division into 31 "articles" of varying length and detail. That said, there is no hard and fast rule for how it should be used. How you choose to employ the study to amplify your prayer life is between you and the Lord (as mentioned in Author's Notes, page 9). Our only request—in fact, our plea—is that you would undertake the study **prayerfully**. Ask God to illuminate your mind, to prepare your heart, and to quicken His words of truth to penetrate deeply, transforming your inward self by the power of His Holy Spirit.

Needless to say, we believe that the book will be of greatest benefit to you if you invest the time needed to look up scripture references and to read further about the meanings of defined words. (Otherwise, why would we include these elements?) However, some pains were taken to craft each article so that it can be read on its own. As strongly as we desire to encourage our brothers and sisters to explore God's Word more often and with sharper focus, we also want this extended examination of prayer to be accessible.

The Concluding Exhortation

As is true of so many things in life, with this study, "You will get out of it what you put into it." If you breeze through this book in one sitting, your time will not be wholly devoid of profit. The Lord's Word does not return to Him void, but always accomplishes that for which it was sent (Isaiah 55:11). But if you commit yourself to spending approximately one month of your life in concerted cultivation of a more ardent prayer life, the Holy Spirit *will* come alongside and assist you, and our Father will bring fruit from your dedication. Some of the words of Christ in John's Gospel capture this truth perfectly:

> "I am the vine, you are the branches. He who abides in Me, and I in him, bears much fruit, for without Me you can do nothing. If anyone does not abide in Me, he is cast out as a branch and is withered; and they gather them and throw them into the fire, and they are burned. If you abide in Me, and My words abide in you, you will ask what you desire, and it shall be done for you. By this My Father is glorified, that you bear much fruit; so you will be My disciples" (15:5-8).

Abide in Jesus and draw closer to Him through His Word and through prayer. And when you ask the Father to mold and refine you into a strident prayer-warrior, He will.

We encourage you, dear Christian soldier, to "pursue righteousness, godliness, faith, love, patience, gentleness. Fight the good fight of faith, lay hold on eternal life, to which you were also called and have confessed the good confession in the presence of many witnesses" (1 Timothy 6:11-12). Jesus did not mislead us. He never promised that this fight would be anything less than strenuous: "In the world you will have tribulation; but be of good cheer, I have overcome the world" (John 16:33). As one who was extremely familiar with the trials involved in spiritual warfare, Paul recorded a truth along the same lines:

> "Therefore we do not lose heart. Even though our outward man is perishing, yet the inward man is being renewed day by day. For our light affliction, which is but for a moment, is working for us a far more exceeding and eternal weight of glory, while we do not look at the things which are seen, but at the things which are not seen. For the things which are seen are temporary, but the things which are not seen are eternal" (2 Corinthians 4:16-18).

Most of the time, we behold the unseen realities of the spiritual realm through the knowledge of them that is provided by God's Word. As we remain sensitive and attentive to the leading of the Holy Spirit, He brings additional awareness of some of those invisible and eternal truths. Knowing that the things we see are only temporary, we *need* to avoid becoming preoccupied with the cares of this world. "You therefore must endure hardship as a good soldier of Jesus Christ. No one engaged in warfare entangles himself with the affairs of this life, that he may please him who enlisted him as a soldier" (2 Timothy 2:3-4).

If, like Joshua, you desire to please your Commander, Jesus, then you must be careful to refrain from becoming ensnared by the trivial aspects of this life. Jesus expressed this wisdom, among other places, in "The Parable of the Soils." "The seed is the word of God," He explained, then described one of the types of soil on which it is cast: "Now the ones that fell among thorns are those who, when they have heard, go out and are choked with cares, riches, and pleasures of life, and bring no fruit to maturity" (Luke 8:11,14). The snares of life rob believers of fruitfulness. They also inhibit Christian soldiers from engaging in effective combat against the enemy.

A vibrant prayer life—one that translates to success on the spiritual battlefield—requires time, focus, and diligence. But all of these necessary factors will be compromised if you permit yourself to become overburdened with concerns that have no *eternal* significance. In the context of this discussion, the late Pastor Ray Stedman presented an observation that is both pertinent and poignant[6]. He noted that this life can be compared to a dot, no larger than the period at the end of this sentence. Eternity, by contrast, would be a continuous line without beginning or end. We must choose whether we will live for the dot or the line; for the temporary world that we can see or the everlasting life that our Father promises us. When the dichotomy[7] is phrased this way, the choice seems rather straightforward. But how often do we, by our actions and daily decisions, choose the dot?

We conclude with an exhortation that any devoted Christian can heartily speak to any other saint; one that captures our earnest desire for any believer who might engage in this study on prayer:

> "Now may the God of peace who brought up our Lord Jesus from the dead, that great Shepherd of the sheep, through the blood of the everlasting covenant, make you complete in every good work to do His will, working in you what is well pleasing in His sight, through Jesus Christ, to whom be glory forever and ever. Amen" (Hebrews 13:20-21).

We sincerely hope and pray that this book will benefit you considerably as you cultivate the practice of continuous, biblical Christian prayer.

---

[6] poignant (C): affecting one's feelings sharply or keenly
[7] dichotomy (O): division into two parts or kinds

The Logistics of Biblical Prayer: How, Where, and When to Pray

Day 1 — Prayer Positions and Postures

Most Christians find that, with time, they develop a preference for praying with their bodies in a particular position and arranged in a consistent posture. Some choose to pray while kneeling, with their heads bowed and their eyes closed, in a sort of conventional configuration. Others find that arrangement to be too rough on the knees. They elect instead to sit or even to stand, still with the head facing downward in an attitude of deference and with the eyes closed to minimize distractions. Some saints squat down and sit on their feet, touching their foreheads to the ground in front of them between their hands, with their palms pressed flat. Still others opt for total prostration, lying flat on their stomachs with their arms and legs outstretched. The variations of position and posture are virtually unlimited.

Perhaps it would help at this point to differentiate between positions and postures, since some people might suppose them to be essentially equivalent. Position concerns the orientation of a person's body with respect to surroundings: standing, sitting, kneeling; lying down—face down, face up, on the side. By comparison, posture pertains to the arrangement of individual body parts relative to the rest of the body: head bowed; eyes closed or open; hands together or raised heavenward. In truth, the distinction between position and posture is not huge, nor is it terribly significant, but there is one.

With these considerations in mind, what does the Bible have to say about the matter? Whatever we may do already, if God's Word prescribes a particular way that we are expected to situate ourselves while praying, then, as His children, we certainly want to conform to our Father's will. In other words, is there a *right* way, and by extension are there *wrong* ways, to configure our bodies while praying? For answers to these questions, let us explore some of the scriptural instances in which believers are described with regard to how they prayed.

Samuel the Prophet was referring to David when he told King Saul, "The LORD has sought for Himself a man after His own heart, and the LORD has commanded him to be commander over His people, because you have not kept what the LORD commanded you" (1 Samuel 13:14). David was considered a man after God's own heart. When he later "pleaded with God" for the life of the child that resulted from his adultery with Bathsheba, he "fasted and went in and lay all night on the ground" (2 Samuel 12:16). Elsewhere, the character of

David is confirmed in an excerpt from the Book of 1 Kings, which also describes his son and successor on the throne, Solomon. Speaking to Solomon, the Lord said, "I have given you a wise and understanding heart, so that there has not been anyone like you before you, nor shall any like you arise after you.... So if you walk in My ways, to keep My statutes and My commandments, as your father David walked, then I will lengthen your days" (3:12,14). At the dedication of the completed temple, Solomon proclaimed aloud an extended prayer, "kneeling on his knees with his hands spread up to heaven" (1 Kings 8:54).

Another king of Judah and servant of God, Hezekiah, is described in some detail in 2 Kings:

> "And he did what was right in the sight of the LORD, according to all that his father David had done.... He trusted in the LORD God of Israel, so that after him was none like him among all the kings of Judah, nor who were before him. For he held fast to the LORD; he did not depart from following Him, but kept His commandments, which the LORD had commanded Moses. The LORD was with him; he prospered wherever he went" (18:3, 5-7).

Although Hezekiah does not have quite the name recognition of David or Solomon, he was clearly just as much a man after God's own heart as they were. While lying on his deathbed, he "turned his face toward the wall, and prayed to the LORD" (2 Kings 20:2). The passage does not indicate that he asked God to extend his life, but the Lord responded immediately, granting the king another fifteen years (verse 6).

Returning to David, a long passage in 1 Chronicles records what the humble shepherd-psalmist prayed when "King David went in and sat before the LORD" (17:16). The self-effacing[8] prayer that he offered while sitting in God's presence poignantly revealed the man's heart, which was devoted to the Lord. A bit farther on in the same book, David addressed the whole "assembly" of his subjects: "'Now bless the LORD your God.' So all the assembly blessed the LORD God of their fathers, and bowed their heads and prostrated themselves before the LORD and the king" (29:20).

Daniel, the humble prophet, was faithful and obedient to the Lord in an historical setting in which such fidelity could easily result in execution. He was called the "servant of the living God" by King Darius, who subsequently became convinced that Daniel's God was the true God (Daniel 6:20). The prophet's prayer practice is recorded in the book bearing his name. "And in his upper room, with his windows open toward Jerusalem, he knelt down on his knees three times that day, and prayed and gave thanks before his God, as was

---

[8] self-effacing (O): tending to avoid the notice of others; humble

his custom since early days" (6:10). Daniel was a man of prayer first. His close relationship with the Lord facilitated all of the other ways in which he served God: prophet, kings' counselor, interpreter of dreams (recall John 15:5-8).

David, Solomon, Hezekiah, Daniel: these are just a few examples, all drawn from the Old Testament, of believing men who were committed to the Lord, and who prayed often and earnestly. Many more could be cited from both testaments of the Bible. For our purposes, though, these should suffice. Standing, sitting, kneeling, lying down, prostrate, hands clasped or outstretched, head bowed or gazing skyward, speaking audibly or silently mouthing words like Hannah: it seems that the positions and postures we adopt while praying are not prescribed to us in God's Word (1 Samuel 1:12-13). But if these aspects of prayer are left to our discretion, does that mean, in effect, that anything goes?

The simplest answer to that question is...not exactly. What do all of the examples described have in common? The common denominator among them should be able to provide us with some helpful guidance to improve our own prayer habits. The quality that applied to all of these godly people was the condition or attitude of their hearts. Or, to put it another way, what they did outwardly with their bodies reflected the inward realities of their hearts.

David spent the night laying on the ground because of the overwhelming remorse that he felt for his sin. One senses that if it were possible for him to force himself even lower, he would have seized the opportunity. Solomon knelt with his hands spread to the Lord as a manifestation of the genuine awe that he experienced when presented with the majesty of God. Hezekiah's body was failing, so he had to remain lying down, but his life clearly demonstrated his complete devotion to honoring God. And Daniel exhibited profound humility and dependence upon the Lord, as well as a keen longing for the homeland that God had given to his people. Through the positions and postures that they assumed while praying, we can perceive some part of what was in their hearts.

The same principle applies to *our* prayer practices. We should embody outwardly what is true of our inward selves. God does not listen more closely if we are kneeling instead of sitting. He is not more inclined to grant our requests if we present them while prostrated than He would be if we were standing. And if we consistently pray with our eyes closed, let it be from a sincere desire to spend time in communion with our Lord, without unnecessary distractions; not because we *assume* that is what we are supposed to do. He sees our hearts, anyway: naked, illuminated, unadorned. If the outward does not match the inward, He is not deceived.

Most parents love when their children seek them out, wanting to spend time with them. There are occasions, though, when the parents are too busy or preoccupied, so the children's timing becomes an issue. Parents have deadlines, appointments, obligations, and commitments that compete with their desire to spend time with their children. God has no such distractions. He is **never** too busy, **never** pulled in too many different directions. If we strip away any hint of negativity, then multiply the desire of parents to spend time with their children by a factor of infinity, we still will be nowhere near to approximating how much our Father desires us to commune with Him, through prayer. Let us come to Him with our **hearts** prostrated, humble, devoted, full of thanksgiving and adoration. And let the *external* arrangements of our bodies, whatever they may be, accurately represent *internal* realities.

Day 2 — Places for Prayer

We turn to the Bible for instruction from God regarding *how* our bodies should be situated when we pray, as we explored yesterday. In like manner, there is certainly no better place to search if we want to discover **where** we are supposed to pray. For some Christians, the objection might spring immediately to mind that, since we have the Holy Spirit dwelling inside each of us, we can pray anywhere. It is not necessary for us to relocate to a particular place in order to communicate with the Lord. Does not the Epistle to the Hebrews exhort us to "come boldly to the throne of grace, that we may obtain mercy and find grace to help in time of need" (4:16)? In fact, that book examines at length the access to God that Jesus obtained for all of His brethren through the work that He finished in obedience to His Father. So the question could fairly be posed, "What is there to discuss?" For answer, let us investigate what the Word of God teaches on the subject.

One prominent example from the Old Testament of a place to which believers went for the express purpose of prayer was the temple, the habitation of God's presence among His people. And that was exactly as the Lord willed: "For My house shall be called a house of prayer for all nations" (Isaiah 56:7). (Incidentally, it is interesting to note here that God did not confine the use of His "house" for that purpose strictly to the Hebrews. Instead, *all* nations were invited to pray there as long as they acknowledged the One True God. Isaiah 56:1-8 makes this perfectly clear. This is one of many indications in the Scriptures that God's marvelous plan of salvation was always destined to extend beyond the nation of Israel to incorporate the Gentiles.) Jesus used this verse from Isaiah's prophecy to rebuke those who were exploiting the temple as a venue for commercial enterprises, thereby transforming a holy site into a "den of thieves" (Mark 11:17; refer to Jeremiah 7:11).

One of Jesus's statements, recorded in John's Gospel and referred to in the others, was at once a bold proclamation of His deity and a cause of total befuddlement[9] to His adversaries. In an exchange with the Jews, "Jesus answered and said to them, 'Destroy this temple, and in three days I will raise it up'" (John 2:19). Prior to Christ's Incarnation, the physical temple in Jerusalem was the single place on earth where God sovereignly elected to make His presence reside. But Jesus indicated, in effect, "I am the presence of God among you. My body is the temple in which the Lord your God dwells, and I have power over life and death" (see verse 21). If the Jews whom He was addressing had ears to hear, they would have understood that He was claiming to *be* God.

---

[9] befuddlement (O): confusion, stupification

Before He physically departed this earth, Jesus promised that He would send the Holy Spirit to inhabit and to help all those who believed in Him (John 14:16-18). Since all genuine Christians have the Holy Spirit within them, they are "children of God" and can pray to Him as easily as crying out "Abba, Father" (Romans 8:14-16). They are not required to journey to a temple to pray because their individual bodies are temples of the Holy Spirit (1 Corinthians 6:19). But that does not mean that material structures are wholly without worth as places to which believers can withdraw explicitly for the purpose of prayer. To underscore this fact, let us refer to the experience of David.

David was a man after God's own heart, as we read yesterday (1 Samuel 13:14). He was a man in whom God's Spirit dwelt (16:13). Overwhelmed by sorrow and remorse because of His affair with Bathsheba, he pleaded with the Lord not to take His Spirit from him (Psalm 51:11). That, of course, would be impossible if the Holy Spirit was not *in* David in the first place. But since he *did* have the Spirit within, David could (and did) pray anywhere. Many of the psalms that he composed are heartfelt prayers set to music. Some of them were written in remote and desolate locations, far from Jerusalem. And yet, despite the privilege that he enjoyed and that all saints share, David felt impelled to go in and sit before the Lord, presumably in the temple, and pray to Him there (1 Chronicles 17:16-27). Clearly, the temple still held considerable value for David as a place for prayer, even though he was not *required* to go there for that purpose.

Drawing a parallel to our experience as Christians, a comparable truth applies. Although it is not necessary for us to travel to a church building in order to commune with God, a church is nonetheless a great place to go for that reason, either kneeling behind a worn, wooden pew; seated on a modern, padded chair; or standing at a rail, gazing through stained glass: most churches provide an excellent atmosphere for prolonged and undistracted prayer. They do this by deliberately cultivating a calm environment that fosters meditation and communion with the Lord. God's Spirit is a Spirit of peace and order, so anywhere His Spirit resides, those qualities should be apparent. And just as the individual Christian is a "temple of the Holy Spirit," so also is each church congregation a "temple of God" where "the Spirit of God dwells" (1 Corinthians 6:19; 3:16).

The best instruction that we could receive regarding places for prayer—and anything else, for that matter—comes from Jesus Himself, both in the recorded examples of His own practices and in His teaching on the subject. In a scene from Mark's Gospel that can be called characteristic of Jesus' prayer habits, "He went out and departed to a solitary [or deserted] place; and there He prayed" (1:35). A few chapters farther on, after He sent His disciples away in a boat on the Sea of Galilee, "He departed to the mountain to pray" (6:46). Over in Luke's Gospel, we read, "So He Himself often withdrew into the wilderness and prayed" (5:16). A solitary place, the mountain, the wilderness: an obvious theme runs through these different passages, and others could be included that reiterate the refrain created by these verses. Evidently, Jesus preferred to go somewhere secluded, by Himself, to spend time alone in communion with His Father.

When He was teaching His disciples how to pray, He instructed them to do something along the same lines as His own tendencies. "But you, when you pray, go into your room, and when you have shut your door, pray to your Father who is in the secret place; and your Father who sees in secret will reward you openly" (Matthew 6:6). For those who have both the ability and the opportunity to do this, it is a wonderful way to spend some quality time alone with the Lord. That is why some contemporary Christian books encourage saints to establish "prayer closets" in their homes; dedicated, private spaces used exclusively for prayer. Needless to say, not everyone can construct such closets, but the idea and its aim are both sound, nonetheless.

Centuries before Christ's birth, Daniel's custom was very similar to what Jesus described. During a terribly troubling time in his life, when his survival was threatened by a hostile conspiracy, he returned home and went into his upper room. After opening the windows on the side of the room that faced toward Jerusalem, he knelt down and prayed to God (Daniel 6:10; we touched on this verse yesterday). He was not interested in calling attention to himself. Rather, his sole concern was to communicate with the Lord; the only one, he knew, who could help him in his present, dire situation.

Many people lack the ability to withdraw into a private room, close the door, and be alone with God. In other words, their circumstances prohibit them from following Christ's instructions. Jesus Himself said, "Foxes have holes and birds of the air have nests, but the Son of Man has nowhere to lay His head" (Luke 9:58). Lack of a permanent residence could be one of the reasons that He went to secluded outdoor settings for the purpose of prayer. Then again, even those who do have access to a private room or prayer closet might prefer to venture to peaceful, natural sites to spend some time praying. In fact, numerous locations throughout the world have received the label "God's Cathedral" — Yosemite Valley and the island of Kaua'i being just two examples. Typically these are areas of superlative[10] beauty in which the splendor of God's Creation is plainly displayed. Such scenes seem to lend themselves freely to contemplation of the Lord's infinite majesty; or, alternatively, to prayer.

We may not always understand why certain aspects of the world function the way they do. But most Christians who have walked with the Lord for numerous years will have experienced the capacity of awesome natural settings to foster or even encourage concentrated and prolonged prayer. The specific place does not necessarily have to be as picturesque as the Sierra Nevada Mountains or the

---

[10] superlative (C): of the highest degree or quality

Hawaiian Islands for the effect to operate. The most important properties seem to be that the site is relatively unchanged from the way God made it, and that the person praying is more or less alone. In the musical "prayer" that David offered in Psalm 19, he fluidly connected these different elements. In it he extolled[11] the grandeur of God's Creation—His general revelation. Then he praised the magnificence of God's Word—His special revelation. Finally, David concluded in the last section with an earnest plea for the Lord to make him righteous in thought, in word, and in deed. The *intent* of his prayer, if not exactly the details of its content, is very much like a prayer that any New Testament Christian might present.

So what is the essential takeaway from all of this? Are we still basically at the same place where we began, supposing that where we pray is, for the most part, irrelevant? It is certainly true that we can pray anywhere, having the Holy Spirit of God residing inside each of us. Turning again to David, he established the latter fact emphatically:

"Where can I go from Your Spirit?
Or where can I flee from Your presence?
If I ascend into heaven, You are there;
If I make my bed in hell, behold, You are there.
If I take the wings of the morning,
And dwell in the uttermost parts of the sea,
Even there Your hand shall lead me,
And Your right hand shall hold me" (Psalm 139:7-10).

There is **nowhere** we can go where God is not. Or, to state this truth positively, *everywhere* we may go, God is. As Paul declared, "in Christ Jesus our Lord ... we have boldness and access with confidence through faith in Him" (Ephesians 3:11, 12). That access is not limited in any way by geography. After all, Paul and Silas prayed while confined in an inner prison, with their feet fastened "in the stocks" (Acts 16:24).

Bearing these facts in mind, it is nevertheless true that some places are more *conducive* to concerted prayer than others. And since our aim is to become effective prayer-warriors on the spiritual battlefield, our commitment should be to choose locations, as often as we can, where we are able to spend time with the Lord in uninterrupted and focused prayer. We must resolve not to become discouraged when the enemy attempts to thwart our efforts in this regard, as he certainly will. We must persevere, we must be diligent, and we must ask the Holy Spirit for help as we devote ourselves to incorporating these habits into our regular prayer practices.

---

[11] extolled (O): praised enthusiastically

Day 3 — Times of Prayer

We have seen that the posture of our bodies when we pray is left to our discretion, according to the Bible. And we have observed that whatever configurations we employ should be honest reflections of the conditions and the contents of our hearts. Then we examined the scriptural precedents concerning *where* believers chose to pray. These, too, are open to our choice, though some environments are clearly more conducive to prayer than others. As our third and final consideration in this section, let us explore what God's Word teaches about **when** we should pray.

As with the previous article, an objection might immediately surface in the mind of any learned Christian, which may sound something like this: "The Bible instructs us to 'pray without ceasing,' 'praying always with all prayer and supplication in the Spirit' [1 Thessalonians 5:17; Ephesians 6:18]. If that's what we're commanded to do, then surely *when* we're supposed to pray isn't open to discussion." Of course it is true that we need to obey whatever God's inspired Word directs, so an important distinction needs to be made before we continue. A pronounced difference exists between the *type* of prayer that we engage in when we are praying continuously and what we do when we set aside a period of time to spend in focused and fervent prayer. ("Praying Without Ceasing" is addressed on day 19.)

Our experience of Christian living should readily affirm the difference between these two broad categories of prayer. With the Holy Spirit indwelling us, we can pray while traveling to and from our jobs; while working; while cleaning our homes or preparing a meal; while cutting the grass or bathing or exercising or painting the garage. We can pray anywhere and at any time. But the Scriptures describe another kind of prayer, recording numerous examples in both testaments of devoted believers faithfully engaging in that type of prayer.

One of the most perfect passages to be found in the whole Bible, with regard to this topic, is located in Psalm 55. Its significance is amplified further by its relevance to the larger theme of participation in spiritual warfare:

> "As for me, I will call upon God,
> And the LORD shall save me.
> Evening and morning and at noon
> I will pray, and cry aloud,
> And He shall hear my voice.
> He has redeemed my soul in peace from the battle that was against me,
> For there were many against me.
> God will hear, and afflict them,
> Even He who abides from of old" (verses 16-19).

When David wrote that he would pray "[e]vening and morning and at noon," his statement could be understood in two different ways. First, the whole description could be taken as a single unit, used as a poetic device to signify that he would pray *all day*. In the Jewish method of timekeeping, a day began at sundown, proceeded through the night and the following daylight hours, and ended at the next sundown. Thus, evening and morning and noon could be intended to indicate one whole day. Alternatively, each piece could represent a discrete time period. That approach would mean that David purposefully reserved three times during the day when he would enter into concentrated prayer before the Lord. Of these two interpretations, the second understanding seems preferable for three reasons.

Jewish custom in the centuries before Christ included specified times of day for prayer. These periods were typically associated with the activities of the temple, though not exclusively. Various scriptures mention this practice, even among the nascent[12] Christian community: "Now Peter and John went up together to the temple at the hour of prayer, the ninth hour" (Acts 3:1). The "ninth hour" was reckoned from sunrise, and would have been around 3 p.m. This "hour of prayer" was historically connected to the offering of sacrifices at the temple, though Peter and John obviously were not there for that purpose.

Another reason to interpret David's statement as a reference to three separate time periods is that such a view aligns with specific practices recorded elsewhere in the Bible. For example, in the now-familiar scene from the Book of Daniel, the devout prophet prayed three times a day in his upper room, "as was his custom since early days" (6:10). Granted, the passage does not indicate that those three times were morning, noon, and evening. But in light of Daniel's personal piety and evident devotion to Israel's God, it is not an unreasonable assumption. Daniel apparently recognized the tremendous value—in fact, the necessity—of spending time with the Lord at regular intervals, apart from all of the distractions, the preoccupations, and the responsibilities of everyday life.

A third reason to interpret "[e]vening and morning and at noon" as a description of three distinct periods is that it harmonizes with good sense. Consider the (roughly) cyclical nature of human life. Generally speaking, we allocate approximately eight hours per day for sleep, eight hours for work, and the remaining eight hours for miscellaneous purposes. In other words, we divide the days more or less into thirds. (Granted, many people in the modern world conform to a very different pattern of life from this one. But often that is because they sacrifice sleep and work long hours—both of which are harmful to long-term health.) In view of this natural rhythm, it seems appropriate to space our "prayer sessions" in a corresponding manner.

---

[12] nascent (C): coming into being

Taking this nominal structure as our guide, we can begin the day in a focused time of prayer and communion with the Lord, following our period of sleep—ideally, about eight hours. If we also conclude each day with a similar time of prayer, then we will have two concentrated periods of prayer every day, separated by roughly eight hours. Then if we interject a third session at some point between the two, depending upon our circumstances, with time we will develop the custom of praying three times a day—just like Daniel and David. Perhaps this third session could be on our lunch-breaks at work. Or it might be immediately after we return home from work, before we attend to the affairs of our households. The conditions of our lives will inevitably influence when this third time of prayer occurs. But it is extremely important that we include such focused prayer in our daily practices.

An obvious challenge to the framework just described applies to a large number of contemporary Christians. Many of us feel that we are simply too busy to commit to such practices. ("Busyness" is discussed at length on day 29.) Segregating ourselves from other people and from the demands of life to spend an extended time in focused prayer seems unrealistic in the modern world. There are simply not enough hours in the day. Many of us are struggling just to keep our heads above water, working ourselves raw to make ends meet. Where are we supposed to find the time to spend an hour or two alone with the Lord every day? This challenge touches on two supremely important concerns that relate to Christian living generally, to prayer specifically, and to the subject of this book: *priorities* and *spiritual warfare.*

If we are sincere Christians, then God is both our Savior and our Lord. When we receive the salvation and the redemption made possible by Jesus, we simultaneously surrender our wills to Him (1 Corinthians 6:19-20; Galatians 2:20; Ephesians 4:20-24). But our flesh furiously resists being dominated and desires to be in control. When we relinquish[13] control of our lives—such as we have—to the Lord, our flesh immediately begins striving to regain control; to throw off His yoke. In the words of Paul the Apostle,

> "I say then: Walk in the Spirit, and you shall not fulfill the lust of the flesh. For the flesh lusts against the Spirit, and the Spirit against the flesh; and these are contrary to one another, so that you do not do the things that you wish.... And those who are Christ's have crucified the flesh with its passions and desires. If we live in the Spirit, let us also walk in the Spirit" (Galatians 5:16-17, 24-25).

---

[13] relinquish (O): to surrender possession of; to give up

Paul explained exceptionally well the contention between the flesh and the Spirit in Romans 7-8. And that theme is repeatedly addressed in numerous places throughout the Scriptures. Simply stated, when we give priority to one, the action of the other within us is suppressed. As Paul declared, "For those who live according to the flesh set their minds on the things of the flesh; but those who live according to the Spirit, the things of the Spirit. For to be carnally [fleshly] minded is death, but to be spiritually minded is life and peace. Because the carnal [fleshly] mind is enmity against God..." (Romans 8:5-7).

By definition, we can choose to give priority to the flesh or to the Spirit, but never both. And yet, the mind of the flesh is an enemy of God. It opposes Him, His purposes, and everything He values. That being the case, when we were "bought at a price" and became Christ's, our flesh was crucified along with Jesus, whose blood paid the cost of our deliverance (1 Corinthians 6:19-20). As far as we are concerned, our flesh is dead. Anything that our flesh might compel us to do, we should reject or disregard as though it is nothing more than the spasm of a corpse. Instead, we should focus our minds on matters of the Spirit, orienting our lives and how we use our time around those things that are important to Him. At the same time, we should deliberately search for and eliminate anything in our lives that we recognize to be fleshly in character. To that end, we can and should *ask* the Holy Spirit to provide us with discernment and with eyes of understanding to distinguish between "the things of the flesh" and "the things of the Spirit." If our hearts are sincere in our expressed desire to "walk in the Spirit," then He will empower us to make the appropriate adjustments in how our time is structured.

We see that the time we devote to focused prayer reflects the relative priority that we assign to the flesh or the Spirit. But how does this connect to spiritual warfare? Recall (from the prologue) that "friendship with the world is enmity with God" (James 4:4). "Whoever therefore wants to be a friend of the world makes himself an enemy of God. Or do you think that the Scripture says in vain, 'The Spirit who dwells in us yearns jealously'?" (verses 4-5). This is a similar idea to the flesh striving against the Spirit, only more personal, and more directly applicable to spiritual warfare. When we fail to make time each day for concentrated prayer, *in effect* we demonstrate friendship with the world. And though few of us would conceive of failing to pray as acting like God's enemy, in reality they amount to the same thing.

To establish this point more clearly, consider the matter in a secular context. A soldier in uniform is sent to a battlefield by the commanding officer. The soldier has everything necessary to do the job required: armor, boots, helmet, shield, sword, and training. But when called upon to engage the enemy, the soldier protests that there are too many reasons *not* to fight: the harvest has nearly arrived; my roof needs repair before the rains come; a family member has taken ill; a major business arrangement is almost finalized. These excuses will carry no weight with the commander, who will interpret the soldier's refusal to fight as dereliction [14]of duty. To put it another way, a soldier who will not obey orders and fight as directed is, in reality, little better than an enemy combatant. Both types of people frustrate the commander's efforts (which arise from responsibility) to overcome the opposition and win the engagement.

Using a similar analogy to encourage his son in the faith, Timothy, Paul commented, "No one engaged in warfare entangles himself with the affairs of this life, that he may please him who enlisted him as a soldier" (2 Timothy 2:4). If we become entangled "with the affairs of this life" to such an extent that we are incapable of contributing effectively to the (spiritual) war effort, our Commander will be displeased. He calls us to *use* what He has given us to participate in the ongoing warfare "against principalities, against powers, against the rulers of the darkness of this age, against spiritual hosts of wickedness in the heavenly places" (Ephesians 6:12). When we neglect this duty because we are too preoccupied with concerns of this life, we act—in effect, though not in purpose—like His enemy.

If we recognize the profound value of effective and fervent prayer in the life of every Christian, then it is absolutely critical that we prioritize prayer every day. Regardless of the commitments and distractions that our lives might include, we need to set aside regular periods of time to spend exclusively with the Lord—like David, Daniel, Jesus, and many others. We need to "seek those things which are above, where Christ is, sitting at the right hand of God. Set your mind on things above, not on things on the earth. For you died, and your life is hidden with Christ in God" (Colossians 3:1-3). Assuming that our professed devotion to Christ is sincere, we should be willing to make any necessary adjustments in our circumstances and our schedules so that we can allot discrete times to earnest prayer each day.

Before we leave the subject of when Christians should pray, there is one more specific occasion for prayer that should be highlighted: *before meals*. In the Bible, we find abundant precedents for the practice of praying and giving thanks before meals. A brief survey of a selection of passages should be enough to establish the importance of praying at these times.

Using only seven loaves of bread "and a few little fish," Jesus fed "four thousand men, besides women and children" (Matthew 15:34-38). "And He took the seven loaves and the fish and gave thanks, broke them and gave them to His disciples; and the disciples gave to the multitude" (verse 36). Later, when Jesus sat at a table with His disciples for the Last Supper, "He took bread, blessed and broke it, and gave it to them" (Luke 24:30).

---

[14] dereliction (CO): abandoning, forsaking, or neglecting

In one of many harrowing[15] experiences that Paul had during his missionary journeys, he and his shipmates were tossed wildly about on tempestuous[16] waters, "driven up and down in the Adriatic Sea" (Acts 27:27). Paul confidently assured the others that they would not be harmed, and encouraged them to take some food for their nourishment (verses 33-34). "And when he had said these things, he took bread and gave thanks to God in the presence of them all; and when he had broken it he began to eat" (verse 35).

Apart from these biblical anecdotes, there is also in Paul's counsel to Timothy a more doctrinal statement of the same precept that the stories illustrate. "For every creature of God is good, and nothing is to be refused if it is received with thanksgiving; for it is sanctified by the word of God and prayer" (1 Timothy 4:4-5). What does this scripture teach us? When we set ourselves to eat whatever God has supplied for our nourishment, we should always pause first to thank the Lord. In this way, we acknowledge Him as our Provider and we express our appreciation for what He has given us. We also sanctify the meal, ensuring that whatever it contains can be consumed without offending our consciences.

Based on what Jesus did Himself; on the examples of saints that are recorded in God's Word; and on the explicit and inspired teachings of the Scriptures, we should develop the habit of praying before every meal, large or small. As we observe with Jesus and Paul, these prayers need not be elaborate or prolonged, but they should occur at each meal. With time, dedication, and a bit of discipline, we can cultivate the practice of praying morning, noon, and evening (nominally), as well as before meals. By doing so, we can remain in regular communication with our Lord, looking to the hand of our loving Father for direction and sustenance. Additionally, in our common role as soldiers on a spiritual battlefield, praying regularly will help to keep us in close accord with our Commander's orders as He conducts His army.

---

[15] harrowing. (O): distressing, tormenting
[16] tempestuous (O): stormy, full of commotion

Various Aspects of Christian Prayer: What to Pray

Day 4 — Thanksgiving

If it is even possible to create an exhaustive list of everything that Christians should include in their prayers, it is almost certainly inadvisable, nonetheless. Prayer should never become a kind of "to-do" list from which we mark off individual items as they are addressed. Instead, our times of prayer should be among the sweetest and most rewarding moments that we experience on any given day. If the reasons why that is so are not already apparent, they will be discussed in greater detail later in the book. For now, we will focus intently in this section on five components that should be included in any well-developed prayer practice: thanksgiving, confession, praise, intercession, and supplication (or petition).

Before we examine thanksgiving more closely, though, one proviso[17] needs to be inserted: The five elements of full-bodied prayer listed above should be well-represented in a saint's prayer life *as a whole*. In other words, it is not necessary every time we pray to ensure that we cover each of these categories. It is not as though our prayers will not "count" or will be less meaningful if we neglect to include one or more of these divisions on any given occasion. We need to remember what we are doing when we pray. We are coming before the throne of Almighty God the Creator, in the Spirit, through the access obtained for us by Jesus Christ. No part of us is in any way concealed from His perfect understanding. Paul spoke to this truth in his Epistle to the Romans:

> "Likewise the Spirit also helps in our weaknesses. For we do not know what we should pray for as we ought, but the Spirit Himself makes intercession for us with groanings which cannot be uttered. Now He who searches the hearts knows what the mind of the Spirit is, because He makes intercession for the saints according to the will of God" (8:26-27).

Consider how profound this truth is! One of the three Persons of the Godhead dwells inside all authentic Christians! And whenever those children of God approach their Father's throne, the Spirit comes alongside and communicates what limited human beings are unable to express themselves. He knows us infinitely better than we know ourselves. In fact, He knows us perfectly. When we pray to Him, we are telling Him what He already knows. So if any of our individual prayers are somehow "incomplete," we need not be concerned that

---

[17] proviso (O): something that is insisted upon as a condition of an agreement

we are failing in some way, as long as our prayer practices are *generally* well-developed.

The same assurance applies when we consider *why* we make a priority of setting aside times for (preferably) undistracted prayer each day. Needless to say, the content of specific prayers will vary depending upon the *reason* that motivated us to pray. For example, when we are embroiled in a heated spiritual battle, our prayers might be composed mostly of intercession and supplication. By contrast, if we are prompted to pray simply because we are moved by how wonderful and gracious the Lord is, then our prayers may consist largely of praise and thanksgiving. As long as our prayer habits include all of the relevant aspects *as a whole*, there is no real cause for concern.

In light of these guiding principles, we need to be careful not to allow our prayer sessions to become formulaic. When our prayer practices begin to resemble a formula or an itemized list, something is terribly wrong. "Alright, I've covered thanksgiving and confession well enough. Now I'll throw in a smattering of praise and a little intercession before moving on to the real reason I'm praying—petition." Few if any of us would actually say these things to ourselves. But the mentality that we display in and through our prayers might be all too similar to the one portrayed. Thus, while we must be mindful to incorporate all aspects of fully-orbed prayer in our prayer habits generally, we should also be attentive to prevent our times with the Lord from becoming mechanical. He both desires and deserves our utmost sincerity.

With these considerations lending structure to our studies, let us explore in greater depth what the Bible teaches about thanksgiving. We will begin with a couple of excerpts from Paul's epistles. "[B]e filled with the Spirit, speaking to one another in psalms and hymns and spiritual songs, singing and making melody in your hearts to the Lord, giving thanks always for all things to God the Father in the name of our Lord Jesus Christ" (Ephesians 5:19-20). In his closing directions to the church in Thessalonica, Paul commanded, "in everything give thanks, for this is the will of God in Christ Jesus for you" (1 Thessalonians 5:18). "[G]iving thanks always for all things..."; "in everything give thanks...": these instructions seem pretty straightforward and definitive. In fact, it would be difficult to state the matter more explicitly than Paul did. When are we ordered to give thanks? Always and in everything. For what do we give thanks? For all things. And why are we directed to give thanks? Because it is God's will.

But the Bible has much to teach on the subject of thanksgiving besides "Do it because I said so." In reality, if that was all God's Word said about the issue, it would still be sufficient to constitute a command of action, since the Scriptures carry the *authority* of their Author (2 Timothy 3:16). But there is more. Consider, for example, one of the observations that Paul made in the well-known first chapter of his Epistle to the Romans. Describing a class of wicked idolaters, he noted that "although they knew God, they did not glorify Him as God, nor were thankful, but became futile in their thoughts, and their foolish hearts were darkened" (verse 21). While commenting on the qualities and behaviors that showed these people to be justly deserving of criticism, the apostle included the charge that they were not thankful.

Paul's damning narrative in the first chapter of Romans discussed the legacy of humankind from the time of creation until the turning point in history that was the Incarnation of Christ (verse 20). Using equally critical terms in a letter to Timothy, he prophetically described the sort of people who would inhabit the world in the days leading up to Jesus's Second Coming:

> "But know this, that in the last days perilous times will come: For men will be lovers of themselves, lovers of money, boasters, proud, blasphemers, disobedient to parents, unthankful, unholy, unloving, unforgiving, slanderers, without self-control, brutal, despisers of good, traitors, headstrong, haughty, lovers of pleasure rather than lovers of God, having a form of godliness but denying its power. And from such people turn away!" (2 Timothy 3:1-5).

One could hardly imagine a more fitting description of the world in the 21st century, which many learned Christians believe does indeed represent "the last days." But notice, about a third of the way through the series of ungodly attributes, Paul's inclusion of "unthankful." With Timothy, we are commanded to "turn away" from such people. Clearly, the matter of thankfulness (in the heart) and thanksgiving (in prayer) is very important to the Lord in His relations with humanity.

Recognizing that we are supposed to *be* thankful and to *express* that appreciation to God, what happens when we do not feel particularly thankful? Are we then to give thanks anyway, when our hearts are not in it? The simplest answer to the latter question is…yes and no. If our hearts are genuinely ungrateful, but we proceed to thank God in prayer because that is what the Bible commands us to do, then our actions resemble those of the Pharisees, which Jesus flatly condemned:

> "These people draw near to Me with their mouth,
> And honor Me with their lips,
> But their heart is far from Me" (Matthew 15:8).

Realistically, there is no point in telling God anything that does not reflect the true content of our hearts. Do we think that He is deceived? Moreover, He wants us to be honest with Him. We should always remember that God is not only our Creator and our Lord; He is also our Father. And as our loving Father, He encourages us to bare our hearts to Him, candidly acknowledging what He already knows is there.

Giving thanks pharisaically[18] when we are not actually thankful has no place in a Christian's prayer life. But there is another sense in which we *should* give thanks anyway, even when our hearts are not in it. In order to appreciate the difference between the two senses, we have to distinguish between the fleeting emotions that we experience and the content of our hearts through time. To help us with this, we might compare the difference here to that between *getting* angry and *being* angry. We could look at other pairings, such as joy versus happiness or contentment versus satisfaction, but we will use anger. It also seems fitting to employ anger for this illustration because anger and thanksgiving so often work against each other.

Anger in the sense of becoming angry is a normal human emotion that everyone has to deal with from time to time. Not only is it universal in human experience, but it also has a necessary role to fill in some circumstances. For example, Jesus felt "righteous indignation" when He purged the temple of moneychangers who had turned God's "house of prayer" into a "den of thieves" (Matthew 21:12-13). His anger was altogether just and appropriate. This type of anger has an animating and invigorating property connected with it that can be helpful when combating injustice or in comparable pursuits.

Some years ago, clerical authorities attempted to discover how widespread the priestly abuse of children was in the Roman Catholic Church. Many of the investigators pursued their appointed task with a fervor that was fueled, at least in part, by anger. They were genuinely outraged by what they unearthed. Here again, their anger was both just and appropriate. In fact, heavy criticism was levied against some priests and lay investigators who did not appear to be *angry enough* about what was revealed.

Contrasting with anger of this type, anger in the sense of *being* angry is characteristic of the "old man." Concerning our former selves, Paul challenged the saints to "put off ...the old man which grows corrupt according to the deceitful lusts" (Ephesians 4:22). And "put on the new man which was created according to God, in true righteousness and holiness" (verse 24).

> "'Be angry, and do not sin': do not let the sun go down on your wrath, nor give place to the devil... And do not grieve the Holy Spirit of God, by whom you were sealed for the day of redemption. Let all bitterness, wrath, anger, clamor, and evil speaking be put away from you, with all malice" (verses 26, 30-31).

---

[18] pharisaically (O): behaving in a hypocritical and self-righteous manner

When anger resides in the heart and festers there, it provides the devil with opportunities to sow seeds of dissipation and further wickedness. This type of anger reflects a condition of the heart that opposes the work of the Holy Spirit and is completely incongruous [19] with the type of people that the Father desires all of His children to be. A quick review of the assorted attributes of "the fruit of the Spirit" that are recorded in Galatians 5 should be sufficient to establish this point (verse 22). Anger would be obviously misplaced if included in that series, but would be right at home among "the works of the flesh" that are recounted in verses 19-21. Thus we see that, while all Christians *become* angry at various times and for different reasons, we should never *be* angry for long.

Having examined how the temporary emotion of anger differs from the ongoing condition of being angry, let us return to the subject of today's focus: thanksgiving. In light of what we have observed, it becomes easier to see how we can still *be* thankful Christians even when we may not *feel* particularly thankful. One type of thankfulness describes the character of our hearts, while the other refers only to a passing emotion. When our circumstances are extremely trying and it seems that everything is going against us, we may not feel especially grateful. But in such situations—in fact, in all situations—our hearts can remain thankful and we can still "[give] thanks always for all things." When the attitude of our hearts is one of sincere thankfulness, we acknowledge the sovereignty of God in any and all circumstances. We demonstrate belief of what He has said and promised. And we express trust in His immutable[20] ability and unwavering commitment to accomplish the work that He has begun in us (Philippians 1:6).

Sometimes when we are brought through trials in life, we can tend to lose sight of those amazing and unchanging truths for which we should be continuously and deeply thankful. But Jesus never misled His followers regarding what the Christian life would entail. "In the world you will have tribulation; but be of good cheer, I have overcome the world" (John 16:33). Paul echoed this fact in his Epistle to the Philippians: "For to you it has been granted on behalf of Christ, not only to believe in Him, but also to suffer for His sake" (1:29). Many other passages could be cited that convey essentially the same truth (see, for example, 2 Timothy 3:12).

Our lives of following Jesus, walking in the Spirit, obeying the commandments of God, and fighting with the enemy on a spiritual battlefield are going to be hard. There will be trials. There will be tribulation. There will be hardships. We will be hated by the world. We will be persecuted and reviled. We will suffer. But in spite of all this, we have hope, we have peace, and we have countless causes to be extremely thankful. To help us to reorient our vision and to focus on the thanksgiving that is rightly due to our Lord, here is a handful of truths

---

[19] incongruous (O): not suitable or harmonious
[20] immutable (O) : unchangeable

that apply to all genuine Christians. These are "true truths," to borrow a phrase from Francis Schaeffer, that are as certain as God's Word accomplishing His purposes (Isaiah 45:22-23; 55:11):

1. God loved us while we were spiritually dead in our trespasses and sins. Because of that love, He sent His only begotten Son to suffer the wrath that we deserve and to die in our places (John 3:16; Romans 5:6-11; Ephesians 2:1-2).

2. Saved, redeemed, and adopted by the God of the universe as His own children, we have all received His precious gift, the Holy Spirit (Romans 8:14-17; 1 Corinthians 2:12; 2 Corinthians 1:21-22; Ephesians 1:13-14; Colossians 1:13-14; 1 John 3:1-2).

3. Eternal life resides in each of us as a present and irrevocable reality. Though our physical bodies wear out and eventually perish, we will live on with our Lord for all eternity (John 5:24; Romans 11:29 with 1 John 2:25; 5:11-13; 1 Corinthians 4:16; 2 Corinthians 5:1-8).

4. Whatever adversity we have to endure in this life will fade into insignificance when compared to the blessed glory that awaits us (Romans 8:18; 1 Corinthians 2:9; 2 Corinthians 4:17-18).

5. At every moment in life, in every circumstance and situation, He is with us, and He promises to help us. Not only are we never alone, but our constant companion is the omnipotent [21]Creator and Sustainer of the whole universe (Deuteronomy 31:6, 8; John 14:15-18,33; Colossians 1:15-17; Hebrews 1:1-4; Psalm 139; Proverbs 3:5-6).

6. Everything happens for a reason, and God shapes the courses of our lives to align with His immutable purposes. There are no accidents. Nothing supersedes[22] or exists beyond the sovereignty of God (Matthew 10:29-31; Romans 8:28).

7. Among the last words that Jesus spoke—as recorded in Scripture—was a sure and joyous promise: "Behold, I am coming quickly" (Revelation 22:7; also verse 20).

In light of all these marvelous truths, how can we neglect to pour out our hearts in a torrent of gratitude to our loving and gracious Father? Or, to put it another way, how can we sin against God by failing to thank Him for all that He does, has done, and promises to do? When we withhold our thanks from Him, who

---

[21] omnipotent (O): having unlimited power; all-powerful
[22] supersedes (C): displaces, sets aside, renders unnecessary

justly deserves as much as we can give, we sin (James 4:17). Though we should always thank God regardless of how we feel, how much better it is to thank Him with a heart that overflows with sincere appreciation! As we consciously cultivate prayer habits that are both effective and fervent, let us take care to include thanksgiving as a constant feature in our prayer practices. Certainly we are commanded to give thanks always, but beyond that, we have **so much** for which to be thankful!

Day 5 — Confession

Sin separates human beings from God. The undeniable truth of that statement should be apparent to any rational, Christian mind. A detailed theological study of the holiness of God would easily fill several volumes—and has. But even without delving into such a thorough review of His holiness, the distance that sin generates between humans and God can also be demonstrated logically.

God is **perfectly** holy, without blemish or impurity of any kind. In fact, our English word "holy" is completely inadequate to describe the attribute of God's character that we mean to identify when we use the term "holy". The concept that we attempt to communicate through that word is but a faint shadow of the superlative [23] holiness of God. We might compare this to the way that the earthly temple was only an echo in time and space of the heavenly reality (Hebrews 9:24, as well as the rest of chapter 9). To state this in another way, some aspects of who God is reflect in human experience, but only imperfectly, as copies or shadows. He alone is the great I AM, the unique self-existent One. The Apostle Paul referred to this truth in one of his epistles:

> "For we know in part and we prophesy in part. But when that which is perfect has come, then that which is in part will be done away.... For now we see in a mirror, dimly, but then face to face. Now I know in part, but then I shall know just as I also am known" (1 Corinthians 13:9-10, 12).

Elsewhere, the seraphim that Isaiah the Prophet saw worshiping the Lord expressed the insufficiency of the word *holy*:

> "Holy, holy, holy is the LORD of hosts;
> The whole earth is full of His glory" (6:1-3; see also Revelation 4:8).

These angels had to declare the word three times just to impart some sense of God's supreme holiness! He is holy beyond expression; holy beyond imagining; holy beyond our capacity to comprehend.

We must first appreciate what is meant by the observation "God is holy" before we can grasp properly the ramifications[24] of sin. In other words, a sober and honest appraisal of God's holiness should impress upon us just how terrible our sins truly are. That is exactly what happened to Isaiah:

> "Woe is me, for I am undone!
> Because I am a man of unclean lips,

---

[23] superlative (C): of the highest degree or quality
[24] ramifications (C): branches, divisions, or parts of a subject

And I dwell in the midst of a people of unclean lips;
For my eyes have seen the King,
The LORD of hosts" (6:5).

Our sin produces a condition of unholiness in us that creates separation between us and the Lord, like a spiritual wedge forcing us apart.

Holiness and unholiness cannot dwell together. Far beyond any analogy to oil and water or to opposite magnetic poles, holiness and unholiness could more accurately be compared to light and darkness. For the two to coexist is altogether impossible—period. Consequently, in order for unholy human beings to draw near to a holy God, something must be done to rectify their unholiness. They need to be made holy. But therein lies the problem. Humans are utterly powerless to make themselves holy, being enslaved by the sinful inclinations to which all are subject. Paul elaborated this fact at length in his Epistle to the Romans (especially chapter 7) and elsewhere, so in the interest of conserving space, we will not explore it here.

Since human beings are fundamentally incapable of making themselves holy, it stands to reason that, if they are going to be made holy, the required remedy must be supplied by God. And that He did through His only begotten Son, Jesus. This truth is central to the Christian Gospel. Since humans could not save themselves, God the Father enabled their salvation by offering His Son, the only sacrifice that could satisfy the demands of God's perfect justice (Hebrews 7:25-27). This component of the gospel incorporates two foundational doctrines, both of which relate to the subject of confession: **justification** and **sanctification**.

In justification, the Lord "declares righteous" a person who sincerely believes and trusts in Jesus Christ for deliverance from the penalty of sin (Romans 8:29-30; 1 Corinthians 6:11). This principle was captured memorably by the Apostle John: "If we confess our sins, He is faithful and just to forgive us our sins, and to cleanse us from all unrighteousness" (1 John 1:9).

From this verse (as elsewhere), it is evident that forgiveness goes hand in hand with being made righteous. But forgiveness requires honest acknowledgment and confession of our sins. Notice that John made his assurance conditional: "If we confess our sins...." And the reverse principle is also implied in this conditionality. That is, if we refuse to confess our sins, then we will not be forgiven nor cleansed "from all unrighteousness."

The importance and the effects of confession, forgiveness, and cleansing from unrighteousness concern more than justification —salvation from the **penalty** of sin. They also relate to sanctification, which has been described as salvation from the **power** of sin. Sanctification is a gradual and progressive process that continues throughout a Christian's life. As saints are sanctified, they are made *more* righteous and *more* holy through the work of the Holy Spirit and through the study of Scripture. Paul referred to this lifelong development in godliness in his Epistle to the Romans: "And do not be conformed to this world, but be transformed by the renewing of your mind..." (12:2). As the Holy Spirit applies and empowers the truths of God's Word, the mind is renewed and the believer is transformed. And such transformation proceeds toward greater holiness and righteousness. We can see this spelled out, in a way, by looking briefly at the Greek word that is translated "sanctification": *hagiasmos*. The Greek term for "holy" is *hagios*, so one way we might render *hagiasmos* is "holy-ification"— making holy. Obviously, this rendition takes some liberty with language, but it also communicates accurately the essence of the term.

Another biblical concept that refers to the process of transformation which Christians undergo is conversion. Simply defined, "to convert" is "to change from one form or use or character to another" (*Oxford*, "convert"). Compare that to the definition provided for "transform": "to make a great change in the appearance or character of" (*Oxford*, "transform"). We can see that they are quite similar. As applied to the Christian life, conversion is the change from unholiness to holiness. It is the change from a life dominated by the sin nature to one that is set apart and surrendered to the Lordship of Christ (Romans 12:1-2). When the Apostle Peter was preaching in Jerusalem at a place called Solomon's Porch, he connected conversion to another important concept: **repentance**. "Repent therefore and be converted," he commanded, "that your sins may be blotted out, so that times of refreshing may come from the presence of the Lord" (Acts 3:19). Repentance signifies turning *away* from the sins being acknowledged combined with turning *toward* God. And obviously, in order to turn away from sins that are being acknowledged, those sins have to be acknowledged, which is confession. In other words, repentance implies confession.

Most people probably already know more or less what the word "confession" means. But to prevent any misunderstanding about how it is used in the Bible, let us briefly review the definition. According to the *Oxford American Dictionary,* to "confess" is "to state formally that one has done wrong or has a weakness." This is an adequate definition, as far as it goes, but it fails to capture the fullness of how the term is used in Scripture. To the information expressed by the *Oxford* definition, *Vine's* adds the important fact that such admission is "the result of inward conviction." This conviction is one aspect of the work of God's Spirit within us. He illuminates the eyes of our understanding so that we can recognize the gravity of our sin, but never with the purpose of causing us to despair or become discouraged. Instead, awareness of how our sin offends His holiness is always aimed at drawing us back into close communion with Him.

When we confess our sins to Him, we honestly and humbly acknowledge the reality of our transgressions. We concede our guilt and recognize that we are utterly lost apart from His grace. In this way, the spiritual wedge of sin that separates us *from* Him is removed *by* Him and we are enabled to draw near *to* Him again. As His servant James commanded in the book that bears his name,

> "Therefore submit to God. Resist the devil and he will flee from you. Draw near to God and He will draw near to you. Cleanse your hands, you sinners; and purify your hearts, you double-minded! Lament and mourn and weep! Let your laughter be turned to mourning and your joy to gloom. Humble yourselves in the sight of the Lord, and He will lift you up" (4:7-10).

James challenges us to allow the full weight of our sins to impress itself upon us. He prompts us to appreciate how horribly offensive our sins are to God's supreme holiness. By experiencing this inward conviction, we should be compelled to confess our sins to the Lord, repent of them, and submit to the sanctifying, converting, transforming work of the Holy Spirit.

To be perfectly clear, repentance requires confession, and confession necessitates repentance. They are indivisible. Both are foundational to forgiveness and critical for conversion. Looking at the matter logically, repentance is *incomplete* without confession, and confession is *empty* without repentance. How can we turn away from sins that we neglect or refuse to acknowledge? Or why would we confess sins to the Lord when we are not resolved to turn away from them? Is God's grace so cheap to us that we would presume upon it through willful sin or through failure to admit our wrongdoing? "Or do you think that the Scripture says in vain, 'The Spirit who dwells in us yearns jealously'?

> "But He gives more grace. Therefore He says:
> 　　　'God resists the proud,
> 　　　But gives grace to the humble'" (James 4:5-6).

Our Lord is truly and abundantly gracious. He readily restores us to intimate relationship with Him when we humbly confess and repent of our sins.

We find numerous examples in the Scriptures that illustrate how closely forgiveness and restoration follow confession and repentance. In Psalm 32:5, David declared:

> "I acknowledged my sin to You,
> And my iniquity I have not hidden.
> I said, 'I will confess my transgressions to the LORD,'
> And You forgave the iniquity of my sin."

Conveying profound comfort and encouragement, in the Book of Proverbs is a memorable description of human experience in relation to God:

"He who covers his sins will not prosper,
But whoever confesses and forsakes them will have mercy" (28:13).

In fact, this proverb could be applied both to the unregenerate[25] and to those who are already Christians. Or, to frame it in different terms, the truth captured in this maxim[26] is relevant prior to justification *and* throughout the process of sanctification. If we try to conceal our sins, then, like David, our "bones" will grow old, God's "hand" will be "heavy upon" us, and our "vitality" will be "turned into the drought of summer" (Psalm 32:3-4). We "will not prosper." But as soon as we confess and repent of (forsake) our sins, the Lord extends His bountiful mercy. He forgives us, removes the wedge between us and Him, and draws us back into closer relationship with Him.

It must be abundantly evident at this point that confession is a critical component of godly living. By extension, so is repentance. And so, too, is prayer. If we want our prayers to be effective and fervent, to avail much, then we must confess and repent of our sins as soon as they come to our attention. We need to embrace the transformative process of "holy-ification" that the Holy Spirit conducts within us. We should ask Him to illuminate our minds to specific sins and sinful habits that we have not yet acknowledged and forsaken. We should also ask Him for the strength to resist the devil, to submit to God and obey His will, and to turn away from those sins that have infiltrated our lives. Certainly, some sins can be very difficult to part with, but **everything** that is contrary to God's holiness has to go. We should remember James 4. We should recall Paul's inspired words in Romans 7-8. And we should make confession a regular element of our prayer practices.

---

[25] unregenerate (O): not reformed or converted to a new way of life; unsaved
[26] maxim (O): a general truth or rule of conduct

Day 6 — Praise

"Praise the LORD!
Praise the LORD from the heavens;
Praise Him in the heights!
Praise Him, all His angels;
Praise Him, all His hosts!
Praise Him, sun and moon;
Praise Him, all you stars of light!
Praise Him, you heavens of heavens,
And you waters above the heavens!" (Psalm 148:1-4).

Yesterday's reading concentrated on the need for confession in our daily prayers. It also emphasized how offensive our sins are to the perfect holiness of God. But dwelling too long on the place that sin continues to occupy in our lives as Christians could cause us to become downhearted, or at least disgusted. "O wretched man that I am!" exclaimed Paul the Apostle. "Who will deliver me from this body of death?" (Romans 7:24). Thankfully, he had the spiritual maturity not to despair, and to answer his own question: "I thank God—through Jesus Christ our Lord!" (verse 25). To lift our spirits after the humbling truths that buffeted[27] us yesterday, we will focus today on a more cheerful aspect of a fully developed prayer practice: **praise**. We should note quickly, however, that this component is just as important as all the others.

Numerous different terms are used in the Bible to indicate praise apart from the word "praise": bless, exalt, extol, glorify, honor, magnify, worship. Each of these verbs, including "praise," expresses a slight variation on the common theme that unites all of them. For example, one Hebrew term that appears frequently is *halal*, which means to "praise," to "celebrate," to "commend," or to "make a show of" someone or something. This word is often combined with a shortened form of the divine name, *Yah*, to produce *halleluyah*, "praise the LORD" (Isaiah 12:2). Both *halal* and *hallelujah* (an alternate spelling) occur many times in the Book of Psalms. By comparison, the Hebrew word that is typically translated "exalt" or "extol" means "to hold high" or "to esteem greatly." (Both "exalt" and "extol" come from the same Hebrew verb, *ruwm* or *rum*.) Elsewhere, the word rendered "magnify" signifies to "make large," to "advance," to "increase," and to "promote." From this brief review of some of their meanings, we see how all of these related concepts can be grouped together under the umbrella of "praise." That, of course, is why they are used as substitutes for the term throughout the Scriptures.

---

[27] buffeted (C): struck with the hand or fist; contended against

In God's Word, it is not uncommon to encounter several of the different expressions of praise occurring in the same passage. And that is especially apparent in the Psalms. A good example of this appears in Psalm 34:

"I will bless the LORD at all times;
His praise shall continually be in my mouth.
My soul shall make its boast in the LORD;
The humble shall hear of it and be glad.
Oh, magnify the LORD with me,
And let us exalt His name together" (verses 1-3).

Bless, praise, boast, magnify, exalt: five separate words indicating praise all appearing in close proximity. This variety can be contrasted with, for example, Psalm 150, in which the word "praise" is featured on every line, and none of the other terms are employed.

Although we commonly associate praise with singing, in reality it can assume different forms: song, dance, music, prose, poetry, painting, and other artistic media can all constitute expressions of praise. Many contemporary saints are unaware that Johann Sebastian Bach was a devout Christian who was ardently committed to using the musical genius he was given for the glory of God. Some of his incredible compositions are purely instrumental, while others incorporate a vocal element. But all of his work, both as individual pieces and taken together, produces a beautiful exhibition of praise to the Lord he adored.

Many other believers praised God in writing or through magnificent paintings, applying their God-given abilities to advance His name. John of the Cross and Gerard Manley Hopkins, to name only two, penned some exquisite poems magnifying the glory of God as manifested in His Creation and His gracious dealings with humanity. And many of the outstanding painters whose names are now enshrined in secular culture were motivated solely by a desire to exalt the glory of the Lord. What the world often calls "religious impulses," they would have insisted was an earnest resolve to praise the One True God.

David was certainly no stranger to praise in several of its different forms. Many of the psalms were written by him—under inspiration of the Holy Spirit—and they are poetry and song lyrics at the same time. He was also a gifted musician who could play numerous instruments. When David and his men recovered the ark of the covenant from the Philistines and escorted it back to Jerusalem, the king was overcome with joy. He was so flooded with gladness that it burst out of him. "Then David danced before the LORD with all his might..." (2 Samuel 6:14). And "Michal, Saul's daughter, looked through a window and saw King David leaping and whirling before the LORD" (verse 16). In this remarkable scene, David publicly praised God by dancing exuberantly[28] before Him, unconcerned about what the people might think of him (verses 20-22).

Of all the different ways in which God's people might praise Him, prayer is probably the most personal and intimate. As we have read previously, when we pray to our Lord, we approach His throne of grace in the Spirit, through the free access that Jesus obtained for all Christians (Hebrews 4:16). In effect, we are "face to face" with God, like Moses was on Mount Sinai, speaking directly to the Almighty. No more personal encounter can be imagined.

Turning again to the Psalms, we find some important instructions that relate to this act of coming before God's throne:

"Make a joyful shout to the LORD, all you lands!
Serve the LORD with gladness;
Come before His presence with singing...
Enter into His gates with thanksgiving,
And into His courts with praise.
Be thankful to Him, and bless His name" (100:1-2, 4).

So what is expected of us when we come before Him, according to these inspired verses? Singing, thanksgiving, and praise. Thanksgiving we have already covered, so let us concentrate on the other two.

As we have seen, singing—in the way it appears in the Psalms—is a type of praise. (Not *all* singing is praise, certainly, and much modern "music" that pretends to worship God is really quite carnal.) But praise also arises in numerous other forms. Depending upon our situations, singing while we are praying might be unwise or even impossible. But if our circumstances permit us to "[c]ome before His presence with singing," then so much the better.

Consider what happened in a Philippian jail, as recorded in the Book of Acts: "But at midnight Paul and Silas were praying and singing hymns to God, and the prisoners were listening to them. Suddenly there was a great earthquake, so that the foundations of the prison were shaken; and immediately all the doors were opened and everyone's chains were loosed" (16:25-26). Of course, we should not assume that a cause-and-effect relationship exists here. In other words, the scripture does not explicitly indicate that the earthquake occurred *because* these two men were "praying and singing hymns to God." Still, we know that "the effective, fervent prayer of a righteous man avails much" (James 5:16). We also know that God desires praise from us when we enter "into His courts." We should not be surprised, therefore, when marvelous things happen as we pray earnestly and frequently and in accordance with God's will.

---

[28] exuberantly (C): copiously, super-abundantly, in high spirits

If we are not able, or perhaps not inclined for whatever reason, to sing when we come before the Lord in prayer, we can still praise Him in other ways. We might simply speak to Him with unscripted expressions of adoration, exalting Him for who He is and for what He does, has done, and promises to do. We could also read, slowly and deliberately, the text of one of the many psalms of praise, or another passage of Scripture that magnifies the Lord's glory. We can praise Him in a general way, perhaps for the beauty of His Creation or the attributes that He possesses in such majestic perfection. Or we might praise Him for something specific, such as His intervention in a trying situation or His provision of a pressing need—ours or someone else's.

Apart from any of His particular acts, God **deserves** to be praised simply for who He is. He is God, the only true God, the great I AM, the Creator, and beside Him there is no other (2 Samuel 7:22; Psalm 86:8-10; Isaiah 46:8-10).

"For the LORD is great and greatly to be praised;
He is to be feared above all gods.
For all the gods of the people are idols,
But the LORD made the heavens.
Honor and majesty are before Him;
Strength and beauty are in His sanctuary" (Psalm 96:4-6).

"You are worthy, O Lord,
To receive glory and honor and power;
For You created all things,
And by Your will they exist and were created" (Revelation 4:11).

When we also contemplate His countless and wondrous deeds, praise should spill from our hearts and pour from our lips as easily as breathing. To that point, *every* breath we take is a gift from God. We occasionally acknowledge that fact, but few of us actually appreciate its magnitude.

Consider for a moment that every breath of every creature on the whole earth, land and sea and air, is supplied continuously by the gracious providence of God (Acts 17:24-25). If He chooses, He can discontinue the breath of a specific creature or of an entire species, according to His purposes and His perfect sovereignty:

"These all wait for You,
That You may give them their food in due season.
What You give them they gather in;
You open Your hand, they are filled with good.
You hide Your face, they are troubled;
You take away their breath, they die and return to their dust.
You send forth Your Spirit, they are created;
And You renew the face of the earth" (Psalm 104:27-30).

Moses grasped these truths well. He captured them succinctly[29] in his parting instructions to the Israelites near the end of his life: "Therefore know this day, and consider it in your heart, that the LORD Himself is God in heaven above and on the earth beneath; there is no other" (Deuteronomy 4:39). In view of who God is and what He does, Psalm 150 (and the Book of Psalms) appropriately concludes with a command that applies to all of us:

"Let everything that has breath praise the LORD.
Praise the LORD [hallelujah]!" (verse 6).

Hopefully at this point the place of praise in every saint's life is well understood. No sincere Christian will deny that the Lord is absolutely and uniquely worthy of all praise. In our times of prayer, we strive to minimize distractions and spend an extended period at the foot of God's throne, communing with Him. Let us also allow ourselves the time for free expression of an outpouring of praise. Whatever form our praise assumes, let us bless His name, exalt His virtues, and glorify Him for the wonders He has wrought. Let us honor Him as the King of kings and Lord of Lords, magnify His grace in the awesome gift of our salvation, and "worship the LORD in the beauty of holiness" (Psalm 96:9; also see Revelation 19:16). Let us praise Him with the absence of embarrassment or self-consciousness that David displayed. As part of our regular prayer habits, let us devote some of the time that we spend with the Lord simply to praising Him.

For anyone who may desire to incorporate readings from the Psalms as heartfelt praises in personal prayer practices, here is a sampling of psalms that are well suited to the purpose:

- General Praise: to "hold high" God's character
  Psalms 8, 19, 29, 92, 95-98, 103, 104, 139, 145, 148, 150

- Specific Praise: to praise the Lord for particular actions, attributes, or gifts
  Psalms 33, 36, 66, 105, 111, 113, 117, 135, 136, 146, 147

---

[29] succinctly (O): expressed briefly and clearly; concisely

Day 7 — Intercession

Intercession could be described as the "work" of prayer, in a manner of speaking, though not in any negative sense. This type of prayer involves petition or entreaty[30] *in favor of others*: individuals or groups; Christians or the unregenerate. Intercession can *feel* like work because, to be genuine, it must be completely selfless. As a result, there is no self-interest motivating us to engage in it. When we act out of potential or probable benefit to ourselves, in reality we are only obeying the impulses of our carnal natures. In other words, self-interest comes naturally to us.

But acting selflessly is an expression of love. This is not the emotional kind of love that the world usually intends when using that word. Instead, this is a volitional[31] and self-sacrificial love that is an aspect of "the fruit of the Spirit" (Galatians 5:22). Such *agape* love is the kind that God demonstrates toward His Creation, particularly in giving His Son as a sacrifice for our sin (see Romans 5:8). We have read previously that "the flesh lusts against the Spirit, and the Spirit against the flesh; and these are contrary to one another" (Galatians 5:17). In a comparable way, the self-denying love of God is opposed to the self-interested type of love that comes to us naturally.

Intercession can feel like work because it is a manifestation of the *agape* love implanted in our hearts by the Holy Spirit. As the Apostle Paul wrote to the Romans, "...the love of God has been poured out in our hearts by the Holy Spirit who was given to us" (5:5). With the Spirit indwelling us, we are enabled to exhibit God's type of love. We can deny ourselves and display love for others by petitioning the Lord on their behalf. But this intercession will continue to feel like work, at least some of the time, for as long as we reside in these bodies and our flesh persists in striving against the Spirit. For this reason (among others), we need to heed Paul's counsel:

> "For...our old man was crucified with Him, that the body of sin might be done away with, that we should no longer be slaves of sin. For he who has died has been freed from sin.... Likewise you also, reckon yourselves to be dead indeed to sin, but alive to God in Christ Jesus our Lord....
>
> Therefore, brethren, we are debtors—not to the flesh, to live according to the flesh. For if you live according to the flesh you will die; but if by the Spirit you put to death the deeds of the body, you will live" (Romans 6:5, 6, 11; 8:12-13).

How do we subdue the pressures of our flesh that drive us to act out of self-interest and not self-sacrificially? By the Spirit. Or, to phrase the matter in

---

[30] entreaty (O): an earnest or emotional request
[31] volitional (O): made according to one's own will (a choice or decision)

different terms, how do we consistently demonstrate God's love for others by interceding faithfully on their behalf? By the Spirit. "And those who are Christ's have crucified the flesh with its passions and desires. If we live in the Spirit, let us also walk in the Spirit" (Galatians 5:24-25). Think about what it means for the flesh to be "crucified." If those "passions and desires" were nailed to a cross, then how can we heed them any longer?

So far we have seen how intercessory prayer can *feel* like work because it involves self-sacrifice: a denial of self-interest; a choice to consider our flesh dead by crucifixion. But intercession can also **be** work in a literal sense. When we intercede, we choose to entreat the Lord in favor of others through an application of will. If that exercise of will were something that we only had to do once, and that single choice would then carry through the duration of our prayer, then intercession would not *be* work, however it may feel. We could simply decide to petition God on behalf of a particular person or group—for instance, our national government—then pray for as long as we desired about different aspects of our subject. Such prayer could still be essentially selfless, so it might *feel* like work, but it would not really *be* work. As virtually all Christians can agree, however, the will does not operate that way.

One of the great challenges of intercessory prayer is that it requires continual renewal of the conscious and self-denying choice to entreat the Lord in favor of other people. More than any of the other facets of fully-formed prayer, intercession entails an almost continuous application of our wills. In other words, not only must we choose to intercede on behalf of others, but we must also *keep* choosing to persist with that selfless prayer. Such is the strength of opposition that we encounter from our own flesh and from our spiritual adversaries that our wills swiftly falter. Our self-interest almost immediately reasserts itself. And that being the case, we are forced to renew, more or less continually, our resolve to bring the concerns and the welfare of other people before God's throne.

All of this might seem like unnecessary hair-splitting. But it is important for us to understand that intercession is basically the *work* of a well-developed prayer life so that we engage in the practice with our "eyes" open. Many Christians recognize the value of "effective, fervent prayer" (James 5:16). But when it comes to cultivating that kind of prayer in their own lives, they are thwarted by obstacles and the resistance that they must overcome. Some perceive the usefulness of composing a "prayer list" of individuals and groups for whom they desire to intercede regularly. But when they try to put those lists to use, they become discouraged by the antagonism of both their flesh and their spiritual enemies. As a result, they only make it partway through their prayer lists before they discontinue their petitioning out of sheer exasperation.

This experience of aborted attempts at intercessory prayer—or one similar to it—is not uncommon. But we have to keep in mind that our past frustrations and failures when trying to use prayer lists do not mean that such lists are ineffectual[32] in themselves. On the contrary, they can be (and usually are) an excellent method for helping to sustain our focus and to return our attention to the task of interceding when something diverts us. Recall from our study on day 2, "Places for Prayer," that a "prayer closet" or a relatively secluded natural setting can be of tremendous benefit. Such places enable us to be alone with the Lord, with minimal distractions. And just as choosing an appropriate location can serve to *minimize* distractions, creating and using a prayer list can help to *counteract* distractions when they do occur.

We simply need to remember that the barriers to prolonged intercession are inherent to the act of interceding. There is no getting around them—at least, not without the aid of the Holy Spirit, as the Bible attests. Even as we commit to interceding for other people, "...the Spirit Himself makes intercession for us with groanings which cannot be uttered. Now He who searches the hearts knows what the mind of the Spirit is, because He makes intercession for the saints according to the will of God" (Romans 8:26-27). Consider what profound relief this short statement supplies! The Holy Spirit, who dwells within all of God's children, knows us infinitely better than we know ourselves. And He instantaneously communicates the complete content of our hearts through His indivisible oneness with the Father. What awesome assurance and comfort this should be to us! Bearing these truths in mind should help us to maintain the proper attitude when we entreat the Lord in favor of others. And the correct frame of mind, paired with an orderly prayer list, will assist us in persevering with intercessory prayer, whatever our flesh and our spiritual adversaries might do to try to defeat us. ("Persistence in Prayer" is discussed on day 18.)

Let us accept the rather self-evident biblical truth that intercession is a critical component of any fully-formed prayer practice. And let us also acknowledge that intercession is one of the most demanding or even difficult types of prayer in which Christians might engage. For whom and for what, then, are we supposed to intercede? Do we simply ask God to transform all the hearts of the unregenerate in the world and leave the rest to Him? Obviously that is not a serious question. But to provide some substance to our petitions, let us examine what the Scriptures teach regarding the practical dimensions of intercessory prayer. We will begin by reviewing those *people* for whom God's Word directs us to intercede.

In a poignant[33] scene from Luke's Gospel, Jesus warned Peter about some troubling events that would soon transpire:

"And the Lord said, 'Simon, Simon! Indeed, Satan has asked for you, that he may sift you as wheat. But I have prayed for you, that your faith should

---

[32] ineffectual (O): not answering its purpose or sufficient to produce an effect
[33] poignant (C): affecting one's feelings sharply or keenly

not fail; and when you have returned to Me, strengthen your brethren'" (22:31-32).

In this remarkable statement, Jesus, an individual, indicated that He had interceded for Simon Peter, another individual and an apostle (a saint). Specifically, Christ prayed for Peter's faith to be sustained when he was tried by the enemy. Elsewhere, Jesus petitioned His Father on behalf of all His disciples (John 17). And in the most *selfless* intercession imaginable, He prayed for the men who crucified Him (Luke 23:34). How many of us would do the same?

Turning from our Savior to "the least of the apostles", Paul proclaimed in his Epistle to the Romans, "Brethren, my heart's desire and prayer to God for Israel is that they may be saved" (10:1; also see 1 Corinthians 15:9). Here Paul, an apostle of Jesus Christ, wrote about praying for a large group of non-Christians, collectively known as "Israel." In particular, he entreated the Lord to **save** them, indicating further that this request stemmed from an earnest desire within his heart. (Recall what he wrote earlier in the letter about "He who searches the hearts"—8:27.) To understand a bit more clearly how this declaration might relate to our own experience, we can take a little liberty with the language: "Brethren, my heart's desire and prayer to God for [Americans] is that they may be saved." And other broad categories of unbelievers could also be substituted with equal validity.

How desperately we should plead for our Sovereign Lord to work in the hearts of our unregenerate countrymen! How we need Him to spur them to repentance and to ignite a revival in our nation, which increasingly opposes Him!

> "Revival brings the searching of hearts on the part of professed Christians, a radical transformation of individual, domestic, and social life, when the Spirit of God is poured out in reality and power…. We should pray for a revival because we cannot endure the dishonor of God caused by the worldliness of the church, the sins of unbelievers, and the proud unbelief of the day…. We should pray for revival so that God may be glorified by the outpouring of His Spirit on the church of Christ…. It is surely time for the Lord to work, for men have made void His law. The voice of the Lord given in the written Word is made void both by the world and the Church" (Torrey 33,64,65,83; also read Psalm 119:126).

Roughly half of Paul's epistles begin with statements that he and his companions interceded for the churches or individuals to whom those letters were addressed (Ephesians 1:15-19; Philippians 1:3-5,9-11; Colossians 1:3,9-11; 1 Thessalonians 1:2; 2 Thessalonians 1:11-12; 2 Timothy 1:3; Philemon 4-6).

Since it is not necessary to prove that God's children are supposed to intercede for their brothers and sisters, let us review instead *what* the first Christians prayed in favor of their brethren. By doing so, we can develop a concrete idea of what we should ask the Lord on behalf of saints in the modern day. But in view of the number of passages which could be cited here, we will include a selection of particularly illustrative examples. And since they are all rather lengthy, we will record them together in sequence and discuss their contents afterward:

> "Therefore I also...do not cease to give thanks for you, making mention of you in my prayers: that the God of our Lord Jesus Christ, the Father of glory, may give to you the spirit of wisdom and revelation in the knowledge of Him, the eyes of your understanding being enlightened; that you may know what is the hope of His calling, what are the riches of the glory of His inheritance in the saints, and what is the exceeding greatness of His power toward us who believe..." (Ephesians 1:15-19).

> "For this reason I bow my knees to the Father of our Lord Jesus Christ, from whom the whole family in heaven and earth is named, that He would grant you, according to the riches of His glory, to be strengthened with might through His Spirit in the inner man, that Christ may dwell in your hearts through faith; that you, being rooted and grounded in love, may be able to comprehend...the love of Christ which passes knowledge; that you may be filled with all the fullness of God" (Ephesians 3:14-18,19).

> "And this I pray, that your love may abound still more and more in knowledge and all discernment, that you may approve the things that are excellent, that you may be sincere and without offense till the day of Christ, being filled with the fruits of righteousness which are by Jesus Christ, to the glory and praise of God" (Philippians 1:9-11).

> "For this reason we also do not cease to pray for you, and to ask that you may be filled with the knowledge of His will in all wisdom and spiritual understanding; that you may walk worthy of the Lord, fully pleasing Him, being fruitful in every good work and increasing in the knowledge of God; strengthened with all might, according to His glorious power, for all patience and longsuffering with joy; giving thanks to the Father who has qualified us to be partakers of the inheritance of the saints in the light" (Colossians 1:9-12).

All of the petitions recorded here can be prayed *by* any Christian *for* any Christian—individually or corporately[34]. And these are in addition to any *specific* issues, concerns, and trials among our brethren for which we entreat the Lord. Undeniably, the body of Christ would be vastly more unified and

---

[34] corporately (O): characteristic of being united in a group

more effective in the world if all of God's true children sincerely prayed this way for each other. In the modern church, one of the principal reasons that we do not have God's power operating in, among, and through us—to the degree that we could—is that we either fail to ask or we ask amiss (see James 4). If we would but ask in faith with true hearts, "laboring fervently... in prayers" on behalf of God's family, undoubtedly we would be amazed by the awesome working of the Lord that we would witness (Colossians 4:12). ("Faith as a Prerequisite to Prayer" is examined in detail on day 11.)

Summing up much scriptural teaching on the subject of intercession, Paul wrote to his "son Timothy":

> "Therefore I exhort first of all that supplications, prayers, intercessions, and giving of thanks be made for all men, for kings and all who are in authority, that we may lead a quiet and peaceable life in all godliness and reverence [or dignity]. For this is good and acceptable in the sight of God our Savior, who desires all men to be saved and to come to the knowledge of the truth" (1 Timothy 1:18; 2:1-4).

For those who are *not* saved, we should ask that they will "come to the knowledge of the truth" and become Christians, trusting Jesus as their Savior and surrendering to Him as their Lord (remember John 14:6). For those who *are* saved, we can pray for everything that we covered from Paul's epistles, as well as for individual needs and requests. And for all who occupy positions of authority, we should petition God to direct those people in such a way as to preserve liberty and justice in a well-ordered society. Obviously, these categories are very broad. We will have to follow the Spirit's guidance in discerning exactly for whom we should intercede, as well as specifically how to entreat the Lord on their behalf.

Paul's encouragement to Timothy should impress upon us just how important intercessory prayer truly is. Granted, "all men" is a tremendously large group, encompassing[35] all of humanity. Some refinement of our prayer lists will inevitably have to occur as our prayer practices become more regular and habitual. But the Holy Spirit will help us to determine both the subjects and the content of our entreaties with time and consistency. Plus He helps us, anyway, wherever we come up short in our prayers, beyond compensating for our deficiencies by interceding for us. We simply need to persevere in praying for other people, even though it may feel like work, and even though we might become frustrated by the efforts of our flesh and our spiritual adversaries to defeat us. As we have seen, committing to this type of prayer requires self-denial, which is an aspect of *agape* love—godly love.

---

[35] encompassing (CO): surrounding, encircling, enclosing

We will conclude this exploration of intercession with a final word from Paul, whose inspired writings have largely shaped our investigation of the subject: "Let nothing be done through selfish ambition or conceit, but in lowliness of mind let each esteem others better than himself. Let each of you look out not only for his own interests, but also for the interests of others" (Philippians 2:3-4). When we adopt a Christ-like approach of service to other people, instead of the carnal attitude of putting ourselves first, it becomes much easier to intercede in favor of "all men" and women as part of our daily prayer practices.

For convenience and ease of reference, the entreaties from page 61 were simplified into the following list. When interceding, we can ask the Lord to:

- give Christians "the spirit of wisdom and revelation in the knowledge of Him."
- enlighten "the eyes of…understanding" of fellow believers.
- provide His children with knowledge of…
  - ➤ "the hope of His calling."
  - ➤ "the riches of the glory of His inheritance in the saints."
  - ➤ "the exceeding greatness of His power toward us who believe."
- grant to His sons and daughters...
  - ➤ "to be strengthened with might through His Spirit in the inner man [or woman]."
  - ➤ "that Christ may dwell in [their] hearts through faith."
  - ➤ that they will be "rooted and grounded in love."
  - ➤ that they "may be able to comprehend the love of Christ which passes knowledge."
  - ➤ that they "may be filled with all the fullness of God."
- expand the love of the body of Christ so that it will "abound still more and more in knowledge and all discernment."
- order believers' hearts to "approve the things that are excellent."
- make His people "sincere and without offense till the day of Christ."
- fill our brethren "with the fruits of righteousness which are by Jesus Christ, to the glory and praise of God."
- instruct Christians in "the knowledge of His will in all wisdom and spiritual understanding."
- direct His children to "walk worthy of the Lord, fully pleasing Him."
- guide believers to become "fruitful in every good work."
- ensure that the saints are always "increasing in the knowledge of God."
- fortify the body of Christ so that it is "strengthened with all might, according to His glorious power, for all patience and longsuffering with joy."

These intercessions were excerpted from Ephesians 1:15-19; 3:14-19; Philippians 1:9-11; Colossians 1:9-12.

Day 8 — Supplication or Petition

Charles Haddon Spurgeon is credited with saying that "God has given to mankind a license to beg." His observation highlights an important point. The Lord does not simply *invite* His children to bring their requests to Him. Much more than that, He *commands* us to ask Him for our needs and for the longings of our hearts. But of all His commandments, this one should be the easiest to obey. Asking for what we need and want comes naturally to us. And Mr. Spurgeon's statement hints at that fact. We are already predisposed to seek the fulfillment of our desires, the thinking goes. So once we are reconciled to God through Jesus Christ, our Father throws open the door for us to deliver all of our requests to Him (see Romans 5:10-11).

Before we explore what the Bible records concerning supplication and petition, we should briefly address the distinction between the two terms. Granted, they *are* very similar, which is why we are discussing them at the same time. Yet they are not synonymous[36]. As a general statement of the difference, we can say that supplication is a *type* of petition, while petition is not necessarily supplication. They are translated from discrete Greek words, each of which carries separate connotations[37]. "Supplication," both in the biblical Greek and in English, conveys a sense of emotional intensity. It implies earnestness, zeal, or even desperation, none of which are indicated by the word "petition." When used as a verb, that term just means "to ask"— again, in both Greek and English. Strictly on the basis of these definitions, we can already begin to appreciate how they differ from each other. But the distinction between the two words becomes even more apparent when we look at examples of how they are used in Scripture.

The Epistle to the Hebrews elaborates in marvelous detail on the High Priesthood of Jesus, "who, in the days of His flesh, when He had offered up prayers and supplications, with vehement cries and tears to Him who was able to save Him from death, and was heard because of His godly fear..." (5:7). The way that the phrase "prayers and supplications" is used in this passage, it becomes apparent that supplications are a different *type* of prayer. Otherwise the phrase would be needlessly redundant. That understanding combines with the mention of "vehement cries and tears" to communicate the intense emotion associated with supplication. In addition to these indicators, the specific *phrase* "prayers and supplications" is peppered generously throughout the Bible. Such widespread use of that particular pairing helps to emphasize further the distinctiveness of supplication as a type of petition.

---

[36] synonymous (C): having the same meaning
[37] connotations (O): implied meanings in addition to the primary meanings

Contrasting with the earnestness of supplication, an appearance of the word "petition" in 1 John 5:14-15 can be considered representative of how it is used in Scripture: "Now this is the confidence that we have in Him, that if we ask anything according to His will, He hears us. And if we know that He hears us, whatever we ask, we know that we have the petitions that we have asked of Him." ("Prayer According to God's Will" is addressed at length on day 15.) In this passage from one of the Apostle John's epistles, "petitions" is used as a blanket reference to represent in a general way all requests that we make of the Lord: "whatever we ask." The tone of John's statement also lacks any of the emotional vigor that we identify with supplication. Although the truth that he spoke of is certainly wonderful and profound, he wrote about it in something like a matter-of-fact style.

The clear distinction between supplication and petition is well evidenced in both testaments of the Bible. In other words, the difference of meaning is present in *both* the Hebrew and Greek originals. To observe the raw emotion and, frequently, the acute distress that supplication implies, we need to look no further than the Book of Psalms:

> "To You I will cry, O LORD my Rock:
> Do not be silent to me,
> Lest, if You are silent to me,
> I become like those who go down to the pit.
> Hear the voice of my supplications
> When I cry to You,
> When I lift up my hands toward Your holy sanctuary" (28:1-2).

> "Out of the depths I have cried to You, O LORD;
> Lord, hear my voice!
> Let your ears be attentive
> To the voice of my supplications" (130:1-2).

Undoubtedly, many Christians can easily relate to the feelings expressed by these impassioned musical prayers. And that is precisely the point. That is why the Psalms resonate at such a deep level with so many saints. The full spectrum of human emotion is reflected in a variety of ways in that book.

Anyone who has studied what the Scriptures chronicle of the life of David will not be surprised by how many of the psalms are attributed to him. In the course of his life, he experienced the loftiest highs as well as the most agonizing lows. That being the case, we can usually locate a poem among those he composed that directly targets the feelings we are having at any given time. In fact, it is remarkable just how closely David's life of walking with the Lord harmonizes with the peculiar challenges of living as an obedient Christian in the modern age.

Psalm 143 is a particularly striking example of this correlation[38]. The whole psalm is essentially one extended supplication, though it does incorporate the actual term as well. In the inspired words that David penned, he probably intended real people when he referred to "the enemy" and his "enemies" (verses 3,4,12). But with the biblical understanding that God has revealed to us of who our *true* enemies are, many of us can echo what David wrote with equally intense feelings:

> "Hear my prayer, O LORD,
> Give ear to my supplications!
> In Your faithfulness answer me,
> And in Your righteousness.
> Do not enter into judgment with Your servant,
> For in Your sight no one living is righteous.
> For the enemy has persecuted my soul;
> He has crushed my life to the ground;
> He has made me dwell in darkness,
> Like those who have long been dead.
> Therefore my spirit is overwhelmed within me;
> My heart within me is distressed....
> Answer me speedily, O LORD;
> My spirit fails!
> Do not hide Your face from me,
> Lest I be like those who go down to the pit....
> Deliver me, O LORD, from my enemies;
> In You I take shelter....
> In Your mercy cut off my enemies,
> And destroy all those who afflict my soul;
> For I am Your servant" (verses 1-4,7,9,12).

In the context of spiritual warfare and the field of battle on which we fight, our enemies are indeed formidable[39]. They are fierce and violent and full of intense contempt for God and His people. To whatever extent they are allowed, they will "persecute" and "afflict" our souls. They will seek to overwhelm our spirits and cause our resistance to wither. And they will strive to crush our lives "to the ground," if possible. The situation seems dire when we only consider what we are up against and nothing else. And that is exactly what "the enemy" desires! He wants us to become so "distressed" that we despair of victory and withdraw from the battle.

But Christian soldiers have assets that are far superior to anything the enemy might deploy. For one thing, the Eternal God, the Sovereign and omnipotent

---

[38] correlation (O): a systematic comparison or connection
[39] formidable (O): inspiring fear or awe; difficult to overcome

Lord of the universe, is our "shelter." As long as we take refuge in Him, our defenses against the assaults of our adversaries are impervious[40] to attack:

> "'No weapon formed against you shall prosper,
> And every tongue which rises against you in judgment
> You shall condemn.
> This is the heritage of the servants of the LORD,
> And their righteousness is from Me,'
> Says the LORD" (Isaiah 54:17).

The Almighty turns the weapons of our spiritual enemies, bending and blunting and breaking them, leaving us unharmed (but not unchanged). Though we, His "servants," engage in clamorous[41] warfare, He shields us from sustaining any serious wounds. More than that, He blankets us with *His own* righteousness. Among other things, that means we cannot be killed! We become, in a word, immortal. (To be clear, we are speaking here of **spiritual** wounds and death). And as if that is not enough sweetness to satisfy His boundless grace, He goes a step further and adopts His "servants" as His own children! (Romans 8:29; Ephesians 1:3-6).

What is a common reaction among children when they are threatened or scared? They cry out for their father to help them! Just as God has brought us into His family, He has also opened a way for us to call to Him when we are assailed by the enemy and his wicked minions. "For you did not receive the spirit of bondage again to fear, but you received the Spirit of adoption by whom we cry out, 'Abba, Father'" (Romans 8:15). In David's poetic supplications in the Psalms, he called for the Lord, his Father and ours, to rush to his aid in the midst of his distress. He knew from Whom his salvation came (see, for example, Psalm 27). His Father was his sole protector and deliverer, his shelter and his rescue. Just the "sight" of his Father's face was a tremendous comfort to his "persecuted soul." "Do not hide Your face from me," he pleaded.

Charles Spurgeon expressed these truths beautifully in his characteristically grand style:

> "The longing desire of an afflicted child of God is once more to see his Father's face. His first prayer is 'Oh that I knew where I might find Him—who is my God—that I might come even to His seat!'

---

[40] impervious (O): cannot be penetrated
[41] clamorous (C): noisy, boisterous

God's children run home when the storm comes on. It is the heaven-born instinct of a glorious soul to seek shelter from all ills beneath the wings of Jehovah" ("Effective Prayer" 3).

As we established earlier in the book, every human being is present on the spiritual battlefield on one of only two sides. And for those of us who "fight the good fight of faith" as God's children, the help of our Omnipotent Commander is but a prayer away (1 Timothy 6:12; also Psalm 46).

Recall the imaginary battlefield from the Prologue. A Christian soldier kneels amid the tumult of war and mouths words silently, and suddenly a staggering volley of projectiles streaks through the sky. At the same time, brilliantly flaming chariots and horses stream forward and surround the kneeling figure. As is probably apparent by now, the prayers that the afflicted soldier uttered were supplications and petitions. And the imagery of that scene illustrates how readily the Lord responds when His children cry to Him:

> "The eyes of the LORD are on the righteous,
> And His ears are open to their cry….
> The righteous cry out, and the LORD hears,
> And delivers them out of all their troubles.
> The LORD is near to those who have a broken heart,
> And saves such as have a contrite spirit.
> Many are the afflictions of the righteous,
> But the LORD delivers him out of them all" (Psalm 34:15,17-19).

Our Father God, the Almighty, hastens to the help of His children when we "cry out" to Him: He is "near," He "hears," He "delivers," He "saves." But as verse 18 declares, the condition of our hearts when we pray is critically important.

Consider well the following truth: If the attitude of our hearts when we petition the Lord is not humble and dependent and surrendered, then, *in effect*, our hearts are telling God that we do not need His help at the same time that we are asking for it. In such circumstances, can we really expect to receive what we request? If we encounter an apparently homeless person begging for money while wearing designer clothes and gold jewelry, how likely is it that we will provide any assistance? In a comparable way, when we ask the Eternal God for anything, we need to ensure that our hearts are correctly prepared:

> "As a petitioner coming into court does not come there without thought to state his case on the spur of the moment, but enters into the audience chamber with his suit well prepared, having also learned how he ought to behave himself in the presence of the great one to whom he is appealing; so it is well to approach the seat of the King of kings as much as possible with premeditation and preparation, knowing what we are about, where we are standing, and what it is which we desire to obtain. In times of peril and

distress, we may fly to God just as we are, as the dove enters the cleft of the rock, even though her plumes are ruffled; but in ordinary times we should not come with an unprepared spirit..." ("Effective Prayer" 7).

So wrote Mr. Spurgeon in a sermon of 1866. In his typically astute fashion, he conveyed through analogy how necessary it is to approach the Lord with our hearts and spirits properly prepared, as much as possible. (Reflect on what Psalm 143 indicates about David's heart and spirit.)

James echoed this principle in a passage that we touched on previously: "Yet you do not have because you do not ask. You ask and do not receive, because you ask amiss, that you may spend it on your pleasures" (4:3). In the words of R.A. Torrey, "Prayer is God's appointed way for obtaining things. The reason we lack anything in life is due to neglect of prayer.... The true purpose in prayer is that God may be glorified in the answer. If we ask any petition merely to receive something to use for our pleasure or gratification, we 'ask amiss' and should not expect to receive what we ask" (7,63). Gathering all that we have studied about supplication and petition to this point, we are now able to state a categorical[42] truth about these types of prayer: **that** we ask is imperative, yet **how** and **why** we ask are also important.

We will conclude our examination of these aspects of fully-formed prayer, as well as this section of the book, with a sobering observation. Certainly, it is easy to see how we stand to benefit from these components of prayer. We have an undeniably powerful motivator, in the form of self-interest, compelling us to present our requests to the Lord. But beyond that factor, there is the inescapable truth that God's Word commands us to ask: "Be anxious for nothing, but in everything by prayer and supplication, with thanksgiving, let your requests be made known to God; and the peace of God, which surpasses all understanding, will guard your hearts and minds through Christ Jesus" (Philippians 4:6-7). In another excerpt from Paul's discourse on "the whole armor of God," central to our theme of spiritual warfare, he concluded his inspired directives with a call to prayer: "...praying always with all prayer and supplication in the Spirit, being watchful to this end with all perseverance and supplication for all the saints..." (Ephesians 6:18). (Note in passing the appearance in both passages of the phrase "prayer and supplication.") Other scriptures that reinforce the commandment to ask will be cited in tomorrow's lesson, "The Model Prayer," in which that theme is briefly revisited.

Do we really need any encouragement to submit our requests to God? It seems more likely that we would need to be discouraged from devoting *too much* time to asking, at the expense of other types of prayer. Still, supplication and petition are important dimensions of a mature and fully-developed prayer practice. As such, these elements of prayer are altogether essential if our prayer habits in

---

[42] categorical (O): absolute, unconditional

general are going to be both effective and fervent. The plain truth of the matter is that, without these aspects of prayer well represented in our lives, we have virtually no hope of "pulling down strongholds" of the enemy (2 Corinthians 10:4). We will not achieve victories on behalf of our Commander, the Lord Jesus Christ. In such circumstances, our effectiveness as Christian soldiers would be severely diminished. But through petition and the awesome power of God that we solicit, there is no telling what marvelous wonders the Almighty will work in and through us. "There is always an open ear if you have an open mouth. There is always a ready hand if you have a ready heart. You have but to cry and the Lord hears; nay, before you call He will answer, and while you are speaking He will hear" ("True Prayer" 22).

General Considerations Concerning Prayer

Day 9 — The Model Prayer

Over the past eight days, we have constructed a stout framework of prayer practice. For the sake of illustration, we might compare that structure to an ordinary suburban residence. We erected exterior walls, attached a roof system, and installed doors and windows in the first three days: The Logistics of Biblical Prayer. With those pieces in place, our building was strong and sealed up against the "weather." But on their own, those basic elements hardly constituted anything that could be considered a *home*. Much more was still needed for the edifice to serve in that capacity. So in the five subsequent days, we divided the interior space into individual "rooms": Various Aspects of Christian Prayer. We called those distinct areas thanksgiving, confession, praise, intercession, and supplication or petition. We might compare those to the separate spaces that commonly occur in many residential buildings: kitchen, bathroom, bedroom, living (or sitting) room, and perhaps a study or a den.

At this point, with all of the "rooms" defined in our imagined prayer house, the inside of the structure is beginning to resemble a standard, humble dwelling. And it would probably fulfill that purpose in a pinch. But more is still required for this partitioned shell to feel like—and to become—a true *home*. Throughout the next sixteen lessons, we will bring in the furnishings, attach the fixtures, and connect the appliances that will transform this simple edifice into a genuine home. By the end of day 24, we should have arrived at a thorough understanding of what effective and fervent prayer entails. And if we have adhered faithfully to everything that we have unearthed from God's Word along the way, then we should be in a position to approach the final section, "Obstacles to Effective Prayer," with a fully-formed and vibrant prayer practice already in place.

The Model Prayer that Jesus taught to His disciples functions as a perfect bridge between the previous section and the current one. It contains references to the various aspects of prayer in a concise and memorable package. In fact, so much significance is represented by that one prayer that it could easily fill up an entire book by itself. For our purposes, though, we will try to do justice to The Lord's Prayer in a single lesson. And we begin by reviewing the text of The Model Prayer as it appears in Matthew's Gospel:

> "Our Father in heaven,
> Hallowed be Your name.
> Your kingdom come
> Your will be done
> On earth as it is in heaven.

Give us this day our daily bread.
And forgive us our debts,
As we forgive our debtors.
And lead us not into temptation,
But deliver us from the evil one.
For Yours is the kingdom and the power and the glory forever. Amen"
(6:9-13).

Before we examine the specific content of the prayer more closely, however, a few general observations need to be included. First, Luke's Gospel informs us that Jesus taught this prayer to His disciples in response to their request: "Lord, teach us to pray, as John also taught his disciples" (11:1). Theirs was a perfectly legitimate petition, and one that *should* be presented by all genuine Christians in the modern era. As Mr. Spurgeon observed, "Prayer itself is an art which only the Holy [Spirit] can teach us. He is the giver of all prayer. Pray for prayer. Pray till you can pray. Pray to be helped to pray. And give not up praying because you cannot pray, for it is when you think you cannot pray that you are most praying" ("Effective Prayer" 13). And R.A. Torrey agreed: "The earnestness that we work up in the energy of the flesh is a repulsive thing. The earnestness created in us by the Holy Spirit is pleasing to God. Here again, if we desire to pray correctly, we must look to the Spirit of God to teach us how to pray" (27). The accomplished work of Christ enables us to approach God in prayer in the first place. Then the Holy Spirit, whom the Father sends in Jesus's name, teaches us *how* to pray as we grow in our respective relationships with Him (John 14:26). And this brings us to our second general observation.

When Jesus responded to His disciples' request, He specifically instructed them, "In this manner, therefore, pray…" (Matthew 6:9). Jesus was teaching His disciples **how** to pray, not **what** to pray. The importance of recognizing that truth cannot be overestimated. The Lord's Prayer is not some kind of magical incantation that grows in power and effectiveness through repetition. In fact, Jesus directly denounced the tendency to use repetition in the futile and groundless hope of being answered: "And when you pray, do not use vain repetitions as the heathen do. For they think that they will be heard for their many words" (verse 7; also refer to 1 Kings 18:20-39).

In the centuries since Jesus walked the earth, such "vain repetitions" in prayer have infiltrated some segments of professing Christians. Some people repeat The Lord's Prayer numerous times. Others use another prayer such as the so-called "Jesus Prayer" or the once-popular "Prayer of Jabez" (1 Chronicles 4:10). Understand, saints, true sons and daughters of the Almighty: Repeating a particular prayer again and again is un-Christian. It is contrary to the teachings of Scripture. And, more to the point, it is **evil.** Before anyone protests these facts, a third observation needs to be inserted, which is related to the second.

Praying persistently is altogether different from using "vain repetitions." ("Persistence in Prayer" is discussed on day 18.) Vain repetition involves saying the same words over and over, like a spell or an incantation. Such pagan practices have no place in biblical Christianity. But that does not mean that reciting the words of The Lord's Prayer, for example, is *inherently* wicked. Nor is it sinful to pray about the same issue repeatedly through the course of time, which is persistence. We must appreciate the critical distinctions among repeating prayers, praying repeatedly, and using vain repetitions. That statement might seem a bit confusing, so let us clarify the difference by looking briefly at a few examples.

If we conclude a church gathering by speaking together the words of The Lord's Prayer, then we are repeating a prayer. By comparison, if we pray every evening with our spouses for the welfare of our children, then we are praying repeatedly. Nothing is wrong with either of these scenarios. But if we utter the words of The Jesus Prayer—"Lord Jesus Christ, Son of God, have mercy upon me, a sinner"—dozens of times in succession, then we are guilty of vain repetitions. We need to know that, in such instances, our prayers will *not* be heard. Scripture is positively pellucid[43] on that point.

Throughout His Word, God makes undeniably clear that His people are to be *set apart* from the world. They are to be holy. They are to be sanctified. Nowhere in the Bible does the Lord condone His people adopting pagan religious customs to be used in worshiping Him. God, and *only* God, prescribes how His people are permitted to approach Him, and what forms of worship are pleasing to Him. This truth is so manifestly evident in both the Old Testament and the New that we will not bother to prove it with citations from Scripture. As a rule, whatever practices and traditions professing Christians may have mingled with authentic, biblical Christianity over the centuries, God's standards have not changed. Moreover, His standards **do not** change! (Malachi 3:6; James 1:17). He alone establishes what is and is not acceptable to Him.

For us to grasp this truth fully is extremely important. Some people hold the mistaken belief that The Lord's Prayer has some kind of extraordinary power. They suppose, usually because they were taught, that reciting The Lord's Prayer a certain number of times somehow elicits favor from God, or that it is effective for absolving[44] a sinner of iniquity. Beloved brothers and sisters, all such teaching is utterly false! It is not only *un*biblical, it is *anti*biblical! The only one pleased by such practices is Satan—and mightily pleased he is, too. Consider how terribly sad this is! These poor people think that they are addressing God in a manner that garners His favor, when in reality their "vain repetitions" grieve the Lord and gladden the devil (refer to Proverbs 28:9).

---

[43] pellucid (C): perfectly clear; transparent
[44] absolving (O): clearing of blame or guilt

The Lord's Prayer is a **model**. It is a paradigm[45] or pattern that indicates what *types* of elements should be included in our prayers, not necessarily the specific words themselves. And that being the case, by analyzing the content of Jesus's prayer, we can learn some valuable truths that will help to make our practices more mature and fully developed—more effective and fervent. We will begin by looking at the salutation[46] in verse 9: "Our Father in heaven...."

What does Jesus teach us by addressing His prayer to "Our Father"? For one thing, He acknowledges that all genuine Christians are His brothers and sisters, sons and daughters of God. Paul confirmed this fact, among other places, in his Epistle to the Galatians: "For you are all sons of God through faith in Christ Jesus.... And because you are sons, God has sent forth the Spirit of His Son into your hearts, crying out, 'Abba, Father'" (3:26; 4:6). As the adopted children of God, the Father, our relationships with Him are not like those of servants to their masters, much less of slaves to their "owners." He does not require us to convince or to cajole[47] Him. Rather, He invites us to come freely to Him, as a loving father welcomes the companionship of his children.

Jesus affirmed, "For your Father knows the things you have need of before you ask Him" (Matthew 6:8). We do not draw near to Him so that we can bring something to His attention of which He is unaware. God knows us *perfectly* (Psalm 139). He knows all of our needs better than we do. Mr. Spurgeon expressed this point in a very compelling way: "There is no need for prayer at all as far as God is concerned, but what a need there is for it on our own account! If we were not constrained to pray, I question whether we could even live as Christians. If God's mercies came to us unasked, they would not be half so useful as they now are, when they have to be sought for; for now we get a double blessing, a blessing in the obtaining, and a blessing in the seeking. The very act of prayer is a blessing" ("Effective Prayer" 14). Think about the profound truth that is communicated here! Our Father does not *need* us to pray, as though His knowledge is somehow incomplete or His hands are restrained from acting (Isaiah 59:1). Prayer is for *our* benefit! The need for prayer is a means of cultivating close relationships between the Father and His children. At the same time, it is a channel through which He continuously showers them with blessings.

We should take care not to stumble into the pitfall of thinking of our Father in heaven as little more than a spiritual or celestial abstraction[48] of an earthly father. In reality, the similarities between human fathers and God the Father are few. With that said, one quality that they both possess, to *infinitely* different degrees, is a loving desire to bless their children with good things. As Jesus stated, "If you then, being evil, know how to give good gifts to your children,

---

[45] paradigm (O): something serving as an example or model of how things should be done
[46] salutation (O): words of greeting; an expression of respect
[47] cajole (CO): to coax; to persuade gradually
[48] abstraction (O): a theoretical rather than practical or material idea

how much more will your Father who is in heaven give good things to those who ask Him!" (Matthew 7:11). Our Father does not have to be pressured or manipulated or pestered into answering our prayers. In fact, all such efforts would be foolish and futile. God's love is altogether selfless, His power unlimited, His knowledge infinite. He invites us—no, stronger than that, He implores us to come to Him, welcoming the approach of His children with sublime love: "Consequently…we shall be humble yet bold petitioners, humbly importuning mercy through the Saviour's blood. We shall not have the reserve of a slave, but the loving reverence of a child, yet not an impudent, impertinent child, but a teachable, obedient child, honouring his Father, and therefore asking earnestly, but with deferential submission to his Father's will" ("Effective Prayer" 9-10).

At first reading, the second line of The Lord's Prayer appears to be an exclamation of praise. In reality, however, "Hallowed be Your name" declares something much different from the initial impression. The verb tense of "Hallowed" in the inspired Greek is *imperative*, meaning that the words could be rendered something like the following: "May Your name be hallowed." And since the term "Hallowed" is somewhat antiquated[49] and might be unfamiliar to many modern readers, we could take the liberty of simplifying the language a bit. "Hallowed" means to be treated as set apart; honored as holy; revered as sacred. By combining these adjustments into a single petition, we can express the second line of The Model Prayer according to the sense of the original Greek and using modern vocabulary: "May Your name be treated as set apart and sacred."

But what does this signify in practice? Do we really expect that the Lord's name will be regarded this way while the world remains in its present state? Of course not! Speaking of society in general, it must be apparent to every serious Christian in the 21st century that God's name is handled with less reverence as time passes. A disturbing number of people habitually use His name profanely, as a curse or in taking rash oaths, without so much as a second thought. But we know perfectly well how *God* views such abuses of His name because He explicitly stated His position: "You shall not take the name of the LORD your God in vain, for the LORD will not hold him guiltless who takes His name in vain" (Exodus 20:7). The third commandment is just as valid and applicable in our day as it was when first spoken by the Almighty. And yet, it is obeyed even less today than it was at that time. That being so, how can we sincerely repeat the intent behind the second line of The Lord's Prayer?

The answer to that question relates to the meaning of "Hallowed be Your name." God's name will be treated as set apart and sacred when, and *only* when, His kingdom has come upon the earth. Very simply defined, a "kingdom" is the area over which a king has dominion. In other words, "king's dominion"

---

[49] antiquated (O): old-fashioned; out of date

becomes "kingdom" through the verbal butchery that commonly occurs with language over time. We can see here how the petition in line two of The Lord's Prayer connects directly to line three: "Your kingdom come" (verse 10). When Jesus prayed "Hallowed be Your name," He was asking that the Father would make His name to be treated as set apart and sacred, as it will be when His kingdom is established on earth at the Second Coming of Christ (Zechariah 14:9). (This is illustrated in much Bible prophecy that is beyond the scope of this book; for example, Revelation 17-22.) "Father," Jesus prayed in effect, "bring to this earth Your supreme kingdom that You have promised. And make Your name to be treated as holy, the name above all names" (see Romans 14:11; Philippians 2:9-11; Hebrews 2:5,8).

Notwithstanding that the ultimate fulfillment of lines two and three must await the Second Coming of Christ, there is a sense in which His name is *already* hallowed and His kingdom has *already* come. Jesus is King in the hearts of all who are genuinely His. In our day, that designation refers to all **authentic** Christians (Psalm 74:12; Isaiah 33:22; 1 Timothy 1:17). Many call Him Lord who are not surrendered to Him in loving obedience of His commandments. Thus He is not their King, and they are not true Christians (see Matthew 7:21-23). All who are sincerely saved should already strive to serve Him as their King and keep His commandments, including hallowing His name.

The same principle of partial fulfillment that we observe in lines two and three also applies to the next two lines of The Model Prayer—four and five:

"Your will be done on earth as it is in heaven" (verse 10).

These lines together comprise a single petition. In heaven, God's will is obeyed perfectly. That must be the case because no sin can remain in the presence of His superlative[50] holiness (recall Isaiah 59:2). When Lucifer exalted himself and sinned against the Most High, he was cast out of heaven to the earth (Ezekiel 28:14-17). No taint or contamination of rebellion against God's will is or can be tolerated in His heavenly realm. So is it possible for the same perfect level of obedience to be manifested on earth, where wickedness and every form of perversion abound and Satan's influence appears to be growing daily? Obviously not. But if that standard of adherence to God's will is not presently attainable, then why would we pray for it? Why did Jesus pray for it?

God's will is "done" when His commandments are obeyed. (Different aspects of God's will have to be taken into consideration in this regard, but we will not address them here. "Praying According to God's Will" is examined on day 15.) So for God's will to be done on earth in the same way that it is done in heaven, what needs to happen? The answer, as before, is that God's kingdom must be established on the earth. To the extent that Christians currently obey their

---

[50] superlative (C): of the highest degree or quality

Father's commandments, His will *is* done on earth, so there is a partial and shorter-term dimension to this petition in The Lord's Prayer. But the complete reality of it—the ultimate and perfect fulfillment—arrives only when God's kingdom comes to this earth, with all that it entails, according to the Scriptures. Thus, expanding the modified prayer of Jesus that we inserted earlier, it might read something like this: "Father, bring to this earth Your supreme kingdom that You have promised. Make Your name to be treated as holy, the name above all names. And cause Your will to be obeyed here in the same way that it is in heaven."

Line six of The Model Prayer might seem unnecessary were it not for the fact that Jesus Himself included it: "Give us this day our daily bread" (verse 11). Our Father promises in His Word to provide for our needs, so why should we ask Him for what He has already assured us He will supply? Remember that The Lord's Prayer is a *model*. By incorporating this petition, Jesus taught the importance of bringing **all** of our needs before the Father—not just the requirement of "our daily bread." In doing so, we cultivate and demonstrate an attitude of humble dependence on the Lord for everything we receive. Moreover, asking our Father to supply our needs serves to nurture a thankful heart, which is both necessary and fitting for every genuine child of God. Consider the character of heart that is evidenced in Psalm 123:

"Unto You I lift up my eyes,
O You who dwell in the heavens.
Behold, as the eyes of servants look to the hand of their masters,
As the eyes of a maid to the hand of her mistress,
So our eyes look to the LORD our God,
Until He has mercy on us" (verses 1-2).

When we recognize and appreciate the fact that *everything* we receive from our Creator is a gift of His grace, our hearts should overflow with abundant gratitude (Acts 17:25; James 1:17). And asking God to supply all of our needs as they occur helps to maintain both the correct mental state and a proper heart attitude.

Before we move along to the next portion of The Lord's Prayer, let us look briefly at two other facets of Christ's humble petition: He addressed only *immediate needs* and He used *simple language*. Here again we may defer to the brilliance of Mr. Spurgeon:

"It is not necessary in the [prayer] closet to ask for every supposable good thing; it is not necessary to rehearse the catalogue of every want that you may have, have had, can have, or shall have. Ask for what you now need, and, as a rule, keep to present need; ask for [your] daily bread—what you want now—ask for that. Ask for it plainly, as before God, who does not regard your fine expressions, and to whom your eloquence and oratory will be less than nothing and vanity. You are before the Lord; let your words be few, but let your heart be fervent" ("Effective Prayer" 11-12).

We should take to heart every word of this wise counsel! Petitioning the Father in this way is precisely the approach that Jesus modeled. The next two lines of The Lord's Prayer are very sobering because they concern the related concepts of sin and forgiveness:

"And forgive us our debts,
As we forgive our debtors" (verse 12).

Some versions of the Bible use "trespasses" instead of "debts," but in all cases it is clear that the reference is to sin. The word picture produced by the term "debts" indicates that our sin creates a moral obligation—a debt—that we are unable to repay. And the shocking magnitude of that debt was illustrated powerfully by Jesus in His "Parable of the Unforgiving Servant" (Matthew 18:23-35). (We will examine that parable more closely on day 12, "Forgiveness and Humility.") Asking God to forgive our sins is necessary and sensible, of course. But notice that our forgiveness by God is linked inextricably[51] to our willingness to forgive others for their offenses against us. If we want to grasp the significance of this segment of The Lord's Prayer, then we only need to look to the verses that directly follow the conclusion of the prayer.

After all of the assorted topics that Jesus addressed in His model prayer, to which ones did He return immediately afterward? Sin and forgiveness. "For if you forgive men their trespasses, your heavenly Father will also forgive you. But if you do not forgive men their trespasses, neither will your Father forgive your trespasses" (Matthew 6:14-15). Could that be any more straightforward? Did He leave any space for confusion or misunderstanding? No, Jesus reiterated His point with extreme clarity: "Forgive, or you will not be forgiven!"

But our present subject is not specifically the relationships of people to each other. We are studying "effective, fervent prayer," the sort of mature prayer that "avails much" on the spiritual battlefields of life. We have seen already that confession and repentance are critical components of a fully-formed prayer practice. As Jesus highlighted here, however, confession and repentance will not result in forgiveness for us if we refuse to forgive others. At first reading, that statement sounds contrary to the teaching of the Bible, so consider it from another angle: We cannot withhold forgiveness from others and expect to be forgiven. Moreover, if we desire the kind of prayer life that the Scriptures describe, then we must carefully guard against any failure to "forgive our debtors."

---

[51] inextricably (CO): unable to be disentangled, separated, or sorted out

Moving on to lines nine and ten of The Lord's Prayer, we encounter another pair of connected requests:

"And do not lead us into temptation,
But deliver us from the evil one" (verse 13).

We need to stress here that God *does not* tempt anyone, as James flatly declared in his epistle (1:13-15). The idea behind petitioning God not to "lead us into temptation" in no way suggests that He *produces* the "temptation." The intent, rather, is to solicit the Lord's guidance. We ask Him to direct our steps along a course which will avoid those temptations that are positioned along our paths by the enemy. This is made clear by the second half of the request, in which Jesus asked our Father to "deliver us from the evil one." The word "But" at the beginning of the line indicates that the second line contrasts with the first. In other words, the "temptation" is the work of "the evil one." By leading us not into such "temptation," our Father also acts to "deliver us from the evil one"—and vice versa[52].

Satan schemes and strives constantly to divert us from walking according to God's will. He presents us with an endless array of enticements, trying to lure us into sin (1 Peter 5:8). He knows our weaknesses, our inclinations, the vulnerabilities of our flesh, and what "baits" have been effective against us in the past. Since "we are not ignorant of his devices," we must be watchful and pray for wisdom and direction to navigate a course through the pitfalls that he prepares, without stumbling (2 Corinthians 2:11). To do so, we need to remain always mindful of the nature of our adversaries and of our warfare against them: "For we do not wrestle against flesh and blood, but against principalities, against powers, against the rulers of the darkness of this age, against spiritual hosts of wickedness in the heavenly places" (Ephesians 6:12). Given the terrible forces of evil that are assembled against all Christian soldiers, it is both prudent and necessary for us to seek our Father's divine deliverance.

Lastly, we move forward to take an abbreviated look at the doxology[53] that concludes The Model Prayer:

"For Yours is the kingdom and the power and the glory forever. Amen" (verse 13).

(Some versions of the Bible omit this line for reasons that are beyond the scope of this book. But the New King James Version includes the doxology with valid reason, so we will discuss it.) This statement ascribes[54] glory and praise to God in a meaningful and revealing way. The words themselves appear to be an

---

[52] vice versa (O): the other way around
[53] doxology (CO): a hymn or a set form of words praising God
[54] ascribes (CO): regards as belonging to or characteristic of a person or thing

abridgement or an adaptation by Jesus of a longer doxology that David proclaimed. We find the text recorded in the First Book of Chronicles:

"Yours, O LORD, is the greatness,
The power and the glory,
The victory and the majesty;
For all that is in heaven and in earth is Yours;
Yours is the kingdom, O LORD,
And You are exalted as head over all" (29:11).

Similarities between the two exclamations of praise are certainly easy to recognize. We could explore the parallels at length, including the significance of Christ as the descendent of David as well as the timing of their declarations. But in the interest of wrapping up today's reading, we will content ourselves with pointing out the apparent correlation. Still, more needs to be said to do justice to The Lord's Prayer.

The word "For" at the beginning of line 11 is important in itself. It identifies the basis on which all of the preceding petitions are presented to our Father. "Why do we bring this prayer specifically to *You*, Father? Because 'Yours is the kingdom and the power and the glory forever.' We realize that our prayers should be directed to You, and only to You, for these reasons." Recognizing this truth, what exactly does it mean that God the Father possesses these things?

First, the *kingdom* is God's because He is the "King of kings and Lord of lords" (Revelation 19:16; also Psalms 10:16; 29:10; 95:3; Revelation 17:14; and *many* other passages). Ultimately, **all** dominion is His, whether on earth or in heaven, material or spiritual. He is Sovereign over all, so there is no higher authority to whom we could appeal. (The doxology in First Chronicles expands on this idea.) In accordance with His perfect designs, He permits agents of evil under the headship of Satan to exercise a measure of influence for a limited time. But in no way are those entities able at any time to defy, much less to overrule, the sovereignty of God. Notice, for example, that Satan had to be given permission to afflict Job (1:8-13). Or that, as Jesus related, Satan *asked* to be allowed to "sift" Peter (Luke 22:31).

Second, the *power* belongs to God because He alone is omnipotent—all-powerful. To appreciate better what this means, consider that His power is not merely great beyond measuring or imagining; it is **infinite**. Nothing in the human capacity for abstract thought enables us to dream about beginning to conceive of the awesome extent of His power. And third, the *glory* is His because, quite simply, He is the One True God. There is no other. There is none beside Him (Deuteronomy 4:35; Isaiah 43:10-13; 46:8-10). All glory belongs entirely and exclusively to Him, the Lord Almighty, the Creator, "the blessed and only Potentate" (see 1 Timothy 6:13-16).

In light of these facts, we can see how feckless[55] and foolish it would be for us to present our prayers to anyone *but* God. Why would we appeal to a regional magistrate or a duke when the King invites us to approach Him directly? Or, to frame the question in different terms, why would the sons and daughters of the king address their concerns, their adoration, and their requests to anyone but their father? As Christians, our Father is not just *a* king; He is **the** King. What a privilege it is for us to be able to go straight to the Most High at any time!

Finally, a few words about "Amen." Most Christians—it is probably fair to say—conclude their prayers with the word "Amen." But how many do so with understanding? How many know what the word means, exactly, or why it became customary to end a prayer with it? Without delving too deeply into the linguistic[56] intricacies of Hebrew and Greek, a short explanation of the word's significance is that it was used to mean "so be it." (Compare Numbers 5:22 in the King James Version with the New King James Version.) The term connotes trustworthiness and can also be rendered "surely" or "verily." (Incidentally, the Greek in this case derives from the Hebrew, so they both signify essentially the same thing.)

The Old Testament contains many occurrences of people expressing their agreement with something that was said by responding with "Amen": for example, Deuteronomy 27:15-26; 1 Chronicles 16:36; Nehemiah 8:6. The practice of demonstrating approval in this manner had already become common among the people of Israel by the time of Christ's earthly ministry. Thus, when Jesus concluded His model prayer in this way, He was not instituting a new format. In other words, His model was not a radical departure from, nor a novel approach to, practices that existed before He taught His disciples how to pray. Rather, He perpetuated a custom that was evident among God's people throughout much of their history.

The practice was evidently well-established in the early church by the time of Paul's writing to the Corinthians, a little more than two decades after Christ's ascension. He referred in one letter to people in the congregation saying "Amen" to indicate their agreement with what was said (1 Corinthians 14:16). Elsewhere, in John's vision of the Revelation is a scene which shows that the custom is apparently practiced in heaven also:

> "And every creature which is in heaven and on the earth and under the earth and such as are in the sea, and all that are in them, I heard saying:
> 'Blessing and honor and glory and power
> Be to Him who sits on the throne,
> And to the Lamb, forever and ever!'
> Then the four living creatures said, 'Amen!'" (5:13-14).

---

[55] feckless (CO): worthless, inefficient, feeble, incompetent, irresponsible
[56] linguistic (C): pertaining to languages

And over in 3:14, Jesus is actually *called* "the Amen"! (Think about what that signifies in the light of what the word means.)

Is it absolutely mandatory for us to conclude our prayers with the word "Amen"? Will our prayers be somehow incomplete, or will they not "count," if we neglect to close them in this way? No, of course not. But understanding that God's people have prayed in this manner for at least 3,500 years; appreciating that Jesus continued this custom in His model prayer; recognizing that this practice is evidently followed in heaven: it seems only sensible, a matter of Christian prudence, for us to close our prayers with "Amen" also.

Our study of The Lord's Prayer, as long as it has been, has barely broken through the surface of the mother lode of instruction that could be mined from it. Nonetheless, our examination should be enough to impress upon us the unrivaled importance of consistent and earnest prayer in the lives of all sincere Christians. As Mr. Torrey correctly observed, "A man or woman who does not spend much time in prayer cannot properly be called a follower of Jesus Christ" (9). The Lord taught His disciples *how* to pray in His model prayer. But He also emphasized repeatedly in His teaching how critical avid prayer is to a life of faith, obedience, and service—a Christian life. "Those men whom God set forth as a pattern of what He expected Christians to be—the apostles—regarded prayer as the most important business of their lives" (7-8). Effective and fervent prayer is equally necessary in our time. "Prayer could work as marvelously today as it ever could, if the Church would only take up the call" (106). Let us pray, then, brothers and sisters, Christian soldiers, in accordance with the example established by our Lord Jesus. Let us "be imitators of God as dear children" (Ephesians 5:1). Above all else, let us pray! Amen.

Day 10 — Praying in the Name of Jesus

"Most assuredly, I say to you, he who believes in Me, the works that I do he will do also; and greater works than these he will do, because I go to My Father. And whatever you ask in My name, that I will do, that the Father may be glorified in the Son. If you ask anything in My name, I will do it" (John 14:12-14).

What does it mean to pray in the name of Jesus? Not surprisingly, Charles Spurgeon offered some thoughts that provide a response to this question:

> "'If you need anything of God, all that the Father has belongs to Me; go and use My name.' Suppose you should give a man your cheque book signed with your own name and left blank, to be filled up as he chose; that would be very nearly what Jesus has done in these words, 'If you ask anything in My name I will give it to you....
>
> When you plead the name of Christ you plead that which shakes the gates of hell, and which the hosts of heaven obey, and God Himself feels the sacred power of that divine plea" ("Effective Prayer" 22-23).

These are indeed potent and inspiring words! Elsewhere, R.A. Torrey expressed a similar assessment of the subject, also employing the language of commerce: "To pray in the name of Christ is to pray on the ground of His credit, not mine. It is to renounce the thought that I have any claims on God whatever and approach Him on the ground of Christ's claims" (36-37).

With all three of these statements—from Jesus, Mr. Spurgeon, and Mr. Torrey—we must be extremely careful *not* to take them only at their face values. In the gospel passage, Jesus was not giving His hearers permission to "name it and claim it," as some falsely teach. To avoid this grave error, we need to examine what Jesus said in its proper context. The overall context includes both the *immediate* context in which His instruction appears as well as the *broader* context of what God's Word reveals as a whole. Only by analyzing the Lord's words in context can we truly understand what it means to pray in the name of Jesus.

To begin with, what does the name of Jesus represent? Beyond just a word by which we distinguish one individual from another, a name stands for a person's authority and character. For example, God's name is to be hallowed, as we discussed yesterday, because it refers specifically to Him, and He is perfectly and uniquely holy. As Jesus informed His disciples when issuing the Great Commission, "All authority has been given to me in heaven and on earth. Go therefore and make disciples of all the nations, baptizing them in the name of the Father and of the Son and of the Holy Spirit, teaching them to observe all things that I have commanded you..." (Matthew 28:18-20). In other words, Jesus essentially stated, "On the basis of the complete authority given to Me, I commission you to travel throughout the world as My representatives and make more disciples." Evangelizing, baptizing, and teaching people to observe God's commandments—all in the name of Jesus—mean acting under the umbrella of His authority and in accordance with His character.

We find the same concepts communicated in the Apostle Paul's writing, which is not surprising at all when we consider the scope of his intensive labors as an evangelist:

"Now all things are of God, who has reconciled us to Himself through Jesus Christ, and has given us the ministry of reconciliation, that is, that God was in Christ reconciling the world to Himself, not imputing their trespasses to them, and has committed to us the word of reconciliation.

Now then, we are ambassadors for Christ, as though God were pleading through us: we implore you on Christ's behalf, be reconciled to God" (2 Corinthians 5:18-20).

Doing anything "on Christ's behalf" is to do it in the name of Jesus. The apostles who spread the gospel in service of the Lord's commission preached and taught "on Christ's behalf"—in the name of Jesus. By definition, those who are appointed "ambassadors," in both secular and spiritual settings, never operate under their own authority or primarily in their own interests. Instead, whatever authority they possess is *delegated* to them. Moreover, the interests that they represent are chiefly those of the individuals or the powers who selected them to be "ambassadors." In fact, the Greek word for "authority" that Jesus used in Matthew 28:18 refers to an authority or a sanction[57] that is formally credited to one party by another party that has superior authority (refer to John 14:28).

Although the matter is not stated this way in Scripture, in a sense Jesus was an ambassador of God the Father during His earthly ministry. "I can of Myself do nothing," Christ declared. "As I hear, I judge; and My judgment is righteous, because I do not seek My own will but the will of the Father who sent Me" (John 5:30). Later in John's Gospel, Jesus expanded on the theme of His role as Mediator in a passage that we examined previously:

"I am the vine, you are the branches. He who abides in Me, and I in him, bears much fruit; for without Me you can do nothing…. If you abide in Me, and My words abide in you, you will ask what you desire, and it shall be done for you. By this My Father is glorified, that you bear much fruit; so you will be My disciples.

---

[57] sanction (O): permission or approval for an action or behavior

As the Father loved Me, I also have loved you; abide in My love.
If you keep My commandments, you will abide in My love, just as I have kept My Father's commandments and abide in His love" (15:5,7-10).

Here we behold with beautiful clarity, Christians, what it means to pray in the name of Jesus. The image of the vine and the branches portrays with delightful simplicity the relationship that enables us to ask anything in the name of Jesus while confidently expecting that He **will** grant our request.

In our opening text, Christ proclaimed, "And whatever you ask in My name, that I will do, that the Father may be glorified in the Son" (John 14:13). Jesus always sought to glorify His Father, not Himself. He singlemindedly served His Father's will, not His own. "For I have come down from heaven, not to do My own will, but the will of Him who sent Me" (6:38). He was (and is) a perfect ambassador of God the Father (see John 14:9). When we pray in the name of Jesus, our object likewise should always be "that the Father may be glorified in the Son." If we ask anything in Jesus's name that would not glorify the Father— that is contrary to His will—we can be certain that the Lord will *not* do it. Intuitively, this seems obvious: Jesus never acts in opposition to the Father's will. But however apparent it may seem, this principle is the key to understanding the teachings that we cited from Christ, Mr. Spurgeon, and Mr. Torrey. This is one reason why it is critical that we "abide" in Christ continuously, clinging to God's will and obeying His commandments.

Consider this truth carefully: the confidence and the power of praying in the name of Jesus apply exclusively to those who abide in Christ and live according to God's will. Propelled solely by that biblical fact, we are miles away from "name it and claim it." Moreover, the efficacy of praying in Jesus's name both proceeds *from* intimate relationship with the Lord and contributes *to* an even deeper sense of union. "There is no greater joy on earth or in heaven than communion with God. Prayer in the name of Jesus brings us into communion with God" (Torrey 13). But in order to have communion with our gracious Creator, we must love Him. And if we love God, we will obey His revealed will. The Bible is exquisitely clear on this point:

"If you love Me, keep My commandments....
He who has My commandments and keeps them, it is he who loves Me....
If anyone loves Me, he will keep My word; and My Father will love him, and We will come to him and make Our home with him. He who does not love Me does not keep My words; and the word which you hear is not Mine but the Father's who sent Me" (John 14:15,21,23-24).

Many other passages communicate the same truth. But surely there is no lingering space for confusion here.

Let us receive some practical counsel from Mr. Torrey, who grasped well the integral truths of this subject:

> "For us to abide in Christ...is to renounce all life independent of Christ and constantly look to Him for the inflow of His life into us and the outflowing of His life through us....
>
> We must study His words and let them sink into our thoughts and heart. We must keep them in our memory, obey them constantly in our life, and let them shape and mold our daily life and our every act....
>
> It is not by moments of mystical meditation and rapturous[58] experiences that we learn to abide in Christ. It is feeding upon His word, His written word in the Bible, and looking to the Spirit to implant these words in our heart..."(54,55,56; see also Galatians 2:20; Colossians 3:3).

We should note here that Jesus spoke of sending the Holy Spirit in the context of instructing His disciples regarding prayer in His name. In other words, the action of the Holy Spirit and praying in the name of Jesus are inseparably connected.

The ministry of God's Spirit within each of us is what *enables* us to abide in Christ at all, with everything that such abiding yields. And the reverse is also true. Without the empowering, sanctifying, and transforming work of the Holy Spirit, we have *no* hope of abiding in Christ (Acts 1:8; Romans 15:16; 1 Peter 1:22; Romans 12:2). A scion[59] of the world's poisoned stock can never be grafted onto the pure tissues of Christ the vine. The graft would fail, not having the living water of the Holy Spirit flowing through the diseased and hardened vessels of the lifeless wood. Like Aaron's rod that blossomed and bore fruit, only those branches to which *God* gives new life can be joined to the Root of David, which is Jesus (Numbers 17:8; Revelation 5:5). All other branches are just dead wood, fuel for the fire. "If anyone does not abide in Me, he is cast out as a branch and is withered; and they gather them and throw them into the fire, and they are burned" (John 15:6).

Christ taught that His followers would receive whatever they asked the Father in Jesus's name. But the context of His statements connected them to obeying the Lord's commandments, abiding in Christ, and loving God—which are essentially three different ways of saying the same thing. Additionally, the insights of Mr. Spurgeon and Mr. Torrey are indeed true, and compelling. But only when we understand and comply with the conditions that must be satisfied can we ask *anything* of our Father in the name of Jesus and expect to receive what we request. Only then are we handed a blank "cheque book," to use Mr.

---

[58] rapturous (O): intensely delightful
[59] scion (O): a cutting or twig for grafting; a descendant

Spurgeon's terms. Only then can we "pray on the ground of [Jesus's] credit," as Mr. Torrey wrote. "Delight yourself also in the LORD," David proclaimed, "And He shall give you the desires of your heart" (Psalm 37:4). When the Lord is our "delight," we love Him, abide in Him, and walk according to His will. Moreover, in such circumstances, the desires of our hearts will be whatever pleases Him. Our earnest desire and commitment will be to glorify our Father in heaven, just like Jesus (recall John 15:7).

A very common practice among professing Christians in our day is to close a prayer with something like "...in Jesus's name, Amen." As with the final word "Amen" that we studied yesterday, however, many who conclude their prayers this way out of habit have little or no solid understanding of *why* they say what they do. They use the phrase because it was modeled for them or because they heard purportedly[60] Christian people do it, but they have never actually investigated the topic in Scripture. Certainly, the name of Jesus possesses tremendous power, but not because of anything inherent in the word itself. Strictly speaking, Jesus is not even Christ's real name. When the angel Gabriel visited Mary and told her that she would bear a Son, he instructed her to call the child *Yehoshua*, meaning "Savior" or "Jehovah saved" (Matthew 1:21; Luke 1:26-31). Gabriel undoubtedly communicated with Mary in her native language (Aramaic). But there are probably very few modern, English-speaking Christians who close their prayers with "in Yehoshua's name, Amen." And complicating the matter even further is the fact that the New Testament was inspired and recorded in Greek. In that tongue, "Jesus Christ" is *Iesous Christos.*

The power possessed by Jesus's name—in any language—derives from the fact that His name represents His character and His authority. When we pray in the name of Jesus, then, we plead to our heavenly Father the merits of who *Christ* is and what *He* has done. We acknowledge that we have no merits of our own on the basis of which we might petition God for a specific favor or manifestation of His power. Instead, we depend exclusively on *Jesus's* merits. But as He established quite clearly, His merits—and His name—can only be applied in ways that serve His Father's will; that glorify His (and our) Father.

"If you ask anything in My name, I will do it," Jesus promised (John 14:14). When we approach our Father in His Son's name, let us remember what the Lord meant by "anything." When we conclude our prayers "in Jesus's name," let us do so with understanding. And beyond the immediate considerations related to praying in His name, let us abide in Christ continuously, as fruitful branches joined inseparably to the vine, receiving a constant supply of His life and His power. Let us demonstrate our love for the Lord in action by obeying all of His commandments and seeking always to glorify Him in every aspect of our lives. As thriving branches grafted to the Eternal Vine by the bond of God's

---

[60] purportedly (O): intended to seem; supposedly

limitless love, we will exhibit those qualities in earthly life of what He has made us: children of the Most High, our heavenly Father (Matthew 5:45; Luke 6:35; Galatians 5:22).

Day 11 — Faith as a Prerequisite to Prayer

Christians "are always confident, knowing that while we are at home in the body we are absent from the Lord. For we walk by faith, not by sight" (2 Corinthians 5:6-7). As long as we inhabit these temporary vessels, our mortal bodies, we must journey through life by navigating our courses according to faith (see 2 Corinthians 4:7). We cannot rely on our *physical* senses to guide us as we tread a *spiritual* path. Most of the time, the spiritual realities that relate to our voyages through life remain concealed from all of our physical senses. (Recall the account of Elisha and his servant on the mountainside in 2 Kings 6, as discussed in the Prologue.) Consequently, in order to travel through life in a manner that pleases our Father, we must "walk by faith."

We can illustrate this pilgrimage by imagining ourselves walking through an unfamiliar land; a long and deep valley terminating at the foot of a majestic mountain. Atop that lofty height is the King's palace, a splendid mansion that was fashioned and adorned with wonders beyond description. The King sent His emissary, beckoning us to His home, where He has prepared a stately room for each of us and reserved a seat at the massive table laid out for His wedding banquet. His ambassador found us shackled in chains and enslaved by a cruel tyrant. But he paid the price to liberate us from our hopeless bondage and presented us with personalized invitations, written with red ink in the King's own hand. "What a marvelous and undeserved privilege," we think, "to see the King face to face, to dwell in His house, and to dine with Him!"

But the journey from the toxic mire where His emissary found us to the gilded palace touching the heavens is an arduous one. Many hazards and pitfalls beset the path, false courses branch away into dark and violent places, and fearsome enemies lurk beside the road, waiting to ambush unwary travelers. Complicating the voyage further, a dense and foul-smelling fog chokes the valley, obscuring everything from sight and deadening all sounds. Something in the fog, if fog it is, clouds our wits, so that none of our senses seem to function normally.

When we first began the long journey we were anxious, wondering how we would ever reach our destination. But then we remembered the ancient guidebook that the ambassador entrusted to us, and the helper he sent to assist and instruct us along the way. That guidebook, we soon discovered, emits a piercing white light that appears to be generated within itself. The radiance of it dispels the suffocating fog, illuminating the path before us for a distance of several strides. As we proceeded, we quickly realized that when we adhered closely to what the book told us to do, we avoided most of the snares and traps that were positioned beside the trail.

Pushing forward, however, the road occasionally arrives at a fork, with several possible paths leading away in different directions and disappearing behind the curtain of mist. Some are marked with signposts such as "Shortcut," "Prince's Pavement," or "Ruler's Route." These all sound promising, sometimes even inviting, after the muddy and boulder-strewn course that we have walked. But the guidebook emphatically warns us not to be diverted by any of these alluring roads. It even advises us numerous times that the only trail which leads ultimately to the King's palace is very difficult and narrow, rarely smooth and bordered by savage enemies.

Sometimes, though, the guidebook does not tell us specifically which one of the remaining choices at a crossroads we should follow. Four possibilities are presented; two are eliminated by the book: Which of the two roads left do we take? We turn to the helper for counsel. He assists us in considering the options before us in light of the knowledge and the wisdom that we have gathered along the way. His insights provide greater clarity and direction and a sense of confidence to our thinking.

Reflecting on our trek to this point, we realize that he has accompanied us every step of the way. He came alongside us and supported us in all of our distresses, comforting and encouraging and instructing us at various times throughout our voyage. Even when we were lured away by the deceptive enticements of a supposedly easier road, he was there, gently guiding us back to the correct path. He normally spoke to us in an obtrusive voice, but occasionally we felt the pressure of his hands upon our shoulders, turning our attention away from some diversion that had captured our gaze. At other times, he pointed out something in the guidebook and exhorted us to contemplate its meaning.

Beloved Christians, this is a picture of the journey of faith. And many examples of stout faith are recorded in God's Word, the Guidebook for our individual voyages of faith through the dark and sin-choked valley of life. Anyone familiar with the Bible will probably think immediately of Hebrews 11 when faith is mentioned, and rightly so. That chapter is to faith what 1 Corinthians 13 is to love. Hebrews 11 is a chronicle or litany of many of the luminaries[61] of faith from throughout the Scriptures. But in addition to the accounts of specific believers and their exemplary faith, another theme is woven through the whole chapter. That theme united all of those men and women across time and distance, just as it unifies all genuine Christians in our day; both with each other and with all of God's people across the span of human history.

The theme is introduced in the first verse and revisited later in the chapter: "Now faith is the substance [or realization] of things hoped for, the evidence [or confidence] of things not seen." To dig deeper into the significance of this statement, consider the meaning of the word "faith" in the original Greek. As a

---

[61] luminaries (O): people having much intellectual, moral, or spiritual influence

noun, the Greek term signifies "trust," or it can also be rendered "firm persuasion." The verb form indicates "to believe." Thus, having faith in God means first that we believe everything He has revealed in His Word. Further, we trust that **everything** He has promised to do will certainly be done, without exception. In fact, so *definite* is the whole of God's Word, so truthful are all of His proclamations and prophecies, that events which have not yet occurred in time are occasionally spoken of as though they have already happened (see Isaiah 46:9-10).

To illustrate this phenomenon with a concrete example, consider a well-known passage from the Epistle to the Romans:

> "For whom He foreknew, He also predestined to be conformed to the image of His Son, that He might be the firstborn among many brethren. Moreover whom He predestined, these He also called; whom He called, these He also justified; and whom He justified, these He also glorified" (8:29-30).

Foreknew, predestined, called, justified, glorified: In the Greek, all of these verbs are in the past tense, indicating actions that have already been completed. From God's eternal perspective, outside the realm of time, the whole plan of salvation and all of human history are already finished. He beholds every moment of time, from the first to the last, as a single, instantaneous *now*. But within the sphere of time that corresponds to the material universe, some things have yet to occur. They still reside in what we think of as the future. So certain are they to happen, though, because the Sovereign Lord has ordained them, that He speaks of them as though they have already transpired.

This truth can be a real brain-scrambler. And our purpose here is not to engage in a detailed theological examination of the eternality and the omnipotence of God. But it is important for us to meditate on this truth, to the extent that each of us is able to understand it, because the precept underpins faith at the most fundamental level. Faith believes that every word God has spoken is true (John 17:17). Faith trusts that **everything** God said He will do, He certainly *will* do. When our enemies, our flesh, or our experiences tempt us to question God, wondering how or when He will fulfill the assurances of His Word, by faith we trust Him anyway. That is what it means to "walk by faith, not by sight" (2 Corinthians 5:7). When our senses ("sight") prompt us to doubt God, faith responds with "let God be true but every man a liar" (Romans 3:4). We *hope* for those wonderful things that our Lord has promised in His revealed Word, and by faith we can "look" upon them as though they have already been realized (refer again to Hebrews 11:1). All things that God has promised, though mostly invisible to us now, are nonetheless evident and very real when we behold them through the eyes of faith.

This is the same type of strident faith that was exemplified by the believers whose names are recorded in Hebrews 11. "These all died in faith, not having received the promises, but having seen them afar off were assured of them, embraced them and confessed that they were strangers and pilgrims on the earth" (verse 13). Such faith allows individual Christians to persevere in travelling through the unforgiving terrain of the valley in our illustration. We *believe* everything that the King's Ambassador told us (refer to the "Parable of the Wedding Feast," Matthew 22:2-14). We *trust* the Guidebook and the Helper, relying on what they tell us even when it seems to contradict the observations of our senses (Psalm 119:105; Proverbs 3:5-6; John 14:16,26). Being *firmly persuaded* of the truthfulness of the King's Emissary, the Helper, and the Guidebook, we "walk by faith" through all of the trials and perils and hardships and confusion that we must endure.

And what does the Bible say of those believers who journey through life with this kind of faith? "Therefore God is not ashamed to be called their God, for He has prepared a city for them" (Hebrews 11:16; also see John 14:2; Revelation 3:12; 21:2). The Scriptures describe these men and women as those "of whom the world was not worthy" (Hebrews 11:38). "And all these, having obtained a good testimony through faith, did not receive the promise, God having prepared something better for us, that they should not be made perfect apart from us" (verses 39-40).

At this point, we should have a pretty clear idea of what the word "faith" means as well as how it is embodied in the lives of Christians. How then does this relate to prayer, the central focus of our study? Simply stated, faith is a prerequisite[62] to meaningful prayer. "But without faith it is impossible to please Him, for he who comes to God must believe that He is, and that He is a rewarder of those who diligently seek Him" (verse 6). Note that it is not somewhat challenging or even extremely difficult to please the Lord without faith; it is totally **impossible**. When we come to God in prayer, we are told to "draw near with a true heart in full assurance of faith…" (Hebrews 10:22). Through identification with "…our Lord Jesus Christ, …we have access by faith into this grace in which we stand…" (Romans 5:1,2). In these passages, it is evident how necessary faith is in facilitating prayer.

Using some rather sobering language, James also connected prayer and faith in his epistle:

> "If any of you lacks wisdom, let him ask of God, who gives to all liberally and without reproach, and it will be given to him. But let him ask in faith, with no doubting, for he who doubts is like a wave of the sea driven and tossed by the wind. For let not that man suppose that he will receive

---

[62] prerequisite (O): something required as a condition for something else

anything from the Lord; he is a double-minded man, unstable in all his ways" (James 1:5-8).

In the specific context, James wrote about asking God for "wisdom." But the same condition that he identified undoubtedly still applies if we substitute anything else that the Father is well-pleased to give His children when they ask Him in faith: knowledge, understanding, discernment, boldness, peace, patience, joy, love. Try replacing wisdom in the statement above with any of these godly things and see how the passage reads.

Critical emphasis in the excerpt from James needs to be placed on asking *in faith*. Later in his letter, he revisited the issue of double-mindedness, which literally means "two souls." "Draw near to God and He will draw near to you. Cleanse your hands, you sinners; and purify your hearts, you double-minded" (4:8). We see here, as we have witnessed elsewhere, that "sinners" must be cleansed of their defilement, and the "double-minded" must have their hearts purified, before they can develop a close relationship with the Lord. Otherwise they cannot draw near to God, and He will not draw near to them. And as we have clearly established through our studies to this point, it is **only** through intimate relationship with God that prayer can be effective and fervent—the type of prayer we seek (see James 5:15-16).

Anyone who is both trusting and untrusting, both believing and unbelieving; anyone who is "double-minded" should not expect to experience any kind of power in prayer. Scripture affirms that God is not inclined to grant the requests of those who call Him a liar. "How many prayers are hindered by our wretched unbelief! We go to God and ask Him for something that is positively promised in His Word, and then we only half expect to get it" (Torrey 73).

Recognizing how necessary sincere faith is as a prerequisite to effective Christian prayer, how do we acquire or develop such faith? And how do we know when we have it? The Bible answers both questions directly. "So then faith comes by hearing, and hearing by the word of God" (Romans 10:17). Faith begins with God's Word. We must read it, study it, meditate on it, and internalize its truths in our hearts. We must seek to understand it, and we must believe that *everything* it says is true. "Beware, brethren, lest there be in any of you an evil heart of unbelief in departing from the living God" (Hebrews 3:12). Contrast this "evil heart of unbelief" that departs from God with the heart of faith that is required in order to draw near to Him.

As contradictory as it may sound, there are people who will hear God's Word and yet will not hear it (see Matthew 13:13-15; Acts 28:26-27). To put it another way, *not all hearing is hearing*. The hearing of understanding that generates faith must be supplied by the Holy Spirit. *Only* as He enables a person to receive with understanding the truths of Scripture does that hearing produce faith in the one who hears (see 1 Corinthians 2:10-16). Genuine faith originates in God.

And faith is also expanded, increased, and matured by Him. He uses His inspired Word as an instrument for cultivating the faith of His people (see Romans 12:3; Hebrews 12:2). In light of this knowledge, how imperative it is that we abide continually in God's Word!

And how do we know when we have authentic faith? True faith is realized through the outworking of love (Galatians 5:6). In other words, if our belief, our trust, our firm persuasion is legitimate, then our lives will prove the authenticity of our faith through the love that we demonstrate for God and for other people. "Show me your faith without your works," James challenged, "and I will show you my faith by my works" (James 2:18). James connected faith to works and the Apostle John linked love to obedience, another side of the same coin. "For this is the love of God, that we keep His commandments. And His commandments are not burdensome" (1 John 5:3).

> "Now by this we know that we know Him, if we keep His commandments. He who says, 'I know Him,' and does not keep His commandments, is a liar, and the truth is not in him. But whoever keeps His word, truly the love of God is perfected in him. By this we know that we are in Him. He who says he abides in Him ought himself also to walk just as He walked" (1 John 2:3-6).

If we want to gauge whether or not our faith is genuine, then we should honestly examine ourselves and assess the way we live. Do we keep God's commandments? Do we love sincerely, without hypocrisy or partiality? "Examine yourselves as to whether you are in the faith. Test yourselves. Do you not know yourselves, that Jesus Christ is in you?" (2 Corinthians 13:5). And Jesus declared, "If you love Me, keep My commandments" (John 14:15).

We certainly have a lot to digest regarding faith and its relevance to "effective, fervent prayer." All that we have discussed here barely scratches at the surface of what could be written on this subject. As with The Model Prayer, in fact, this topic could easily produce a book by itself. Hopefully, though, we have established well enough how utterly and inescapably *critical* faith is as a prerequisite to prayer.

> "If we are to have real faith, we must study the Word of God and discover what is promised. Then, we must simply believe the promises of God. Faith must have God's sanction.... Believing what God says in His Word is faith.... If there is no promise in the Word of God and no clear leading of the Spirit, there can be no real faith" (Torrey 46).

Without faith, prayer is *meaningless*. Nothing can be gained by praying to the Lord when we do not believe what He has said; when we do not trust Him to fulfill all that He has promised. *With* faith, however, the awesome power of God that can be manifested in and through us is literally unlimited. As evidence of this, consider the lesson of the withered fig-tree scene in Matthew's Gospel in the light of everything that we have studied today (21:18-22).

Day 12 — Forgiveness and Humility

Strictly speaking, God does not forgive sin. From the first moment of creation to the present, not once in all of history has God forgiven sin. (If you have not thrown the book across the room, please continue reading for an explanation). These declarations might inspire protest, so please read further before forming any opinions or leveling any charges.

God never forgives *sin*, but He does justify *sinners*. In fact, everyone reading these words at this moment is almost certainly a pardoned sinner—also known as a Christian. Unless a person is massively deluded, it is highly improbable that any unregenerate worldling will make it this far into the book. And since Jesus stated explicitly that believing in Him is the only way of salvation, we can proclaim categorically[63] the following complementary[64] truths (John 14:6):

1. Anyone who is a forgiven sinner, in reality and not solely in profession, can be fittingly called a Christian.
2. All *authentic* Christians are undeniably forgiven sinners.

At first reading, this might seem like stating the obvious. But it is essential to understand and to establish the foundation on which all of our conversations related to God's Word must be based. For emphasis, we will include a verse of scripture that is well known to many saints: "For no other foundation can anyone lay than that which is laid, which is Jesus Christ" (1 Corinthians 3:11). **All** discussion of forgiveness must center on Jesus! Anything else—everything else—is completely empty of eternal significance and is entirely unbiblical. On no other basis, and through no one else but Christ, can a sinner be forgiven and cleansed of sin—period.

Assuming that everyone reading at this point is a sincere believer, on what grounds does God pardon sinners? And how is it that He justifies sinners, but never forgives sin? The answers to these two questions are connected. God is able to forgive sinners because He has already *judged* their sin in His Son, Jesus Christ (Romans 3:21-26; 2 Corinthians 5:21; 1 John 2:2). He does not forgive sin; He punishes it. Every sin committed is a transgression of God's moral law (1 John 3:4). This law is a concrete expression of the Lord's standards—His will. And His will is rooted in who He is as the One True God (John 17:3). Just as sin is an intolerable offense against His perfect *holiness*, so also does His perfect *justice* demand retribution for that sin. For that reason, every sin—every transgression of God's moral law—must be punished. Otherwise God would not be perfectly just (Numbers 14:18). Either He punishes the sin by executing His judgment on the offender, or else an adequate substitute must be provided to bear the sentence in the sinner's place. As a gift of His indescribable grace,

---

[63] categorically (O): absolutely; unconditionally
[64] complementary (O): making complete by forming a complement

God the Father supplied a substitute who was qualified to endure the punishment for *all* who humbly and sincerely place their faith in Him, trusting Him for salvation (Ephesians 2:8-9; see also Hebrews 10:4). The only substitute who could possibly serve in that capacity by offering Himself as a sacrifice was the sinless Son of God, the perfectly righteous Jesus.

These truths form the bedrock of the gospel, so almost all genuine Christians are already acquainted with them at some level. Many believers, however, have not thought these subjects through in any real depth. To do them justice, they need to be explored in much greater detail. But such an examination is beyond both the scope of this book and the focus of today's study. Anyone who desires to investigate these topics further should explore the Books of Romans and Hebrews, probably with the assistance of a couple of good commentaries. What we have included here should be sufficient review for our purposes in this lesson.

We have highlighted some of the major elements in the plan of salvation because it is absolutely critical that we have a deep sense and a firm grasp of the *gravity* of our sin. We will not appreciate as we should what it means to be forgiven of our sin as long as we have an inadequate conception of how offensive our sins are to God's holiness. Our transgressions of His moral law, His perfect and unchanging standards, are abominations to Him (for example, Proverbs 6:16-19). "Or do you despise the riches of His goodness, forbearance, and longsuffering, not knowing that the goodness of God leads you to repentance?" (Romans 2:4). Consider the apostle's words carefully. How does "the goodness of God" lead us "to repentance"?

When we recognize how terribly abhorrent[65] our sins are to God, invariably our next thought should be that, according to the demands of justice, we deserve *nothing* but His wrath. Every one of us should be condemned! In fact, without Jesus, we *are* condemned (see John 3:18). Consequently, it would not be unjust in the least for Him to cause the earth to open up and swallow us, as it did all those who allied themselves with Korah in rebellion against Moses (Number 16:31-33). If God removed the breath of life from our nostrils at this moment, as He did with Ananias and Sapphira, no one could accuse Him of injustice (Acts 5:1-11). For a single careless and unintentional act of irreverence, Uzzah was struck dead by the Lord for touching the ark of the covenant (2 Samuel 6:6-7). All of these people's lives ended very abruptly. They were not granted any "second chances" with which they might turn from those sins that provoked God to wrath.

Many modern, professing Christians read about these people in the Bible and suppose, perhaps unconsciously, that things have changed. "Those were different times. God doesn't strike people dead for their sins anymore." Saints,

---

[65] abhorrent (CO): detestable, loathsome, repugnant

the sobering truth we need to receive is that we are *all* Korah; we are Ananias and Sapphira; we are Uzzah. By nature, all of us have rebellious, self-centered, lying, manipulative, presumptuous, irreverent hearts (recall Jeremiah 17:9). When we internalize this fact and attempt to form a realistic notion of our own wickedness, then we can begin to apprehend how "the goodness of God leads...to repentance." We are forced to recognize that we do not in any way merit His goodness. We deserve only condemnation. The fact that He demonstrates His goodness toward us anyway, by grace, impacts our hearts in such a way that we are compelled to turn away from sin and toward God—to repent.

In the first three verses of Romans 2, Paul confronted our tendency to view ourselves as somehow different from those idolatrous worldlings whose actions we condemn:

> "Therefore you are inexcusable, O man, whoever you are who judge, for in whatever you judge another you condemn yourself; for you who judge practice the same things. But we know that the judgment of God is according to truth against those who practice such things. And do you think this, O man, you who judge those practicing such things, and doing the same, that you will escape the judgment of God?" (2:1-3).

Space prohibits a thorough examination of the many potent truths that Paul elaborated in the second chapter of Romans. But taking this passage by itself, there is profound application to our present study of forgiveness and humility.

Jesus indicated the effect that forgiveness has on a sinner's heart in a dialogue over dinner at the home of a Pharisee. Speaking about a woman "who was a sinner" (prostitute), Jesus told Simon the Pharisee, "Therefore I say to you, her sins, which are many, are forgiven, for she loved much. But to whom little is forgiven, the same loves little" (Luke 7:37, 47). As the Lord expressed here, being forgiven impacts the condition of a person's heart in a remarkable way. That is one reason why self-righteousness is so repulsive in God's sight. People who are painfully aware of their sinfulness are well-positioned to experience a powerful transformation in their hearts and minds. And that metamorphosis[66] occurs when the Lord removes their hearts of stone and replaces them with hearts of flesh (see Ezekiel 36:25-27). This sinful woman was primed to have her life radically changed by Christ's intervention—by His touch. The self-righteous, by contrast, do not properly acknowledge their dire need for the salvation that *only* God delivers; and that *only* through Jesus.

Here we encounter the close relationship between forgiveness and humility. And we should note that this connection operates in both directions. To begin with, people who have been forgiven much are often humbled by the knowledge

---

[66] metamorphosis (C): change of form, structure, substance, appearance, character; transformation

of what a tremendous gift of grace God has furnished to them. In other words, being pardoned of much sin generally translates to deeper humility. And the reverse is also true. Those who thought that they were pretty decent people, on the whole, before they "gave their lives to Christ" do not usually exhibit the same profound degree of humility as their grievously sinful counterparts. Of course, this is not to suggest that anyone should sin more so that greater humility will result. This is an observation of what commonly happens, not a description of a model that should be followed. (Recall from the beginning of today's reading that we are specifically addressing people who are already Christians.)

The relationship between forgiveness and humility also works in the other direction, from humility to forgiveness. Those who *are* relatively humble are considerably more likely to recognize their need for God's pardon, and to seek it on *His* terms. The proud, on the other hand, are too blinded by self to perceive that they are utterly condemned apart from Christ. "God resists the proud," quoted James, "But gives grace to the humble" (4:6; also 1 Peter 5:5-6). And Jesus illustrated this principle in the "Parable of the Pharisee and the Tax Collector," found in Luke's Gospel (18:9-14). The self-absorbed Pharisee could only thank the Lord that he was not like the sinners he saw. He did not convey the slightest indication that he was aware of his need for God's forgiveness. The tax collector, by contrast, was overwhelmed by sorrow for his sin and humbly pleaded with God for mercy. We see, then, that just as pride and self-righteousness are linked to unforgiveness, so also is humility essential to forgiveness. And this truth applies whether we are speaking of being forgiven or of forgiving others.

In today's study, our focus is primarily on the critical requirement that we forgive others in order for our prayers to be both effective and fervent. To put it another way, we defer again to Mr. Torrey: "An unforgiving spirit is one of the most common hindrances to prayer. Anyone who is nursing a grudge against another has closed the ear of God against his own petition" (70-71). The truth of this observation quickly becomes apparent when we consider what Jesus taught on the subject of forgiving others for their offenses against us.

In our long exploration of The Model Prayer, we already discussed a couple of verses that pertain directly to the topic before us. After including a range of petitions in His prayer, the Lord revisited the issue of forgiveness: "For if you forgive men their trespasses, your heavenly Father will also forgive you. But if you do not forgive men their trespasses, neither will your Father forgive your trespasses" (Matthew 6:14-15). These declarations are a concise presentation of an important precept for Christian living. And a parable that He spoke, recorded later in Matthew's Gospel, poignantly illustrates that principle through a real-world scenario that we can easily apply to our own experiences.

Simon wanted to know how many times he should forgive his "brother," so he followed the most sensible course and asked Jesus (Matthew 18:21). But he probably got more than he bargained for in the response that he received. Jesus instructed him to forgive, not "seven times" as Simon suggested, but "seventy times seven" (verse 22). This figure was not stated in order to put a definite limit on the number of times that we forgive other people for their trespasses against us. "Sorry, brother, that's 491. I can't forgive you this time." Instead, Jesus's reply indicated, in effect, that our forgiveness should be *unlimited*. This fact is then established forcefully by the "Parable of the Unforgiving Servant" that follows, in verses 23-34. Finally, the Lord further emphasized the point by reiterating the principle in verse 35.

One servant owed his master, the king, the unimaginable sum of "ten thousand talents" (verse 24). Such an incredible figure would be equivalent to approximately sixty million days' wages for an ordinary laborer in those days! (One talent was roughly 6,000 denarii, and one denarius was a day's wage for a common laborer.) To put these numbers in modern terms, it would be like someone who earns $120 per day owing a creditor $7,200,000,000! Needless to say, no servant could hope to repay such a mammoth debt. And the obvious fact that no king would ever loan such a huge amount to any servant is not relevant to the object lesson of the parable. Out of his own grace, prompted by compassion for his sorrowful servant, the king ultimately forgave the man what he owed (verse 27). No sooner had he shown such incredible favor to his desperate servant, however, but that wicked man pressured one of his fellow servants to repay a debt owed to him of "a hundred denarii"—about 100 days' wages (verse 28). Just as he had done with the king, the debtor pleaded with him for patience, and promised to repay the full amount (verse 29). Unlike the king, though, the wicked man refused to forgive the other servant his (relatively minor) debt, and treated him harshly (verse 30).

The parallels that are illustrated by this parable are not difficult to grasp, so we will not belabor the point by examining them in detail. But if we are completely truthful with ourselves, how often do we imitate the wicked servant by withholding forgiveness from another person? Consider the specific *words* of the warning that Jesus issued in verse 35: "So My heavenly Father also will do to you if each of you, from his heart, does not forgive his brother his trespasses." The forgiveness that we are required to render to other people must come *from the heart*. It must be sincere, honest, and genuine. But who will know if we fake it; if we say that we forgive someone while secretly nursing a grudge in our hearts? God will know. He sees our hearts. "And there is no creature hidden from His sight, but all things are naked and open to the eyes of Him to whom we must give account" (Hebrews 4:13; also 1 Samuel 16:7; 1 Kings 8:39; Jeremiah 17:10).

As we study the Bible in depth, we should develop a penetrating and persistent sense of what the Lord did on our behalf in order to make it *possible* for Him to pardon us of our sins, without compromising His justness and holiness (Romans 3:21-26; particularly verse 26). With that sense filling and gripping our hearts, we should be quick to forgive other people for their trespasses against us. Paul noted more than once that we "were bought at a price" (1 Corinthians 6:20; 7:23). Consider the "price" that our Father paid by offering His only Son as a sacrifice for sins, punishing sin in Jesus so that He could forgive wretched sinners like us (2 Corinthians 5:21). And reflect on what it means to have been "bought." He purchased us with the currency of His own righteous blood, which is infinitely more valuable than any earthly treasure. We belong to Him, and we are not our own (1 Corinthians 6:19; also John 17:9-10).

In view of all that *God* has forgiven us, when our King instructs us to forgive others from the heart, how can we fail to obey? "And if you call on the Father, who without partiality judges according to each one's work, conduct yourselves throughout the time of your stay here in fear; knowing that you were not redeemed with corruptible things, like silver or gold, from your aimless conduct received by tradition from your fathers, but with the precious blood of Christ, as of a lamb without blemish and without spot" (1 Peter 1:17-19).

Many more scriptures could be cited in support of the truths that we have explored in today's reading. But authentic Christians will not need to have these points hammered on endlessly. We know already—or we should—that there is no legitimate justification we can give for withholding forgiveness from anyone. Whenever someone wrongs us, perhaps even grievously, God will deal with that person according to His perfect timing (Romans 12:17-21). And how unenviable will be the situation of that individual who trespasses against another person—especially a Christian—and fails to confess and seek forgiveness! "It is a fearful thing to fall into the hands of the living God.... For our God is a consuming fire" (Hebrews 10:31; 12:29; also Matthew 25:40,46). In the meantime, we must pardon the offender and pursue peace. Recall what our central verse states before it mentions the power of "effective, fervent prayer": "Confess your trespasses to one another, and pray for one another, that you may be healed" (James 5:16). Clearly, as Mr. Torrey indicated, unresolved "trespasses" inhibit the efficacy of prayer.

Most of us can at least recognize intuitively that praying to our Father while we harbor unforgiveness in our hearts is rather foolish. "But the wisdom that is from above is first pure, then peaceable, gentle, willing to yield, full of mercy and good fruits, without partiality and without hypocrisy. Now the fruit of righteousness is sown in peace by those who make peace" (James 3:17-18). Meditate on the words in these verses in the light of the subject of today's study. And remember how angry the king became at his unforgiving servant. Do we suppose that our Lord is any less provoked to anger by our refusal to pardon? Ten thousand talents is a pittance[67] compared to the debt that He forgave every

---

[67] pittance (O): a very small amount

one of us. Do we then dare to treat His mercy as a small thing—a triviality—by failing to forgive others for their trespasses? "For judgment is without mercy to the one who has shown no mercy. Mercy triumphs over judgment" (2:13). "Therefore humble yourselves under the mighty hand of God, that He may exalt you in due time, casting all your care upon Him, for He cares for you" (1 Peter 5:6-7).

Day 13 — Prayer Meetings and Unity in Prayer

"For as the body is one and has many members, but all the members of that one body, being many, are one body, so also is Christ. For by one Spirit we were all baptized into one body...and have all been made to drink into one Spirit. For in fact the body is not one member but many.

...But now indeed there are many members, yet one body.... But God composed the body, having given greater honor to that part which lacks it, that there should be no schism [division] in the body, but that the members should have the same care for one another. And if one member suffers, all the members suffer with it; or if one member is honored, all the members rejoice with it. Now you are the body of Christ, and members individually" (1 Corinthians 12:12-14, 20, 24-27).

"And He put all things under His feet, and gave Him to be head over all things to the church, which is His body, the fullness of Him who fills all in all" (Ephesians 1:22-23).

Taken as a whole, all true Christians together comprise the body of Christ. And Jesus is the "head" of that body. As with the head of a healthy *human* body, He directs and manages all of the numerous and often interdependent functions that the body performs. Most of us already know these truths, even if we have not meditated on them in depth. But what does it mean, in *practice*, that Christians collectively constitute Christ's body? We regularly toss around the phrase "body of Christ" in our conversations with other saints, but to what extent do we really internalize the profound significance of that truth? To help us comprehend the mysterious operation of Christ's spiritual body, let us briefly examine a few of the workings of a physical, human body.

Consider how much is involved in something as simple as lifting a glass of water from a table to take a drink. Numerous muscles, several joints, and dozens of bones must all cooperate to grip the glass at the proper pressure, lift it at an appropriate speed, and pour a moderate amount of water into the mouth to be swallowed. These actions require countless nerve impulses, blood-pressure regulation, and respiration to supply oxygen and nutrients to the tissues and remove waste products. They also entail a variety of processes at the cellular level that are too numerous and complicated to describe here. And all of this is necessary just to take a drink of water! Moreover, if one or more of these elements fails to work properly, then the whole sequence is substantially more difficult or even impossible. The human body is truly an astonishing arrangement of intricate systems, each one more amazing and awe-inspiring than the last!

"For You formed my inward parts;
You covered me in my mother's womb.
I will praise You, for I am fearfully and wonderfully made;
Marvelous are Your works,
And that my soul knows very well" (Psalm 139:13-14).

As this psalm attests, David clearly appreciated what a "marvelous" exhibition of God's creative genius the human body is.

Several times in his epistles, the Apostle Paul compared the body of Christ to a human body. Nowhere did he present that comparison more eloquently or in greater detail than in the passage from 1 Corinthians 12 that began today's lesson. Turning to another of his letters, Paul wrote, "For as we have many members in one body, yet all the members do not have the same function, so we, being many, are one body in Christ, and individually members of one another" (Romans 12:4-5). All genuine Christians have been *incorporated* into Christ's body through the indwelling of the Holy Spirit. And we have all been situated within His body according to the perfect wisdom and knowledge of God, as we saw: "God composed the body..." (1 Corinthians 12:24). Each part of the body—every saint—has a "function" to fulfill within the body that is assigned by God. And no particular function deserves more honor or recognition than any other. Instead, all parts of the body are supposed to serve harmoniously under continuous direction from the head, Jesus.

When various members of the body of Christ work together, guided by the head and empowered by the Holy Spirit, abundant spiritual fruit is produced. But for this to occur, an attitude of humility and submission to God's will must be conscientiously maintained by each member. Christians need to be mindful that no single part of Christ's body is sufficient in and of itself to accomplish the purpose that our head ordains for that part of His body. We rely on each other even as we all depend, ultimately, on Him. Hence Paul's admonition in Romans 12: "For I say, through the grace given to me, to everyone who is among you, not to think of himself more highly than he ought to think, but to think soberly, as God has dealt to each one a measure of faith" (verse 3).

After Paul discussed the unity of the body of Christ and the different gifts that God supplies to specific saints, he provided some practical ways to behave like a Christian while serving in Christ's body:

"Let love be without hypocrisy. Abhor what is evil. Cling to what is good. Be kindly affectionate to one another with brotherly love, in honor giving preference to one another; not lagging in diligence, fervent in spirit, serving the Lord; rejoicing in hope, patient in tribulation, continuing steadfastly in prayer; distributing to the needs of the saints, given to hospitality.

...Rejoice with those who rejoice, and weep with those who weep [recall 1 Corinthians 12:26]. Be of the same mind toward one another. Do not set your mind on high things, but associate with the humble. Do not be wise in your own opinion" (Romans 12:9-13,15-16).

This sequence of principles for Christian living includes several admonitions that connect to other passages in Paul's epistles. In particular, we will focus on his instruction in verse 16, "Be of the same mind toward one another."

In order for all of the individual members of the body of Christ to function effectively *as a body*, we Christians need to humble ourselves and strive to maintain unity. This we must do in spite of all the forces that labor endlessly to divide us. One way in which we pursue unity is by dedicating ourselves to being "of the same mind toward one another." To that end, Paul presented some poignant counsel in his Epistle to the Ephesians:

"I, therefore, the prisoner of the Lord, beseech [or exhort] you to walk worthy of the calling with which you were called, with all lowliness and gentleness, with longsuffering, bearing with one another in love, endeavoring to keep the unity of the Spirit in the bond of peace. There is one body and one Spirit, just as you were called in one hope of your calling; one Lord, one faith, one baptism, one God and Father of all, who is above all, and through all, and in you all" (4:1-6).

We are one in the Spirit, united into one body by the Holy Spirit who indwells all authentic Christians. We also see that "the unity of the Spirit" is something that we must *endeavor* to keep. A conscious and continual commitment is required from all of us to maintain the unity that is only possible through His Spirit. Additionally, we witness the quality of character that is necessary to persevere in unity, both in this passage and in the principles that we reviewed from Romans 12.

As Paul elaborated later in Ephesians 4, God supplies the grace to gift the members of Christ's body in various ways. This He does in accordance with His purposes for individual saints, for the church, and for the world at large. His endowments also demonstrate His sovereignty. "God composed the body," as we have seen. The **broad** reason why the Lord constructs the body as He does is "for the equipping of the saints for the work of ministry, for the edifying of the body of Christ, till we all come to the unity of the faith and of the knowledge of the Son of God, to a perfect man, to the measure of the stature of the fullness of Christ" (Ephesians 4:12-13). Our Father wants us to "grow up in all things into Him who is the head—Christ—from whom the whole body, joined and knit together by what every joint supplies, according to the effective working by which every part does its share, causes growth of the body for the edifying of itself in love" (verses 15-16). What a beautiful picture of the church functioning in the way that God desires!

Jesus communicated His profound concern for the unity of His body in a prayer to His Father, shortly before the conclusion of His earthly ministry. In it He interceded on behalf of His disciples and all who would believe in Him "through their word;"

> "...that they all may be one, as You, Father, are in Me, and I in You; that they also may be one in Us, that the world may believe that You sent Me. And the glory which You gave Me I have given them, that they may be one just as We are one: I in them, and You in Me; that they may be made perfect in one, and that the world may know that You have sent Me, and have loved them as You have loved Me" (John 17:20-23).

As Jesus prepared to confront the tremendous trial that He would soon endure, He expressed potent concern for His followers. Among His final words of instruction to them was a commandment to "love one another" in the same way that He had loved them (15:12). He wanted His people to be knit together with cords of love, unified by love through His indwelling presence. And the intensity of His desire was reflected in how He concluded His prayer to the Father, "...that the love with which You loved Me may be in them, and I in them" (17:26).

These considerations relate to the *broad* reasons why God organizes the body of Christ as He does. Now let us narrow our focus. Suppose we say that these broad or general points regarding the structure of the church concern the body itself—its health and cohesion and completeness (recall Ephesians 4:13). Constricting our focus, then, the **specific** purpose for God assembling His body in the way that He does pertains to the *operations* of His body in the world. Humanly speaking, a body that is diseased and debilitated, arthritic and anemic[68], partially paralyzed and impaired by cataracts, will not be able to function as well as a body that is totally healthy. We all know this intuitively, if not from personal experience.

The same principle applies in the case of the body of Christ, as should be evident. When different members of Christ's body all labor toward the same end, with each part doing its bit, the Holy Spirit works powerfully through the body to produce much fruit in the world. Here we should review Paul's stern counsel to the Church at Corinth. But for the sake of space, we will examine only a handful of highlights:

---

[68] anemic (CO): lacking vigor or positive characteristics; sickly, feeble

"For where there are envy, strife, and divisions among you, are you not carnal and behaving like mere men? ...So then neither he who plants is anything, nor he who waters, but God who gives the increase. Now he who plants and he who waters are one, and each one will receive his own reward according to his own labor. For we are God's fellow workers.... Do you not know that you are the temple of God and that the Spirit of God dwells in you?" (1 Corinthians 3:3,7-9,16).

In this specific context, we should note that Paul was addressing Christians who were foolishly contending with each other about nonessential matters. He was not describing *how* the body bears fruit through the agency of the indwelling Spirit. But his observations about the body—its construction and its functioning—still apply to our discussion.

In fact, it is precisely at this point that everything we have considered today regarding the body of Christ intersects with the primary subject of this book—effective and fervent prayer. Since it *is* "God who gives the increase," anything and everything we do that is not in accordance with His will is a waste of time and energy and resources. Whether we work individually or collectively, if the Lord has not sanctioned[69] the end toward which we strive, then we labor in vain:

"Unless the LORD builds the house,
They labor in vain who build it;
Unless the LORD guards the city,
The watchman stays awake in vain" (Psalm 127:1).

On the opposite side of that coin, however, is a joyful certainty that Paul affirmed: "Therefore, my beloved brethren, be steadfast, immovable, always abounding in the work of the Lord, knowing that your labor is not in vain in the Lord" (1 Corinthians 15:58). When our efforts, as individuals and as a church, are "in the Lord," we can *always* rest assured that our "labor is not in vain." Elsewhere, Paul challenged the Philippian church (and us) to "stand fast in one spirit, with one mind striving together for the faith of the gospel" (1:27). Faith in the Lord Jesus Christ with belief in His gospel is one objective toward which we can always work without hesitation, confident of His blessing.

Under the light of these truths, how can we know that our labors are "in the Lord"? And how can we determine if they are *not* blessed by Him? Of course we must humbly seek guidance from God's Word, a treasury of His revealed will:

"Your word is a lamp to my feet
And a light to my path" (Psalm 119:105).

---

[69] sanctioned (O): granted permission or approval

"If we want power in prayer, we must be earnest students of His Word to find out what His will regarding us is. Then having found it, we must do it" (Torrey 31). We should begin by looking for His direction as it is recorded in the Bible. But for this search to be successful, and more generally for our *lives* to be fruitful, we must pray. The Scriptures are saturated with statements to that effect, as we have glimpsed in our survey of the subject to this point. Since our current lesson centers on "Prayer Meetings and Unity in Prayer," however, let us look to the practices of the early church for an example.

After some of Christ's disciples witnessed His bodily ascension to heaven, they received instruction from "two men" who "stood by them in white apparel" (Acts 1:10):

> "Then [the apostles whom He had chosen] returned to Jerusalem from the mount called Olivet, which is near Jerusalem, a Sabbath day's journey. And when they had entered, they went up into the upper room where they were staying: Peter, James, John, and Andrew; Philip and Thomas; Bartholomew and Matthew; James the son of Alphaeus and Simon the Zealot; and Judas the son of James. These all continued with one accord [purpose or mind] in prayer and supplication..." (1:2,12-14).

Here were "the apostles whom He had chosen" striving together with one mind "in prayer and supplication" (verses 2,14; also look again at Romans 12:16). We could justly say that these were the first prayer meetings to occur following Christ's departure from earth. And notice how unified these men were! The Lord desires such unity and commonality of purpose to be evidenced within the church in our day.

As we have seen, prayer groups and meetings are scriptural. Wherever they are possible, gatherings of *sincere* Christians specifically for the purpose of corporate prayer can be both wondrously beneficial and awesomely effective. In addition, the fruits of prayer meetings can profit those who participate in such assemblies just as much as anyone for whom the groups intercede. At this point, a pair of observations by R.A.Torrey can serve to spotlight the underappreciated value of prayer meetings in the biblical mold:

> "If we would only spend more time in prayer, there would be more fullness of the Spirit's power in our work. Many men who once worked unmistakably in the power of the Holy Spirit now fill the air with empty shoutings, beat it with meaningless gestures, because they have neglected prayer. We must spend much time on our knees before God if we are to continue in the power of the Holy Spirit" (16).

> "But, where there is real agreement, where the Spirit of God brings believers into perfect harmony concerning that which they ask of God,

where the Spirit lays the same burden on two or more hearts, there is absolutely irresistible power in prayer" (28).

God does the real work through the agency and power of His Spirit, who dwells in the church as a whole and in saints individually (recall 1 Corinthians 3). But for His power to be demonstrated, we need to pray humbly, earnestly, and steadfastly, as He ordered. We must dedicate ourselves to maintaining the unity of the Spirit, a commitment that inevitably involves sacrifice and self-denial.

Our adversary knows what manner and magnitude of power will operate in and through the body of Christ when we strive together according to the direction of God's Word. Consequently, Satan devotes himself with tremendous zeal and single-mindedness to thwarting the actions of Christ's body in the world. And he knows that when we are preoccupied with challenging each other, we are not focused on fighting him. "The devil hates the church and seeks in every way to block its progress; by false doctrine, by division, and by inward corruption of life. But, by prayer, a clear way can be made through everything" (Torrey 20-21).

We require the Spirit's power and guidance to combat our enemy effectively. And to experience that power revealed in our midst, we must *endeavor* to remain united. "There is a great work to be done in the hearts of men, there is a fierce battle to be waged with spiritual wickedness in heavenly places…. And in these things, it is by prayer above all other means that we shall be able to cooperate with the Captain of the Lord's host" (MacIntyre 33).

> "Therefore, as the elect of God, holy and beloved, put on tender mercies, kindness, humility, meekness, longsuffering; bearing with one another, and forgiving one another, if anyone has a complaint against another; even as Christ forgave you, so you also must do. But above all these things put on love, which is the bond of perfection ['a perfect man'; Ephesians 4:13]. And let the peace of God rule in your hearts, to which also you were called in one body; and be thankful. Let the word of Christ dwell in you richly in all wisdom, teaching and admonishing one another in psalms and hymns and spiritual songs, singing with grace in your hearts to the Lord" (Colossians 3:12-16).

Paul's pastoral counsel here is a beautiful description of a united, loving, **Christian** church body. This kind of church bears much fruit, glorifying the Father in heaven (remember John 15:8). To that purpose we are called; for that work we are sent into the world. As Jesus said, "You did not choose Me, but I chose you and appointed you that you should go and bear fruit, and that your fruit should remain, that whatever you ask the Father in My name He may give you. These things I command you, that you love one another" (15:16-17).

Day 14 — Praying Before the Throne of Grace

Anyone who knows the Bible well probably thinks immediately of Hebrews 4:14-16 when the phrase "throne of grace" is mentioned. Those verses contain a powerful exhortation to approach the Lord in prayer, frequently and without hesitation. We will begin our exploration of "the throne of grace," within the larger context of effective and fervent prayer, by reviewing first what Scripture states:

> "Seeing then that we have a great High Priest who has passed through the heavens, Jesus the Son of God, let us hold fast our confession. For we do not have a High Priest who cannot sympathize with our weaknesses, but was in all points tempted as we are, yet without sin. Let us therefore come boldly to the throne of grace, that we may obtain mercy and find grace to help in time of need" (Hebrews 4:14-16).

In this passage are two operative words that should direct and inform any analysis of its meaning: "then" and "therefore."

The word "then" in the first sentence indicates that what follows is a conclusion based upon the foregoing information. The author of the Epistle to the Hebrews has just occupied almost four chapters—or nearly one-third—of his letter with establishing the supreme *worthiness* of Jesus to serve as our High Priest. Additionally, the writer has emphasized Christ's complete *faithfulness* in that capacity (read, for example, 2:17-3:2). "For this one has been counted worthy of more glory than Moses, inasmuch as he who built the house has more honor than the house" (3:3). In other words, Jesus *created* the office of High Priest. He brought into existence the role of a mediator between God and humanity, so He is certainly deserving of more glory than any earthly occupant of that position. (The High Priesthood of Jesus is one of the central themes of Hebrews and is revisited repeatedly throughout the remainder of the letter, as we will see.)

Under the terms of the Old Covenant, once each year the High Priest would pass through the veil inside the sanctuary of the tabernacle or temple. By doing so, he entered the Most Holy Place, where the ark of the covenant and the mercy seat were housed. Between the two cherubim atop the mercy seat, the Lord God made His presence to reside (Exodus 25:22). Once inside the Most Holy Place, or Holy of Holies, the High Priest would atone for the sins of the nation, God's Chosen People (see Leviticus 16). But to be eligible to perform this rite of atonement (without dying in the process), the High Priest first had to satisfy some extraordinary and stringent[70] requirements. Even when all of this was

---

[70] stringent (C): binding strongly; exact and strictly enforced

completed correctly, the ritual still had to be repeated once a year, every year, in perpetuity[71] (Leviticus 16:29,31). "For it is not possible that the blood of bulls and goats could take away sins" (Hebrews 10:4).

Praise the Lord that from this necessity, among others, Jesus freed God's people when He fulfilled the requirement *permanently* by offering Himself: "Not with the blood of goats and calves, but with His own blood He entered the Most Holy Place once for all, having obtained eternal redemption."

> "For if the blood of bulls and goats and the ashes of a heifer, sprinkling the unclean, sanctifies for the purifying of the flesh, how much more shall the blood of Christ, who through the eternal Spirit offered Himself without spot [blemish] to God, cleanse your conscience from dead works to serve the living God? And for this reason He is the Mediator of the New Covenant, by means of death, for the redemption of the transgressions under the first covenant, that those who are called may receive the promise of the eternal inheritance" (Hebrews 9:12-15).

This is Jesus our High Priest, who will remain High Priest forever because of the sheer perfection of His sacrifice (6:20; 7:26-28).

"We have such a High Priest, who is seated at the right hand of the throne of the Majesty in the heavens, a Minister of the sanctuary and of the true tabernacle which the Lord erected, and not man" (8:1-2). Imagine the scene that is described here! Our High Priest sits "at the right hand of the throne," always able to intercede for us. He *never* needs to satisfy any additional requirement in order to obtain access to God's throne. "But He, because He continues forever, has an unchangeable priesthood. Therefore, He is also able to save to the uttermost [completely or forever] those who come to God through Him, since He always lives to make intercession for them" (7:24-25). How marvelous it is to behold Christ's *perfect* and *permanent* fulfillment of the office of High Priest! And how comforting it should be to us to know that "we have an Advocate with the Father, Jesus Christ the righteous" (1 John 2:1)!

"Seeing then that we have a great High Priest who has passed through the heavens, Jesus the Son of God," what was the conclusion that the author of Hebrews commanded? With that understanding in mind, he challenged, "let us hold fast our confession" (4:14). We know what manner of High Priest we have. And on the basis of that knowledge, we can "hold fast the confession of our hope without wavering, for He who promised is faithful" (10:23). As the word is used here, our confession is the content of our belief: founded on the revealed truth of Scripture; animated and worked out in practice by faith; and empowered by the Holy Spirit who dwells within each of us. To *that* confession we are enabled to "hold fast," this verse affirms, by trusting in the faithfulness of God.

---

[71] perpetuity (C): duration for an indefinite period; lasting forever

Our confidence stems from the Lord's extensive history of absolute faithfulness. That record includes what is written in His Word as well as our own experiences of His faithfulness as we walk with Him. Built upon the bedrock of that certainty, we believe that everything He has promised to do, He *will* do, without exception.

Not for one moment do we need to be concerned that our access to the Father has been suspended or revoked. The pathway to God's throne that was established by Jesus, "the forerunner," He keeps open forever (6:20). With His sinless blood, Jesus pierced the veil that shielded the Most Holy Place from all who were unfit to enter. By His sacrifice, Christ supplied all who truly belong to Him with unrestricted access to approach "the throne of grace" and speak directly to our Eternal Father. What an awesome privilege this is! And how little we appreciate it!

> "Therefore, brethren, having boldness [confidence] to enter the Holiest by the blood of Jesus, by a new and living way which He consecrated for us, through the veil, that is, His flesh, and having a High Priest over the house of God, let us draw near with a true heart in full assurance of faith, having our hearts sprinkled from an evil conscience and our bodies washed with pure water" (10:19-22).

The way lies open. The Mediator, our Advocate, is already there, seated in a place of highest honor. What prevents us from coming, from approaching the throne of God Almighty, where grace awaits? What hinders us most of the time is mentioned in the next verse of our central passage: "For we do not have a High Priest who cannot sympathize with our weaknesses, but was in all points tempted as we are, yet without sin" (4:15). Our profound and sometimes pronounced "weaknesses" inhibit us from entering boldly and without reservation into His presence, coming before His throne. These weaknesses are infirmities or debilities of the body or the mind, including an inability to produce results. The Greek word here translated "weaknesses" literally means "strengthlessness" or "feebleness." That seems relatively straightforward: we are weak, infirm, feeble; we have no strength.

Interestingly, we should also note that the Greek term includes the ideas of sickness, malady, and disease. In other words, the weaknesses that obstruct or restrain us from confidently drawing near to "the throne of grace," "in full assurance of faith," are among the many lingering effects of our *infection* with sin. His idea calls to mind a well-known verse from Jeremiah's prophecy:

> "The heart is deceitful above all things,
> And desperately wicked;
> Who can know it?" (17:9).

The phrase "desperately wicked" here can also mean "incurably sick." Again, the connections among wickedness, strengthlessness, and the lethal disease of sin are evident.

The Apostle Paul wrote poignantly about the shortcomings of his flesh that prohibited him from obeying the law of good that he willed to do:

> "For I know that in me (that is, in my flesh) nothing good dwells; for to will is present with me, but how to perform what is good I do not find. For the good that I will to do, I do not do; but the evil I will not to do, that I practice. Now if I do what I will not to do, it is no longer I who do it, but sin that dwells in me.
>
> ...O wretched man that I am! Who will deliver me from this body of death?" (Romans 7:18-20,24).

Paul recognized and lamented the effects that his infection with sin had on his ability to obey the Lord. "For what I will to do, that I do not practice; but what I hate, that I do" (verse 15). "I *want* to obey God, but I end up sinning instead! What is wrong with me?" he cried. "Who will save me from this horrible, maddening dilemma?"

But then Paul answered his own question: "I thank God—through Jesus Christ our Lord!" (verse 25). God the Father, by the awesome work that He accomplished through Jesus, saved Paul (and us) from the terrible situation that was brought about by the lethal contagion of sin. *His* power succeeded where we had none. Christ's obedience prevailed where we had failed countless times. Even though Jesus encountered all of the same *types* of temptations that we confront, He never sinned. He knows intimately the difficulties and the struggles that we must contend with in life. When He intercedes with God on our behalf, seated beside Him on His throne, He can relate to us because He has walked among us.

Jesus has endured every degree and variety of temptation to which human beings are subject ("in all points"). And how did He achieve this? By *becoming* human! His infinite compassion arises from His heart of perfect love, and it includes the fact that He personally experienced what we all experience:

> "For it was fitting for Him, for whom are all things and by whom are all things, in bringing many sons to glory, to make the captain of their salvation perfect through sufferings. For both He who sanctifies and those who are being sanctified are all of one, for which reason He is not ashamed to call them brethren....
>
> Inasmuch then as the children have partaken of flesh and blood, He Himself likewise shared in the same.... Therefore, in all things He had to be made

like His brethren, that He might be a merciful and faithful High Priest in things pertaining to God, to make propitiation[72] for the sins of the people. For in that He Himself has suffered, being tempted, He is able to aid those who are tempted" (2:10-11,14,17-18).

Jesus is **uniquely** qualified to represent us before the Father. "And having been perfected, He became the author of eternal salvation to all who obey Him..." (5:9). To the regenerate Christian heart, these truths are *wonderful* beyond expression!

"Let us therefore come boldly to the throne of grace, that we may obtain mercy and find grace to help in time of need" (4:16). The word "therefore" in this admonition is significant. It encapsulates[73] all of the information about Jesus as High Priest, His uniqueness and perfect qualification, and the path unto the presence "behind the veil" that He opened, which no one can shut (see Revelation 3:7). Built upon the immovable foundation of that body of truth, we are told, "let us...come boldly to the throne of grace." Everything that normally inhibits us from proceeding confidently into His presence has been taken into account. Jesus has already dealt with *everything* that might hinder us. The way lies open. His spilled blood marks the path. The nails that pinned Him to a cross now hold the door open, so that nothing and no one can close it to those who come to God through Him.

We do not have "boldness to enter the Holiest" because *we* deserve to be there. If access depended upon *our* merit, then the door would be barred against us forever. Our confidence in coming without reservation to "the throne of grace" stems from the belief that **Jesus** deserves to be there. And we are joined to Him like branches to a vine, or parts of a body to the head. Sinful, diseased, and feeble as we are, He says "Come." Whatever objections we may raise, protesting our unworthiness, He bids us "Come." He knows that we are unworthy. He knew our arguments before we thought of them, and still He summons us to "Come."

"My blood has covered all of your sins, your inadequacies, your strengthlessness," He assures us. "Look, the way lies open. Come, beloved, to the throne. Receive mercy and grace to help you in your hour of need. Come, dear saint, for My grace is sufficient for you, and My strength is made perfect in weakness. Come to Me, receive My light and My healing.

"I have been where you are. I understand perfectly what you are enduring, and I have also experienced such trials. I have walked many miles in your shoes. Whatever tempts you, I know the way of escape. Whatever hardship or adversity you face, I can resolve, and I will bring you through it. Whatever need

---

[72] propitiation (O): something that obtains favor or appeases; atonement
[73] encapsulates (O): encloses in a capsule, a defined package

you have, I can supply. Nothing is impossible for Me, and I love you more than you could ever imagine."

"The way lies open, so come."

Day 15 — Praying According to God's Will

"Now this is the confidence that we have in Him, that if we ask anything according to His will, He hears us. And if we know that He hears us, whatever we ask, we know that we have the petitions that we have asked of Him" (1 John 5:14-15). As a point of beginning for studying this characteristic of prayer, if we seek to pray according to our Father's will, then the question we need to ask is, "What is God's will?" Before we proceed to an answer, however, hopefully it will be enough to state that all sincere Christians *should* desire to pray according to His will. (Surely it is not necessary to prove the futility of asking anything that is *contrary* to His will.) In other words, all genuine believers want their prayers to align with the Lord's will, to the extent that they are open to implementing any necessary changes. With that said, in order to understand what God's will is, an important distinction needs to be highlighted.

Throughout the Bible, God's will is pronounced both *subjectively* and *objectively*. Distinguishing between the two hinges on the difference between what the Lord desires or allows to occur and what He sovereignly **causes** to happen. (If this seems a bit confusing, continue reading and it should become clearer.) To illustrate the disparity[74] between God's subjective and objective wills, we will revisit an exceptionally familiar passage of Scripture found in Genesis 2-3.

"And the LORD God commanded the man, saying, 'Of every tree of the garden you may freely eat; but of the tree of the knowledge of good and evil you shall not eat, for in the day that you eat of it you shall surely die'" (Genesis 2:16-17). God the Creator very clearly communicated His will to Adam and Eve, including what the consequences of disobedience would be. And we can be certain that they understood the Lord's will in this matter because Eve reiterated His commandment to the serpent in 3:2-3. No ambiguity or confusion existed. They did not have to "discern God's will" in this regard, as saints throughout history have been compelled to do on various issues. No "ethical dilemma" or "moral quandary" needed to be resolved. The whole situation was painted black and white.

The evidence of Scripture plainly demonstrates that the Lord's will as expressed here was *subjective*—a statement of God's desire. If His will in this respect were *objective*, then it would have been physically impossible for Adam and Eve to take and eat the fruit of the forbidden tree. For them to do so would involve overruling the Creator's sovereign power, which is utterly impossible. The fact that they had a *choice* of whether or not to obey—that they were physically *able* to remove fruit from the tree and eat it—indicates beyond question that God's stated will in this instance must be understood *subjectively*. The Lord declared His desire that they would not partake of that particular tree,

---

[74] disparity (O): inequality, difference

but left them with some freedom concerning which course they would pursue. The same type of subjectivity is evident in the Decalogue, the Ten Commandments that God provided as a succinct presentation of His moral law for humanity (Exodus 20:1-17).

Before we return to our text in 1 John, let us consider another example that illustrates the difference between the subjective and the objective will of God. "In those days Hezekiah was sick and near death. And Isaiah the prophet, the son of Amoz, went to him and said to him, 'Thus says the LORD: "Set your house in order, for you shall die, and not live""" (2 Kings 20:1). The Creator of the universe "gives to all life, breath, and all things" (Acts 17:25). Consequently, when He sends a prophet to tell someone, "You shall die," that person had better pray that the Lord's will in that instance is subjective. If God says, "You shall die," and His will is objective, then death is unavoidable.

In a contrasting scene, "the LORD sent Nathan to David" to confront him about his adultery with Bathsheba and the terrible business with her husband, Uriah the Hittite (2 Samuel 12:1). David then acknowledged his sin, confessing "I have sinned against the LORD":

> "And Nathan said to David, 'The LORD also has put away your sin; you shall not die. However, because by this deed you have given great occasion to the enemies of the LORD to blaspheme, the child also who is born to you shall surely die.' Then Nathan departed to his house."

> "And the LORD struck the child that Uriah's wife bore to David, and it became ill. David therefore pleaded with God for the child, and David fasted and went in and lay all night on the ground" (verses 13-16).

Nathan had already told the king that the child "shall surely die." But David hoped that the Lord's expressed will in the matter was subjective, and therefore open to change. Based on that possibility, he fasted and prayed and pleaded for God to spare the child.

The baby eventually died, and David accepted that the Lord's will had been done. Afterward, he explained his actions to his servants, saying, "While the child was alive, I fasted and wept; for I said, 'Who can tell whether the LORD will be gracious to me, that the child may live?' But now he is dead, why should I fast? Can I bring him back again? I shall go to him, but he shall not return to me" (verses 22-23). While any hope remained, David interceded on his son's behalf. He knew the Lord to be wondrously gracious, as he proclaimed repeatedly in many of his psalms. So David hoped and prayed that the Lord's grace would prevail over His declaration that the child "shall surely die." Once God's will was finalized, however, he accepted and submitted to it, in keeping with his character as a man after God's own heart (see 1 Samuel 13:14; 16:7,12-13).

David hoped that God's stated will would prove to be subjective, and prayed that the outcome would change from what was prophesied. Ultimately, in that instance it was objective, and the child died. By comparison, when Hezekiah was informed by Isaiah (another prophet) that *he* would die, he also wept and prayed. "Then he turned his face toward the wall, and prayed to the LORD, saying, 'Remember now, O LORD, I pray, how I have walked before You in truth and with a loyal heart, and have done what was good in Your sight.' And Hezekiah wept bitterly" (2 Kings 20:2-3). Hezekiah's life displayed the sincerity of his love for God, yet he was still very sorrowful about the prospect of his impending death. Unlike in David's circumstances, however, the prediction of Hezekiah's death *was* subjective. Moreover, the action that God elected to take was explicitly influenced by Hezekiah's prayers and heartfelt sorrow. We know this because God sent Isaiah back to Hezekiah with the report, "Thus says the LORD, the God of David your father: 'I have heard your prayer, I have seen your tears; surely I will heal you.... And I will add to your days fifteen years'" (verses 5,6).

As we have seen, subjective and objective make a world of difference when it comes to praying according to God's will. Having now (hopefully) a clearer understanding of the distinction between the two, let us return to our primary text in 1 John. In the operative phrase there, "according to His will," the word "will" is used *subjectively* (verse 14). Here, the language of *Vine's* may prove beneficial in grasping what that means: In 1 John 5:14, God's will is "being spoken of as the emotion of being desirous, rather than as the thing 'willed'" (*Vine's*, "will," A,1,b). So if it is necessary to ask "according to His will" in order to have "confidence" that "He hears us," how then do we determine His will so that we can be sure our petitions are aligned with it? Are we left in a situation like Hezekiah's or David's, pleading with God but painfully uncertain of His will in the matter?

As a general rule that applies always and everywhere, *God's Word* is a grand repository[75] of His will as it has been revealed throughout history. And that is true in terms of both communication (how He has made known His will) and manifestation (how He has executed His will). Stated more simply, the Bible is an extensive record of God's will operating in the lives of His people and in the world at large. By prayerfully and diligently studying the Scriptures over time, we can acquire a much deeper understanding of the Lord's purposes, plans, desires, and actions—His will. Becoming intimately familiar with the revelation of God's will that He has graciously supplied to humanity—the Bible—provides us with a glimpse into His mind. Lest we become puffed up with pride by the knowledge that He gives us, however, we should remind ourselves of such truths as Isaiah 55:8-9. Whatever He teaches us, even the most learned among us, His mind remains **infinitely** greater than we are capable

---

[75] repository (C): a place or receptacle in which anything is stored

of comprehending. Still, the rule endures: To discern God's will, begin by studying His Word.

With that principle serving as a baseline for discovering the Lord's will, it is encouraging to note that there are places in Scripture where His will is very plainly stated. One perfect example is the Decalogue that we mentioned earlier—the Ten Commandments (Exodus 20:1-17). These ten mandates present God's moral law—His **will**—in a concise and memorable package. No ambiguity or guesswork is involved. Another place where His will is expressed forthrightly is found in 1 Thessalonians: "For this is the will of God, your sanctification" (4:3). And Jesus issued a powerful statement of the Father's will when He told His disciples, "A new commandment I give to you, that you love one another; as I have loved you, that you also love one another" (John 13:34). We can consult other verses of Scripture and scenes from Christ's life to develop a more complete picture of what that kind of love looks like in practice. But His "new commandment" is no less a declaration of God's will than the Ten Commandments that were delivered to Moses. (No proof is really needed of this truth, but it is supported by Jesus's response to the lawyer's question in Matthew 22:35-40.)

Obviously, it is relatively easy to know God's will when He spells it out for us in such plain language. But what about those circumstances that all Christians encounter in which it is not entirely clear what His will is? For example, we are confronted with a choice between two courses of action, and both of them seem to be honorable and worthwhile: Which one does the Lord favor? Or, alternatively, all roads leading away from a point appear to be equally horrible: How do we select the "least worst" of the possibilities? Those of us who are sincerely surrendered to the Lordship of Christ are committed to walking (and praying) "according to His will." But since it is not *always* clear what His will is, sometimes we are constrained to act without much confidence that our chosen path is the one He desires us to follow.

Not surprisingly, God's Word provides counsel that applies to such difficult circumstances. For instance, in his Epistle to the Colossians, Paul included an encouraging and instructive statement describing the content of his prayers:

> "For this reason we also...do not cease to pray for you, and to ask that you may be filled with the knowledge of His will in all wisdom and spiritual understanding; that you may walk worthy of the Lord, fully pleasing Him, being fruitful in every good work and increasing in the knowledge of God..." (1:9,10).

Ability to discern the Lord's will is a byproduct of developing godly wisdom (as opposed to worldly wisdom, which is "foolishness with God"—1 Corinthians 3:19; also see James 3:13-15). *Godly* wisdom is usually acquired gradually over the course of time through the application of "spiritual understanding" to various life experiences (including studies). And our spiritual cognition[76] is empowered and sharpened by the Holy Spirit as we consistently "walk in the Spirit." While we grow in wisdom, the Lord increases our capacity to discern His will. He expands our "knowledge of His will" and molds us more and more into the image of Christ—which is essentially sanctification. Our lives will align more closely with His will as this transformation progresses, so that in time we will "walk worthy of the Lord, fully pleasing Him." We will bear fruit through our works done in and unto the Lord, and we will come to know God more intimately (see Ephesians 2:10).

"Therefore do not be unwise, but understand what the will of the Lord is" (Ephesians 5:17). We see that wisdom and understanding of God's will are close traveling companions, a truth that is repeatedly affirmed in Scripture (much of the Book of Proverbs, for example). "If any of you lacks wisdom," James wrote, "let him ask of God, who gives to all liberally and without reproach, and it will be given to him" (1:5). The Lord *will* teach us wisdom when we ask Him for it in faith (verses 6-7).

We know that God *desires* for His people to be wise because His Word is perfectly clear on that point (for example, Proverbs 4:5,7; Ephesians 5:15-16). So when we petition Him to give us wisdom, according to 1 John 5:14 we are requesting something that is undoubtedly "according to His will." Therefore, we *know* that He hears us, and we can be completely confident that He *will* provide us with the wisdom for which we have asked. Then, as we continue to increase in wisdom, our ability to discern His will in other matters improves. That, in turn, enables us to pray "according to His will" in those areas as well. With time, this whole process will bring us into closer alignment with His will, so that Colossians 1:10 will apply to us. And why does this process foster such conformity to His will? Because "it is God who works in you both to will and to do for His good pleasure" (Philippians 2:13). "God breathes the desire into our hearts; and as soon as the desire is there, before we call He begins to answer (Isaiah 65:24)" ("True Prayer" 14). The Spirit conducts the internal work of transformation (sanctification) that produces growth in Christlikeness and more faithful adherence to the path of God's will.

In order for our prayers to be effective and fervent, both individually and collectively, they must be "according to His will." Intuitively, this makes complete sense. Since God is altogether perfect, *everything* He wills is also perfect. Never is there a better option than the one represented by His will. Our part is to discover His will, seeking it with vehement cries and tears, if necessary, and to embrace and obey it fully once known. Inevitably, perhaps even frequently (at first), situations will arise in which *His* desire is diametrically[77] opposed to our own (think of Jonah). Or His will might leave us

---

[76] cognition (C): the mental processes by which knowledge is apprehended

[77] diametrically (C): like two points at opposite ends of a line passing through the center of a circle

feeling confused, even angry. This is our flesh asserting itself, trying to propel us to prioritize our own desires over God's. We can expect our flesh to offer potent resistance to the Holy Spirit's work of transformation within us (see Galatians 5:16-17). Whenever His will causes us to feel uncertain or vexed or at odds with the Lord's leading, it is never because there is anything wrong with His will. The shortcoming is always ours.

Paul elaborated at length on the role of the flesh in sabotaging both our growth in the Spirit and our obedience of the Father's will. But his counsel is too extensive to delve into here. Instead, we will content ourselves with a simple summary of his own (inspired) composition: "And those who are Christ's have crucified the flesh with its passions and desires. If we live in the Spirit, let us also walk in the Spirit" (Galatians 5:24-25). We must treat our flesh as though it were dead—"crucified," in fact (see Romans 6:6,11). If we yearn for "effective, fervent prayer" that "avails much," then we must *obey* the Lord's will when He makes it known to us. "There must be mingled with acceptable prayer the holy salt of submission to the divine will..." ("Effective Prayer" 12). Obedience will involve sacrifice, self-denial, and some painful choices at times. But we can take these decisions and obey Him with complete confidence that His will is always the best way.

For further reflection, if desired: consider how God's proclamation of impending judgment against Sodom and Gomorrah was an example of His *objective* will (Genesis 18:16-19:29). Then contrast that with the destruction of Nineveh that God decreed to the Prophet Jonah in the book bearing his name. That judgment ultimately proved to be an expression of God's *subjective* will. Similar conditions of wanton[78] depravity existed in both areas, yet one was incinerated and the other spared.

---

[78] wanton (CO): licentious, excessive; lacking proper restraint or motives

Day 16 — Prayer as Planning and Preparation

Yesterday's lesson underscored the necessity of wisdom in discerning and following the Lord's will. Today's reading will continue the theme of wisdom as it pertains to practical Christian living. As we will highlight in our exploration of the subject, earnest prayer during planning and preparation is a feature of the path of wisdom. Not surprisingly, since we will emphasize wisdom, our scriptural support will be drawn largely from the Book of Proverbs, an inspired treasury of wisdom.

Many of us have heard the familiar (though somewhat trite[79]) expression, "Failure to plan is planning to fail." Although it lacks verbal sophistication, there is nonetheless a gem of truth embedded in this unrefined packaging. Generally speaking, sound planning is critical to the success of any endeavor, from the most mundane[80] to the most monumental. In fact, the greater the *scale* of any undertaking—in terms of the size or the complexity or the seriousness and reach of its ramifications—the more important proper planning and preparation become. We may require only a vague list to purchase groceries at the market, but years of ongoing work can be involved in building a skyscraper before ground is broken. Whatever the project or task happens to be, planning is essential to ultimate success. And along the way it is necessary for efficiency of execution and for responsible stewardship of resources. "Failure to plan" may not always equal "planning to fail," but it *is* unwise.

Most of us already plan, in differing ways and to varying extents. Many of us reside and function in an extremely busy and demanding world. Consequently, planning and preparation are crucial to using as fruitfully as possible the time and the material resources that God has entrusted to our management. We plan to leave work by a certain time so we can transport our kids to soccer practice. We plan the meal that we will serve at a gathering of church friends so that we can remember to purchase the required ingredients on our next trip to the supermarket. Some of us might plan to skip certain meals for a month so we will be able to afford our children's school supplies. Others may plan how to fit more shifts into the week, or even a second job, to generate additional income for some burdensome medical expenses. Whether or not we engage in it *deliberately*, we all plan and we all prepare.

The question is, how many of us plan and prepare **prayerfully**? Some of us might pray more or less faithfully about "the big stuff": how much to deposit in Lucy's college fund; what model of vehicle to purchase; whether or not to homeschool the children; involvement with a particular ministry at church. But

---

[79] trite (C): worn by use; used till novelty and interest are lost
[80] mundane (O): dull, routine

the Bible does not teach us to pray about "important" issues and attend to smaller matters ourselves. On the contrary, God's Word is abundantly clear that we Christians are to pray in and for *all things*. Here we will rely on a relatively well-known but nonetheless highly-instructive excerpt from the Book of Proverbs:

> "Trust in the LORD with all your heart,
> And lean not on your own understanding;
> In all your ways acknowledge Him,
> And He shall direct your paths" (Proverbs 3:5-6).

These two verses are heavily laden with wisdom, so we will unpack their precious cargo in pieces.

"Trust in the LORD with all your heart" does not mean "trust Him with the big stuff, but try not to bother Him with trivialities." It means to have complete and unreserved faith in Him (and only Him) in every aspect and eventuality of life, from the greatest to the least. The idea conveyed is a conscious and purposeful dependence on Him, nothing withheld. When we trust the Lord in this way, we are wholly given over to reliance on Him, and never in any circumstance or to any degree trusting in ourselves—or in anyone else, for that matter (see Psalm 118:8-9). If this standard of trust *seems* unattainably high, that is because it is. While we reside in these corruptible bodies and continue to be subject to the inclinations of our flesh, we will never be able to trust the Lord perfectly. We will fail, we will fall short, we will miss the mark, we will gratify the desires of our flesh: In a word, we will sin. But that does not mean that the caliber of trust mandated here ceases to be the ideal to which we aspire. God's standards do not change simply because we fail to live up to them. In fact, they do not change at all.

The second line of the proverb complements and reinforces the first. Part of trusting entirely in the Lord involves a deliberate and exclusive dependence upon *His* understanding instead of our own. To state the obvious, God is our Creator and we are His creations. All of His attributes are infinitely superior to our own. So much greater is He, in truth, that Isaiah 55:8-9, which we referenced yesterday, is still an understatement. It conveys the point, but in reality there is no legitimate basis for comparison between the Creator and His Creation. We could sooner outlive eternity than probe the immeasurable depths of the mind of God. Although it is impossible for our finite minds to comprehend exactly what it means that His understanding is *infinite*, we can at least recognize that it is true. And that being the case, do we suppose that there is some kind of risk included in leaning on His understanding, dismissing our own?

Our Lord is not obligated to provide an account of Himself to us. He is not beholden to us, nor does He owe us an explanation (see Romans 9:21; also, as time permits, Job 38-41). God alone is the Self-Existent One, answering to none, and doing "whatever He pleases" (Psalm 115:3). Our place is not to interrogate Him about His purposes or His plans. The Bible, His revealed Word, affirms repeatedly that all of His purposes and plans are good. He sovereignly causes all things to "work together for good to those who love God, to those who are the called according to His purpose" (Romans 8:28; also 12:2). Those assurances should be sufficient for us, His creations, to silence our questioning. Our part is to believe and to trust the Lord, confident of the eternal truth of His Word, and to lean on *His* understanding. Anything less than this is doubt, which is another name for unbelief (see James 1:6-7). And failure or refusal to believe God is tantamount[81] to calling Him a liar— Him, the very Author and Source of truth (Numbers 23:19; John 14:6; 17:17)! "For what if some did not believe?" Paul inquired. "Will their unbelief make the faithfulness of God without effect? Certainly not! Indeed, let God be true but every man a liar" (Romans 3:3-4).

Having established the attitude that we should have concerning the Lord's ways, the third line of the proverb is where it intersects with our current study, "Prayer as Planning and Preparation." "In all your ways acknowledge Him," verse 6 challenges, with the incentive attached that "He shall direct your paths." ("Direct" here can also mean "make smooth" or "straight.") To rephrase this for clarity, God will smooth out and straighten our paths when we acknowledge Him in all our ways. Planning and preparation involve charting a course that recedes before us into the mists of a nonexistent future. We can attempt to speculate about and anticipate what lies ahead, but only God knows with complete certainty (see James 4:13-16). We develop our plans and prepare based on our educated guesses about what the future holds, but these are imperfect at best. So God comforts us in our confusion and uncertainty with the assurance that *He* will act upon the road before us. He will make it smooth(er) and straight(er). But He wants us to be devoted to Him to the extent that we acknowledge Him in all our ways. To understand better what this looks like in practice, we need to explore the significance of the operative word, "acknowledge." Before we do, though, a couple of qualifications must be inserted.

First, when the Lord smooths and straightens our paths, that does *not* mean that we will not experience adversity, persecution, and other difficulties. We know that God cannot contradict Himself, and Jesus declared plainly that we *will* endure hardships: "In the world you will have tribulation; but be of good cheer, I have overcome the world" (John 16:33). Paul stated a similar fact in his counsel to Timothy: "Yes, and all who desire to live godly in Christ Jesus will suffer persecution" (2 Timothy 3:12). When God makes our paths smooth and straight, He provides direction as well as an increased sense of confidence that the road we tread is the one on which He desires us to walk. "A man's heart plans his way," states another proverb, "But the LORD directs his steps" (16:9).

---

[81] tantamount (C): equivalent to in effect or meaning

God goes before us, casting aside boulders of anxious uncertainty and filling in potholes of second-guessing. He splinters misleading signposts erected by the enemy to divert us from the correct course. And He marks blazes periodically along the trail to guide us on our journey. Nevertheless, the trek remains arduous and requires dedication and perseverance.

The second qualification that we need to bear in mind is that the Book of Proverbs, in general, deals not in concrete promises but in truths that apply in *most* cases. To illustrate this, we will look briefly at an example that is familiar to many biblically-minded Christians, particularly those who are parents:

> "Train up a child in the way he should go,
> And when he is old he will not depart from it" (22:6).

The language makes it sound like a binding principle, a *quid pro quo*[82], with the predictability of a mathematical formula: "Parents, if you do 'A', then 'B' will happen." For that reason, it is perhaps understandable that some well-meaning Christian parents have latched onto this proverb and "claimed" it in their prayers as a promise that God will restore their wayward children. But sadly, not all "prodigal son" stories end with the rebel returning home to the father's waiting arms. As a result, the faith of some parents has been challenged because they felt God had not done what He said He would do (to their way of thinking). But the Book of Proverbs does not conform to a *quid pro quo* framework. And we need to remember that fact as we analyze 3:5-6.

Returning to our exploration of the word "acknowledge," the original Hebrew term has an assortment of meanings. So in order to understand what "In all your ways acknowledge Him" signifies in practice, we need to develop an inclusive sense of those meanings. In passing, however, it is interesting to note how fitting it is that the term has such a range of connotations[83]. For "acknowledge" as an action to pertain to and incorporate *all* of our ways, it must necessarily be adaptable and flexible. The irony here is endearing. We are *acknowledging* the wisdom of God evidenced in the words that the Bible uses, even as we consider one use of the word "acknowledge" in Scripture.

Bible translators should be commended for their selection of the English word "acknowledge" to express most of the prominent meanings of the original Hebrew. Since there is no direct correlation between Hebrew and English in this instance, "acknowledge" is arguably the closest that English has to an equivalent term. As a point of beginning, we acknowledge God when we **thank** Him for everything that He gives us, specifically and as it is given. This requires maintaining a continuous awareness of the fact that *everything* we receive is from Him. Every thing is a dispensation of His faithful and loving providence:

[82] quid pro quo (C): this for that; something given or received in exchange for something else
[83] connotations (O): implied meanings in addition to the primary meanings

clean water to drink and the homes we live in; clothes to cover and protect our bodies and the food that nourishes them (recall Psalm 104:27-29; Acts 17:25; James 1:17).

We acknowledge God when we **affirm** the authority and unchangeable truth of His living and powerful Word. We acknowledge God when we perceive Him working in our circumstances and **recognize** what He does, either in prayer or by reporting His actions to another person—or both. We acknowledge God when we **call attention** to the evidence of His sovereignty displayed in the world. We acknowledge God when we **share** the gospel of salvation with others; when we **confess** how He has graciously provided the way for our ruined relationships with Him to be restored. We acknowledge God when we **obey** Him in spite of the consequences, proclaiming by our lives that His will needs to be served at all times instead of our own. And we acknowledge God when we investigate and **mark** His "fingerprints" in Creation, the signs of His awesome creative genius that are everywhere to be seen.

More could be written, of course, but this should be enough for our purposes. When Scripture instructs the saints to "acknowledge Him" in all their ways, it means **all** of them: every circumstance, every eventuality, every situation; at *all* times and in *all* places. This level of acknowledgment involves cultivating a continuous mindfulness of the Lord. It requires an ongoing awareness that not only "senses" His Spirit working in the world but also communicates continually with Him. (We will examine this type of correspondence in more detail on day 19, "Praying Without Ceasing.") Simply stated, what we have described is an image of walking in the Spirit (recall Galatians 5:16). It portrays a steady stride "as children of light (for the fruit of the Spirit is in all goodness, righteousness, and truth), finding out what is acceptable to the Lord" (Ephesians 5:8-10). This type of constant acknowledgment of Him in all ways pictures a journey of faith as "children of God without fault in the midst of a crooked and perverse generation, among whom you shine as lights in the world" (Philippians 2:15). The road is still adorned with all manner of temptations, pitfalls, and enemies lying in wait to ambush us. But when we walk along the trail of life in the way that He desires, acknowledging Him in all ways, He goes before us as our Almighty Trailblazer, our unwearying Forerunner, to smooth and straighten the path ahead.

We needed to emphasize the kind of life to which *all* Christians are called because it bears directly on "Prayer as Planning and Preparation." If we are not careful, our plans and preparations quickly begin to center on ourselves. But selfishness and self-centeredness are not overcome through asceticism[84] or empty rituals. They are counteracted by **surrender**. And that is what Proverbs 3:5-6 depicts: surrender—submission to the Lordship of God. All of our plans

---

[84] asceticism (C): the practice of training oneself to endure severe bodily hardship as a religious discipline

and preparations, like our lives in general, should revolve around *God's* will, not our own. That fact is stressed in this excerpt from Proverbs, and it is repeated throughout Scripture. Not surprisingly, no better example of this can be found than that of the Lord Jesus. He explicitly stated to His disciples, "For I have come down from heaven, not to do My own will, but the will of Him who sent Me" (John 6:38). And Paul spotlighted Jesus's single-minded determination to do the Father's will in his Epistle to the Philippians: "Let this mind be in you which was also in Christ Jesus, who...humbled Himself and became obedient to the point of death, even the death of the cross" (2:5-6,8). Jesus's life on earth concentrated exclusively on serving His Father's will, and our lives should have the same sharply-defined focus.

Since these principles apply to *all* of life, no single example will adequately illustrate what they look like in practice. However, to demonstrate the attitude of heart involved, we will briefly consider two poignant incidents from the life of Christ. The first occurred in the garden of Gethsemane, as Jesus prepared to confront the terrible ordeal that He knew was imminent (Matthew 26:36-46). "He began to be sorrowful and deeply distressed" (verse 37). Peter, James, and John accompanied Him as He ventured into the garden, and "He said to them, 'My soul is exceedingly sorrowful, even to death. Stay here and watch with Me'" (verses 37,38).

Luke's account of this scene reveals just how excruciating it was for Jesus. "And being in agony, He prayed more earnestly. Then His sweat became like great drops of blood falling down to the ground" (22:44). The language used here is not figurative, as some have suggested. During periods of exquisite stress, the body can become so flooded with stress hormones that capillaries[85] near the skin's surface can rupture. Small quantities of blood then mix with sweat released by the sudoriferous (sweat) glands in a condition known as *hematohydrosis*. It appears that the person is literally "sweating blood." (How appropriate that Luke the physician would include this medical fact.)

Knowing what awaited Him, Jesus "went a little farther and fell on His face, and prayed, saying, 'O My Father, if it is possible, let this cup pass from Me; nevertheless, not as I will, but as You will'" (Matthew 26:39). Although Jesus asked to be spared from the unimaginable horror of His Passion, He still subordinated[86] Himself obediently to the Father's will. And that is precisely the attitude of heart that we need to have as we conceive and develop *all* of our plans and preparations. We pray about everything—trusting, leaning on, and acknowledging Him—then we submit ourselves to obeying His will, whatever it is. While planning and preparing must include prayer, obedience is equally

---

[85] capillaries (O): the very fine blood vessels that connect veins and arteries
[86] subordinated (C): considered or treated as of less importance or weight than something or someone else; made subject to

important. All of these actions are individual parts of a whole. And that whole is a Christian life that glorifies and pleases God.

A second example from the life of Christ that underscores the necessity of "Prayer as Planning and Preparation" returns us to Luke's Gospel. Jesus "went out to the mountain to pray, and continued all night in prayer to God. And when it was day, He called His disciples to Himself; and from them He chose twelve whom He also named apostles" (6:12-13). Consider the enduring significance of those selections! Think about how those twelve men figured into the events that followed, with respect both to the Passion of Christ and to establishment of the church after Jesus ascended. And what did Jesus do before He chose them? He prayed *all night*, indicating clearly how necessary prayer is when we are faced with momentous decisions. "When any crisis of life is seen to be approaching, we should prepare for it by a season of very definite prayer to God…. Many temptations come upon us suddenly and unannounced. All that we can do is lift a cry to God for help then and there. But, many temptations of life we can see ahead of time, and, in such cases, the victory should be won before the temptation really reaches us" (Torrey 78,81).

Has the point been made? Simply stated, Christian living is prayerful living. "For the beauty of nature, the fellowship of the good, the tender love of home; for safe conduct in temptation, strength to overcome, deliverance from evil; for the generosity, the patience, the sympathy of God; and for ten thousand thousand unobserved or unremembered mercies, let us unweariedly bless His Holy Name" (MacIntyre 21). As we pray continually throughout each day, we should acknowledge the Lord in all our ways, leaning on Him exclusively and trusting Him completely. This type of trusting, leaning, and acknowledging is absolutely *essential* to effective and fervent prayer. In all of our planning and preparing, while we walk the narrow road through life as children of God and soldiers in the army of the Lord, the only way we can "bear much fruit" and do what is "acceptable to the Lord" is to proceed in prayer.

Day 17 — Prayer and Fasting

"But you, when you fast, anoint your head and wash your face, so that you do not appear to men to be fasting, but to your Father who is in the secret place; and your Father who sees in secret will reward you openly" (Matthew 6:17-18).

Among the many instructions that Jesus delivered to His disciples in the Sermon on the Mount were a few important points on the subject of fasting. But before we consider what the Lord said *about* fasting, it is worthwhile to note that Jesus introduced His teaching with "when you fast" (verses 16,17). He did not say "if you fast" or "if you feel led to fast," but "when you fast." According to Jesus, fasting is not conditional; it is expected. Fasting is not a relic of the Old Covenant ceremonial religious structure, with its washing and waving, its prescribed and proscribed[87] rituals. Nor is fasting a practice that only zealots or the self-righteous pursue, trying to demonstrate their superior piety by calling attention to themselves as they fast. Jesus addressed such hypocrisy directly in verse 16.

In truth, fasting is as valid in a Christian's life today as it was for the ancient Israelites. For saints to fast in our day is just as appropriate and meaningful as it has been for sincere believers in every generation. For as long as devout men and women have called upon and served the One True God, fasting has featured in their lives to varying extents. Counsel recorded by the Apostle Paul will prove helpful in this regard. He distinguished between what was required under the Old Covenant and the liberty that all saints possess through Christ.

"All things are lawful for me, but all things are not helpful [or profitable]. All things are lawful for me, but I will not be brought under the power of any[thing]" (1 Corinthians 6:12). (Interestingly, in the same context, Paul addressed some pastoral instruction to married couples concerning the issue of sexual intimacy: "Do not deprive one another except with consent for a time," he wrote, "that you may give yourselves to fasting and prayer..." [7:5]. Here he clearly affirmed the practice of fasting as a component of Christian living.) We are no longer bound, as Christians, by the *ceremonial* laws to which the ancient Israelites had to adhere. By contrast, the *moral* law codified[88] in the Ten Commandments continues to apply to all of humanity, Christian and non-Christian alike. So when Paul stated "All things are lawful for me," he was not declaring that it would be permissible for him to worship idols or murder or steal. Instead, he was making a pair of points: first, ceremonial observance had no impact whatsoever on his salvation (see 6:11); second, the fact that he was lawfully allowed to do something did not necessarily mean that he should do it.

---

[87] proscribed (C): forbidden, outlawed, prohibited
[88] codified (O): laws or rules systematically arranged into a code

Confronting a similar issue in the Galatian church, Paul presented the following admonition: "Stand fast therefore in the liberty by which Christ has made us free, and do not be entangled again with a yoke of bondage" (Galatians 5:1). In Christ we have liberty. We are not required to abide by the Old Covenant ceremonial rules and rituals in order to be counted among God's people. We *are* His people because we belong to Jesus. And **no one** can change that fact because no one is powerful enough to remove us from His hand (see John 10:27-30).

Some professing Christians slip into error by including the practice of fasting with the Old Covenant ceremonies. They assume that it does not apply in the so-called "church age." But fasting transcends Old and New Covenants. It is a *timeless* custom undertaken by servants of God who "believe that He is, and that He is a rewarder of those who diligently seek Him" (Hebrews 11:6). And such people have existed throughout humanity's history, from Abel to the present day (verse 4). Fasting attends belief and prayer wherever they occur, without reference to any particular covenant. Specifically regarding the covenant people, Bible scholars recognize that "fasting" had become a common practice among Jews, and was continued among Christians" (*Vine's*: "fast, fasting," A,1,a). Numerous instances of fasting are mentioned in the New Testament, in addition to those occasions that happened before the birth of Christ. For the sake of clarity and simplicity, we can conclude all of this information related to fasting with a single statement: Fasting is a necessary element of obedient and prayerful Christian living.

Since we, as sons and daughters of God, are supposed to fast, we need to understand what constitutes a biblical fast. It may also be helpful to survey some of the different reasons that might propel a person (or group) to undertake a fast. Before we do, however, one critical point must be spotlighted: Fasting never stands alone. Voluntary fasting should *always* be accompanied by abundant and earnest prayer. The concerns or reasons that prompt a fast will vary, but the purpose is always the same. It is a companion to fervent prayer, conveying an intensity of feeling on the part of the individual or group involved. In effect, fasting proclaims, "This matter is more important to me than food!" But without the focused prayer that is supposed to occur at the same time, voluntary fasting is just dieting. Choosing to abstain from food for a period of time, but not for the purpose of ardent prayer, has no spiritual value. It *may* have merit in terms of physical health or benefits to other people, but not spiritual value. By definition, biblical fasting *must* be joined by profuse prayer.

Food was never intended to be the paramount concern in a person's life. Most of us know from experience that some things in life are more important than food. And for Christians, those things should always be the subjects of diligent prayer. Jesus affirmed these truths in His Sermon on the Mount, including this question: "Is not life more than food and the body more than clothing?" (Matthew 6:25). At the beginning of His earthly ministry, when He was tempted by Satan in the wilderness, He responded by repeating a profound truth regarding humanity's relationship to food:

> "And when He had fasted forty days and forty nights, afterward He was hungry. Now when the tempter came to Him, he said, 'If You are the Son of God, command that these stones become bread.'
>
> But He answered and said, 'It is written, "Man shall not live by bread alone, but by every word that proceeds from the mouth of God"'" (4:2-4).

Bread, here representing physical food generally, provides nourishment for the body that sustains all of its cellular processes. But keeping the body alive is not the same thing as life. A person who is physically alive but spiritually dead is not really living. Fullness of life, the abundant life that Jesus came to give, requires spiritual "nourishment" also (see John 10:10).

All genuine Christians have the blessed assurance that "God has given us eternal life, and this life is in His Son. He who has the Son has life; he who does not have the Son of God does not have life" (1 John 5:11-12; also see Ephesians 2:5; Colossians 2:13). And in an inspiring and poignant passage of Scripture, Paul declared, "I have been crucified with Christ; it is no longer I who live, but Christ lives in me; and the life which I now live in the flesh I live by faith in the Son of God, who loved me and gave Himself for me" (Galatians 2:20). Then in his Epistle to the Colossians, he connected our death to sin and new life in Christ with how we conduct ourselves in the present: "If then you were raised with Christ, seek those things which are above, where Christ is, sitting at the right hand of God. Set your mind on things above, not on things on the earth. For you died, and your life is hidden with Christ in God. When Christ who is our life appears, then you also will appear with Him in glory" (3:1-4).

"Set your mind on things above," Paul admonished. Prior to regeneration by the Holy Spirit, people's minds are focused on worldly affairs. But after the Spirit indwells and breathes new life into a person, the mind should be fixed on heavenly matters. Applying this general truth to ourselves, it means that we do not abandon or neglect our earthly responsibilities, but they are not our highest priorities. Our minds should concentrate on godly concerns, in keeping with our commissions as ambassadors for Christ and soldiers in the army of the Lord (remember the Prologue). And that being the case, there are inevitably times when we confront issues of such grave spiritual importance that we voluntarily abstain from food in order to devote ourselves without distraction to fervent prayer. That is biblical fasting. And it is a practice that should be included in every sincere saint's mode of living.

To this point in today's lesson, we have seen that fasting is something all Christians should do. Now let us consider a handful of the reasons that compelled people in the Bible to fast. These can serve to illustrate some of the different motivations that might prompt God's people to fast in our day. To begin with, sometimes fasting is associated with **repentance**. The Prophet Jonah (reluctantly) prophesied the destruction of Nineveh, as the Lord commanded him (Jonah 1:1-3; 3:3-4). The Ninevites heeded this warning, "proclaimed a fast" throughout the city by order of the king, and repented "from their evil way" (Jonah 3:5-10; also read Joel 2:12-18). Additionally, **mourning** and similar periods of emotional intensity are common occasions for prayerful fasting. Remember the moving scene of 2 Samuel 12, wherein King David fasted and pleaded with God not to kill the child that he had conceived in adultery with Bathsheba (verses 13-23; also read Joel 1:13-14).

These examples might give the impression that fasting is only undertaken for negative reasons, but that is not the case. Plenty of affirmative (or positive) motivations for fasting exist, as the Bible indicates. For instance, the Church of Antioch prepared to send out Barnabas and Saul for the work to which the Holy Spirit called them (Acts 13:1-2). The Christians there "fasted and prayed, and laid hands on them," affirming and identifying with their ministry before sending them away (verse 3). Over in 14:23, Paul and Barnabas "prayed with fasting" to **commend to the Lord** the elders they had appointed in the local churches. And, as we read earlier, husbands and wives may abstain from sexual intimacy for a limited time so they can devote themselves to seeking the Lord in fasting and prayer (1 Corinthians 7:5). Elsewhere in Scripture, we find fasting mentioned in the context of **voluntary humbling**. On such occasions, the people of God earnestly sought His **direction** or His **healing**, or they humbled themselves for some other purpose (see Ezra 8:21-23; Psalm 35:13).

All of these reasons for combining fasting with prayer are completely valid for modern saints. But the brief sampling that we have examined is not an exhaustive list. In addition to the various concerns illustrated by these passages, we might cry out to God in profound anxiety or distress. We may experience crushing sorrow over a particular sin. Perhaps we are desperate for answers or a definite course in the midst of uncertainty. We can fast and pray for the blossoming and strengthening of our marriages; for our children and grandchildren (prodigal or not); for a specific ministry that we are involved with or that resonates with the deepest concerns of our hearts; for the millions of Christian martyrs around the world, or for a variety of other reasons. We can fast for one day or one month, individually or corporately, in small groups or entire churches. No prescribed set of *rules* dictates what we must do when we fast. In fact, such a rigid approach would probably fall under the category of "a yoke of bondage," against which Paul cautioned the Galatian church (5:1).

Although no definitive body of rules governs voluntary biblical fasting, several *principles* should steer us in the practice. A few of these we have already discussed, but they warrant repeating. The first is simply that, as Christians, we are *supposed* to fast. Second, any fasting undertaken for spiritual reasons *must* be accompanied by abundant and earnest prayer. Third, while abstaining from physical food to focus on prayer, we need to receive ample spiritual "nourishment" by reading and meditating on the Word of God. We should humbly seek the Lord's will and listen to Him communicate through the Scriptures, with our hearts open to receiving His instruction. Fourth, fasting is intended to be a *liberating* element in a saint's life (read Isaiah 58, if time permits).

We do not fast to demonstrate how pious we are, or because we desire to be esteemed and recognized by others. We do not fast in the mistaken belief that God will grant requests when we fast that He would not otherwise. Is God capricious[89]? Can grace be earned? No, the Lord's favor remains unmerited— grace is still grace—even though we are saved and belong to Him. *When* we fast, we abstain from gratifying the desires of our bodies so that we can concentrate our attention on matters of the Spirit. Primarily, that translates to fervent and focused prayer.

One overarching principle to bear in mind was indicated by Jesus in the passage that opened today's lesson (Matthew 6:17-18). Fasting is supposed to remain between the Lord and us. When we fast correctly, meaning biblically, most people will be completely unaware that we are fasting. God sees the *full* content of our hearts, and He perceives our motives *perfectly* (see Jeremiah 17:10). If our reasons are sound, the Lord knows, and He will respond and reward us according to His good pleasure (1 Chronicles 28:9). However, if our motives for fasting are not honorable, God is not fooled, and He cannot be coerced. For anyone to fast for reasons that are not entirely pure is foolish. The Lord Almighty and All-Knowing cannot be deceived.

On the other face of that coin, the fact that God sees the complete content of our hearts has an undeniably positive aspect. Some Christians, usually for medical reasons, are unable to abstain voluntarily from food for longer than a few hours at a time. For those people, the prospect of fasting for an entire day, let alone more than one, is virtually unthinkable. Does that mean fasting has no role in their lives of faith? Do we suppose that God only honors and rewards fasts that involve abstaining from food? Is our Lord limited, or do we constrain Him in some way to condition His actions and His favor upon what we do? To all of these questions we can respond with one of Paul's favored exclamations: "Certainly not!"

In both the Hebrew and Greek, the words that are translated "fast" in English specifically indicate abstaining from food. So a fast in the Bible, strictly speaking, means to go without eating. But Jesus clearly taught in His Sermon on the Mount, and in some of His parables, that God is more concerned with the attitude of a person's heart than with flawless observance of rituals (see

---

[89] capricious (C): having a disposition or mood inclined to changes of humor or opinion without reason

Hosea 6:6). Pure motives with imperfect execution are more pleasing to Him than perfect observance with a self-serving motive. A poor widow who deposited "two mites" to the temple treasury received praise from Jesus, while the rich who gave of their abundance were not recognized (Mark 12:41-44). She gave *sacrificially*, "her whole livelihood," revealing the content of her heart (verse 44). Jesus commended her, even though the amount of her offering was insignificant, because He perceived the character of her heart. "For the righteous God tests the hearts and minds," a psalm proclaims (7:9). **How** we give reveals the condition of our hearts more than **what** we give. In the same way, *how* and *why* we fast are more important than the particular item from which we abstain. "Every way of man is right in his own eyes," states a proverb, "But the LORD weighs the hearts" (21:2; also see 24:12).

For those Christians who are unable to fast by abstaining from food, other options are available. When we *sincerely* desire to honor the Lord through fasting, He focuses on our hearts, not on the specific thing that we forego. And the sacrifice involved reflects the magnitude of our commitment. This principle applies both to what we give up—whether food or something else—and to the duration of the fast. For one person, abstaining from food for two days might be terribly difficult, and therefore a significant sacrifice. Another Christian may forego television for one month, while someone else might "fast" from social media for the same span of time. (Notice that all of these "fasts" would free up time to spend concentrating on prayer and the Word.) The critical issue is not what we give up and for how long. Instead, the most important criteria for fasting is this: What is in our hearts? The Lord weighs the hearts.

When we fast, let us undertake the practice with mindfulness of its purpose and with hearts devoted to our Lord. Let us remember that we all stand upon a spiritual battlefield. And let us appreciate the role that effective and fervent prayer has in combating the designs and the devices of the enemy. That type of prayer is evident in a Christian life that includes fasting, not out of compulsion, because it is expected, but arising from a sincere desire to seek the Lord earnestly by foregoing certain earthly concerns. As children of light walking in newness of life, our minds should be focused on heavenly, spiritual matters. Any hope that we have of defeating and subduing the forces of darkness arrayed against us flows through the light and power of the Lord, our Commander. With Him we communicate by prayer, and He "speaks" to us through His Word. Has it become evident now how fasting fits into this picture?

Onward, Christian soldiers!

Day 18 — Persistence in Prayer

Persistence in prayer can be challenging for some Christians for several reasons, both conceptual and practical. To begin with, we need to take into consideration the *whole* counsel of God on the subject. Otherwise, we can develop the mistaken impression that the Lord can be pestered into granting our requests. Another line of thought proceeds something like this: Since He knows our hearts perfectly, why not pray about a particular concern or request once and trust Him with the result? Why pray about the same issue or bring Him the same petition repeatedly, since He cannot be coerced? Either it is or is not His will, and our persistence will not alter it one way or another. These are legitimate questions, so to resolve them we will, of course, look to God's Word.

Let us begin by reviewing a passage of Scripture found in Luke's Gospel. As He was instructing His disciples, Jesus delivered a parable about a man who received an unexpected visitor after closing up his house for the night (Luke 11:5-8). His visitor was a friend who wanted to borrow three loaves of bread. And he needed the bread to feed another friend who had stopped at *his* house while on a journey. The first man did not want to leave his bed, disturbing his children in the process, to provide his friend with the bread that he requested. Arriving at the object lesson of the parable, Jesus taught, "I say to you, though he will not rise and give to him because he is his friend, yet because of his persistence he will rise and give him as many as he needs" (verse 8).

Jesus clearly stated that the visitor's petition was satisfied "because of his persistence." At first reading, it seems like the man badgered his friend into giving him what he wanted. But surely Jesus was not instructing His followers to pester the Lord continually until He grants their requests. That sounds too much like trying to bend God's will to our own, which we know is *completely* contrary to Scripture. The essence of Jesus's point in the parable hangs on the significance of the word translated "persistence." So to delve deeper into what He taught, we should begin by mining the meaning of that term.

The Greek word that appears in the NKJV as "persistence" can also be rendered "importunity." That is a rather antiquated[90] term that is not frequently used in our day. Its age is reflected in the fact that it is the word that appears in the 1611 King James (Authorized) Version. According to *Vine's*, the Greek term "denotes 'shamelessness, importunity,'" which is actually more helpful than it might seem. The Greek word is constructed from roots that literally mean "no shame." By consulting our two English dictionaries, *Chambers* and *Oxford*, we can assemble a workable definition for **importunity**: persistence and urgency in requesting or demanding. When we then incorporate the "shamelessness"

---

[90] antiquated (O): old-fashioned; out of date

conveyed by the Greek, we arrive at a solid definition for the word *importunity* as it is used in Luke 11:8: shameless persistence and urgency in requesting or demanding.

We can see easily enough how the actions of the man in Jesus's parable displayed this quality. But are we any closer to resolving our initial questions? The two verses that follow the parable will help us here: "So I say to you, ask, and it will be given to you; seek, and you will find; knock, and it will be opened to you. For everyone who asks receives, and he who seeks finds, and to him who knocks it will be opened" (Luke 11:9-10). The attribute stressed in these verses is **persistence**. In other words, receiving, finding, and opening are *not* emphasized; asking, seeking, and knocking are.

The three operative verbs in Christ's instruction—ask, seek, knock—are in a tense that is not reflected in the English translation. (We should note here that there is good reason for this, as it would sound awkward to the English reader.) As they appear in the Greek, the verbs mean "keep on asking," "keep on seeking," and "keep on knocking." When viewed this way, the shameless persistence that they highlight becomes more apparent. Emphasis is laid on *how* we come to God in prayer, not on what we might get out of it when we do. "We should be careful about what we ask from God. But, when we do begin to pray for a thing, we should never give up praying for it until we receive it or until God makes it very clear and very definite that it is not His will to give it" (Torrey 51). Is it accurate to conclude that God rewards persistence in prayer, as the man "rewarded" his friend's importunity? Yes, God does reward persistence in prayer, but *never* in any way that is contrary to His will. To say that the Lord never contradicts or counteracts His own will is correct, but it is also incomplete. God **cannot** violate His own will.

If some of these themes sound familiar, they should. Persistence is one characteristic of powerful prayer, as are boldness to come before the throne of grace (day 14) and praying according to God's will (day 15). All of these attributes are different aspects of a single entity, like the many facets of a diamond that produce its mesmerizing brilliance and sparkle. Some overlap between the characteristics of prayer inevitably occurs. As a result, the central theme of one day's lesson reappears in the discussion on another day. Of course, this bleedover makes complete sense, since our express aim is to survey the *whole* counsel of God concerning effective and fervent prayer.

To aid our understanding, we have attempted to analyze each quality of potent prayer in relative isolation, to the extent possible. This approach also helps when implementing what we have learned in our own prayer practices. If we give one of Shakespeare's plays to students in the third grade, they will not benefit from it. That is because comprehension and proficiency have to be developed *progressively* over time and with substantial *practice*. For that reason, some overlap always exists from one grade level to the next—it is built into the structure of our educational system. That deliberate overlap assists with retention of concepts, facts, and methods already covered. It also facilitates understanding and application of *new* material. And the same principle applies to our studies of prayer that "avails much." Most of its attributes are so interrelated that they cannot be wholly separated, even when we try to investigate them individually. Needless to say, this is not a serious shortcoming, but it does mean that occasionally some material will sound redundant.

With these observations in mind, let us return to our exploration of importunity. The "shamelessness" conveyed by that word is more or less equivalent to the *boldness* with which we approach the throne of grace. Such confidence in drawing near without reservation can stem from one of two sources: first, knowing that we have an established rapport[91] with the person to whom we are speaking. That relationship permits us the latitude[92] to speak shamelessly without fear of reprisal[93]. The man in Christ's parable addressed his friend as he did *because* he was his friend. And we "come boldly to the throne of grace" for all of the reasons that we examined on day 14; in particular, the relationship that we now have with God through Jesus Christ. He is the Friend and Advocate who provides us with unhindered access to the throne.

The second source of our boldness or shamelessness carries our studies of persistence in prayer a step further. We may also speak confidently and directly when we are *certain* that we are "in the right"; when our position is **objectively just**. If this seems a little confusing, it will become clearer in a moment. To begin, turn to chapter 18 of Luke's Gospel and read the "Parable of the Woman and the Judge" (verses 1-8). We are not told what the widow's "adversary" did to her, but we are given to conclude that she is "in the right." She was legitimately wronged in some way, and her claim is just. As far as we know, she had no previous relationship to speak of with the judge (no rapport), and none is suggested by their exchange. Instead, her importunity, her shameless persistence in demanding justice, derived from her confidence in the *justness* of her position.

The moral illustrated by the parable is relatively easy to grasp (especially since Jesus spelled it out for us). An "unjust judge," "who did not fear God nor regard man," granted the widow's request to spare himself the agitation of her persistence (verses 2,5,6). If an unjust judge will do that, then how much more will a *perfectly* just and loving God "avenge His own elect who cry out day and night to Him" (verse 7)? The elect of God crying out day and night constitutes persistence in prayer. But God does not avenge them *because* of their persistence, strictly speaking. In other words, the intent is not to form a direct parallel between the judge and God (though some teachers mistakenly do). The

---

[91] rapport (O): a harmonious and understanding relationship between people
[92] latitude (O): freedom from restrictions in actions or opinions
[93] reprisal (O): an act of retaliation

Lord does not avenge His elect to spare Himself the nuisance of their importunity, as the judge did. Instead, He avenges them because of what their persistence indicates; what it reflects; what it represents.

The shameless persistence of God's elect refers back to the first verse of chapter 18. There Luke stated directly why Jesus taught His disciples with this specific parable: "Then He spoke a parable to them, that men always ought to pray and not lose heart." Persistence in prayer demonstrates in a practical way that our hearts are invested in what we are saying. It reinforces our insistence that what we are praying for is of genuine and lasting importance to us. "In other words, the prayer which prevails with God is the prayer into which we put our whole soul, stretching out toward God in intense and agonizing desire. Much of our modern prayer lacks power because it lacks heart…. If we put so little heart into our prayers, we cannot expect God to put much heart into answering them…. When we learn to come to God with an intensity of desire that wrings the soul, then we will know a power in prayer that most of us do not know now" (Torrey 26). Persistence in prayer proclaims an "intensity of desire" that cannot be faked. Importunity cannot be counterfeited.

Paradoxically[94], and perhaps most significantly, persistence evidences faith, not a lack of it. Do we sincerely believe that the issue or problem or situation we are confronting *requires* the Lord's intervention? Do we trust that God *will* do everything He has promised to do; that *all* of His assurances will be supported by action? The Apostle John declared that "he who does not believe God has made Him a liar" (1 John 5:10). Would any of us want to accuse God, the very Creator and wellspring of truth, of lying? We have studied previously about the necessity of genuine faith in effective and fervent prayer (on day 11 and elsewhere). Of course, regardless of any other consideration, the Lord knows if our faith is authentic or not. He knows all and sees all (recall 1 Chronicles 28:9).

At the same time, the Bible clearly teaches that sincere faith will always manifest itself through a believer's works (remember James 2:18). Faith without works is empty, pie-in-the-sky spiritualism. Works without faith is lifeless, suffocating legalism. Neither will profit a person with regard to salvation (verses 14,26). And neither will provide any power to a person's prayer to make it more effective and fervent. Faith and works are two halves of a whole, incomplete and ineffectual without each other. Persistence in prayer is a **work** that displays and should emanate from genuine **faith**. Hence Jesus's question at the end of His parable in Luke 18: "Nevertheless, when the Son of Man comes, will He really find faith on the earth?" (verse 8).

To this point in today's lesson, we have considered how persistence exhibits the heart of the person praying. And we have examined how persistence in prayer demonstrates the legitimacy of our faith in a practical way. But one

---

[94] paradoxically (CO): appearing or operating in a manner that suggests the existence of a paradox

additional characteristic of persistence needs to be mentioned: the impact of importunity *on* the person praying. Recall the questions with which we began: Since He knows our hearts perfectly, why not pray about something once and trust Him with the result? Why pray about the same issue or bring Him the same request repeatedly, since He cannot be coerced? Apart from what persistence in prayer reveals *about* us, there is the effect that the need for persistence has *on* us.

The requirement for us to be shamelessly persistent in our prayers serves to condition us to be more dependent upon the Lord. "There is no more blessed training in prayer than that which comes through being compelled to ask again and again, over long periods of time, before obtaining what we seek from God" (Torrey 51). We can interpret the training that He subjects us to in two different ways. To begin with, consider our role as soldiers in the army of the Lord. In an earthly military force, no commander pulls a recruit from civilian life and sends him directly to the front line to engage in combat. To do so would be tantamount[95] to murder. Instead, the raw recruit must first be trained extensively. He must be taught how to fight effectively using the weapons that are provided to him. In addition, his body must be conditioned to withstand the rigorous demands imposed upon him, both in battle and in maneuvering from one place to another. Only after the soldier has undergone proper training in *both* areas is he deployed to combat the enemy.

In a comparable way, when we enter the Lord's army at the moment of our salvation, we are fresh recruits ill-suited for battle. God's requirement for us to be persistent in prayer is one of the methods that He uses to train us. Since prayer is one of the principal "weapons of our warfare," we must be drilled in how to wield it with greatest effect. And the need for importunity is one of the instruments of our instruction. It teaches us how to use prayer skillfully to tear down strongholds and cast down arguments. At the same time, it conditions us so that we can endure the hardships imposed on us by spiritual warfare.

A second way that we can understand the Lord's training concerns how we relate to Him. As we have repeatedly emphasized, God knows our hearts **perfectly**. He knows how easily we are turned aside from following the path of His will. He knows how swift we are to invest confidence in ourselves instead of Him. If we could pray once about an issue or problem or situation and leave it to Him, then we would inevitably come to treat Him like a magic genie in a bottle. But our loving Father and Lord is not in the business of granting wishes. He does not stand by attentively, waiting to exercise His power in gratifying our desires whenever we feel compelled to call upon Him. What a perverse distortion of reality that is!

---

[95] tantamount (C): equivalent to in effect or meaning

God wants us to have **relationships** with Him. In fact, He desires such relationships so deeply that He willingly sacrificed His only begotten Son to restore the relationships which we (humans) sabotaged (1 John 4:9-10). By contrast, what does a genie typically say to the person who releases him (it?) from the bottle? "What is your wish, master?"—or something along those lines. Are we masters over God, that we can compel Him to do our bidding? Absolutely not! The very suggestion of it is utter blasphemy! Our relationships with the Lord are built on **faith**, **hope**, and **love** (see 1 Corinthians 13:13). *We* have faith in *Him*, and that faith is demonstrated (in part) by our persistence in prayer. We hope in Him, meaning that we earnestly expect Him to fulfill *perfectly* all that He has promised to do. That includes responding to our cries when we call upon Him in faith. And we love Him, but only because He first loved us (1 John 4:19).

God's requirement for us to be persistent in prayer is an expression of His love. The Lord Almighty is not Zeus or some other Olympian god. He does not amuse Himself by forcing us to jump through endless hoops in order to appease Him; to avoid incurring His wrath. God **loves** us. He expects us to be persistent in prayer because it strengthens our relationships with Him. The need for importunity maintains our dependency on Him, constraining us to trust in Him and not in ourselves (recall Proverbs 3:5-6). In practice, persistence keeps us coming back to Him, orienting the rest of our lives around Him and the loving relationships that we have with Him.

Resting in the love that our Father has for us, let us cultivate persistence in our prayers. Let us keep asking, keep seeking, and keep knocking, until God either grants our petitions or reveals that they are not aligned with His will. (If it is not already obvious, asking, seeking, and knocking can be remembered easily by forming an acronym with the first letters of the words: Ask, Seek, Knock— A.S.K.) Since he has featured prominently in today's exploration of persistence in prayer, we will give the last word to Mr. Torrey: "Be constant and persistent in your asking. Be diligent and untiring in your asking. God delights to have us 'shameless' beggars in prayer; for it shows our faith in Him, and He is mightily pleased with faith" (12).

For further reflection, if desired: Chapter 9 of the Book of Acts describes Paul's encounter with the risen Lord Jesus as Paul (then Saul) journeyed toward Damascus. After he became a Christian, Paul spent a short time in Damascus before escaping and fleeing to the desert of Arabia (2 Corinthians 11:32-33; Galatians 1:15-17). He spent "three years" there before going "up to Jerusalem to see Peter [or Cephas]" (verse 18). Think about Paul's history as a Pharisee and a persecutor and murderer of Christians. Think about how he came to know Christ, as "one born out of due time" (1 Corinthians 15:8). Then consider how the Lord used him to spread the gospel; to plant churches; to instruct the brethren; to disciple those who would continue his work; to write almost half of the New Testament.

In light of all these things, how does Paul's time in the Arabian desert compare to the "training" that all Christians are supposed to undergo? Paul had mastered the Jewish *religion* with all of its ceremonies and rituals, but he had no real *relationship* with the Lord (see Philippians 3:4-6). What might have been the purpose of Paul's "training" in Arabia? What was God teaching him that he did not already know? How do the answers to these questions apply to us?

Day 19 — Prayer Without Ceasing

"Rejoice always, pray without ceasing, in everything give thanks; for this is the will of God in Christ Jesus for you" (1 Thessalonians 5:16-18). The language that Paul the Apostle used here can seem rather intimidating when we first read it. He employed such terms as "always," "everything"; all of which suggest the existence of an unattainably high standard. Then he slammed the point home when he declared emphatically, "this is the will of God in Christ Jesus for you." He left no ambiguity[96]. Nothing about his statement or its context hints that he was purposefully using exaggeration to underscore the importance of what he was saying. On the contrary, "this is the will of God" is about as concise and forthright as it is possible to be.

When our sinful nature (our flesh) encounters what appears to be an unreachable standard, our tendency is to begin looking immediately for a loophole. "Well," we tell ourselves, "when God said, 'You shall not,' He really meant, 'You should try not to….'" We rationalize[97] away the plain teaching of Scripture, manipulating what it clearly states in order to accommodate *our* inability to live up to it. But we need to recognize that this inclination proceeds from our flesh. Therefore, it is contrary to the Spirit (Romans 7:14,25; Galatians 5:16-17). Again, Paul's instruction was quite explicit: "But put on the Lord Jesus Christ, and make no provision for the flesh, to fulfill its lusts" (Romans 13:14). We can deploy all the verbal gymnastics we like to provide ourselves with a comforting sentiment. But all it amounts to in the end is making "provision for the flesh." "God knows I'm human," we insist. "God loves me as I am." Or the popular modern refrain, "God made me this way, and He doesn't make mistakes." There is no end to the ways in which our flesh will pressure us to dilute or subvert the straightforward revelation of God's will in the Bible.

So that we are not inclined to cut ourselves some slack, in a manner of speaking, a second point needs to be acknowledged. Our tendency to explain away the plain meaning of Scripture is **satanic**, in the most *literal* sense of the word. Consider the strategy that Satan used to tempt Eve. God's command was perfectly clear, as were the consequences of disobedience (Genesis 2:16-17). But when the serpent approached Eve, he probed, "Has God indeed said...?" (3:1). Did God *really* say, "You shall not eat of every tree of the garden?" Satan altered the Lord's express commandment, and at the same time sowed doubt in Eve's mind concerning what God truly meant. And once he formed an opening, he wormed his way in further. "You will not surely die," he assured her, at that point directly contradicting what the Lord had said (verse 4). "For God knows…." In essence, Satan's appeal to Eve was based on the same kind of

---

[96] ambiguity (O): doubtfulness, uncertainty
[97] rationalize (O): to invent a rational explanation of; to find false reasons for irrational or unworthy behavior

watering down of God's will toward which we all tend, owing to our sinful nature. "What did God say? Well, what He really *meant* was...," and a short step later we are being expelled from the garden with Adam and Eve.

If this all seems like it has no relevance to our opening passage from 1 Thessalonians, it will become clearer in a moment. In those three verses, as we noted earlier, Paul used the words "always," "without ceasing," and "everything." When we then observe that he did not necessarily mean "always," "without ceasing," and "everything," it must be understood that we are not just rationalizing because he established an impossibly high standard. Instead, we must remember the principles that always apply to understanding what Scripture means by what it states. And since they pertain to our current study, we will briefly review those principles.

First, a biblical text must always be considered in context. And since the Bible is the authoritative revelation of the One True God, the context of every verse has multiple dimensions:

- the **immediate** context of the grammar and vocabulary used in the original, inspired languages
- the **local** context of points or themes that are developed in neighboring verses
- the **broad** context of the book or epistle in which the passage appears, including its intended recipient(s), the identity of its (human) writer, and the overarching purpose or thesis
- the **historical** context, taking into account cultural norms, customs, idioms[98] of language, and what was happening in the wider world at the time

When we ignore context, we can cherrypick portions of God's Word and cause the Bible to teach almost anything we prefer.

The second guideline is related to the first: We need to receive the *whole counsel of God* on a given subject, from throughout Scripture. One crucial principle emphasized during the Reformation was *Sacra Scriptura sui interpres*, a Latin phrase which translates to "Sacred Scripture is its own interpreter." A diligent, humble, and prayerful student of God's Word can understand what Scripture teaches through what it records by using the Bible itself. (One accessible and instructive guide to mining the treasures of God's Word is *Knowing Scripture*, by Dr. R.C. Sproul—highly recommended.)

With all of this information in mind, let us return to 1 Thessalonians. Since the topic of our present study is "Prayer Without Ceasing," we will narrow our focus in Paul's letter to concentrate on verse 17 and part of verse 18: "pray

---

[98] idioms (C): modes of expression peculiar to a language or dialect

without ceasing, ...for this is the will of God in Christ Jesus for you." The phrase "without ceasing" is an example of Scripture saying something that it does not mean—in a sense. Simply stated, the data communicated by that phrase in *English* do not precisely convey the significance of the inspired *Greek*. In other words, the limitations that are inherent in translation appear in this instance. Sometimes no *direct* correlation of meaning exists between two tongues. Translators have to do the best they can, applying their expertise with the languages, and aided by the Holy Spirit. Hence the need for students of Scripture to consider the immediate context, to grasp as well as possible what the inspired languages taught. For that purpose, a good Bible dictionary is invaluable.

The English phrase "without ceasing" translates a single Greek word. And *Vine's* defines that word in the following way: "the meaning in each place is not that of unbroken continuity, but without the omission of any occasion." The term signifies "unceasingly, without ceasing," and is employed "not [in the sense] of what is not interrupted, but of that which is constantly recurring" (*Vine's*: "cease" B,c). Two particular nuggets of information are uncovered here that help considerably to clarify what is *actually* intended by the phrase "without ceasing": "without the omission of any occasion" and "that which is constantly recurring."

In English, "without ceasing" implies continuousness. It refers to an action that happens on an ongoing basis without stopping. The earth rotating on its axis and revolving around the sun are both continuous actions. The beating of a human heart is not. Hence the difficulty that results from the appearance of that phrase in 1 Thessalonians 5:17. At the practical level, we all recognize that it is simply impossible to "pray without ceasing" in the sense conveyed by the English. No one can pray continuously, without stopping. Only when we understand what the inspired Greek communicates do we *begin*, at least, to imagine how such prayer enters the scope of possibility. Admittedly, the standard established by the Greek is still unsettlingly high. But it is not impossible. In fact, if we take a little liberty with the language, we can craft an instructive statement that accurately relates what Paul meant: "Pray without the omission of any occasion. Make your prayers constantly recurring." (Is it clear now why the translators opted for "without ceasing," despite its limitations?)

Examining the Greek has helped us to develop a somewhat sharper image of what prayer "without ceasing" will look like in a Christian's life. That covers the *immediate* context; the specific wording used in the original. (In the interest of space, we are not going to investigate all of the dimensions of context related to our main scriptural text. Also, we can learn enough about "Prayer Without Ceasing" for our purposes without exhaustively analyzing the contextual details.) To provide ourselves with a more complete picture of how this kind of prayer will appear in practice, let us look briefly at one example from elsewhere in Paul's writing.

At the beginning of his epistle to the Church of Rome, Paul assured the saints there, "without ceasing I make mention of you always in my prayers" (1:9). Needless to say, Paul was not informing those Christians that he prayed for them continuously, without any interruptions or intervals. Such a statement would be obviously nonsensical[99], even if recorded by someone as highly (and deservedly) esteemed as the Apostle Paul. Knowing what we do about the significance of the Greek term that is rendered "without ceasing," we can understand Paul's intended meaning. Calling God as his witness, he desired to impress upon the Roman saints that he prayed for them at every opportunity. He consistently *and* continually interceded for them during the times that he spent in prayer. And those times occurred frequently. Paul's example can serve as a worthy model for all of us as we devote ourselves to engaging in effective and fervent prayer in our own lives of faith (recall 1 Corinthians 11:1).

At this point in today's study, we have established a better understanding of what it means to "pray without ceasing." Now we have a proper framework within which to explore what unceasing prayer will look like in *our* daily practice. One thing we must realize at the outset is that this sort of prayer does not develop overnight. Instead, it requires discipline, time, and the diligent and purposeful cultivation of a godly habit. It requires assistance and empowerment by the Holy Spirit. And it can require perseverance and sacrifice. Becoming the kind of Christian who prays "without ceasing" is far from easy. Such prayer is a **spiritual discipline**, characteristic of precisely the type of servant and soldier that the Lord our Commander calls all saints to be. And that being the case, we must anticipate that both our flesh and our adversary will fight against us every step we take in that direction.

At the same time, however, we have the assurance of Scripture that praying "without ceasing…is the will of God in Christ Jesus." We **know** beyond any question or semblance of doubt that it is God's will for us to pray this way. Therefore, when we ask Him to help us to pray in this manner, we can have complete confidence that He *does* hear us and He *will* grant our request (remember 1 John 5:14-15 and day 15, "Praying According to God's Will"). As Charles Spurgeon wrote, "If you have a divine promise, you need not plead that with an 'if' in it; you may plead with a certainty. If for the mercy which you are now asking, you have God's solemn pledged word, there will scarce be any room for the caution about submission to His will. You know His will. That will is in the promise; plead it" ("Effective Prayer" 17). To highlight the amazing power in this truth, read 1 Thessalonians 5:16-18 and 1 John 5:14-15 together.

---

[99] nonsensical (O): not making sense, absurd, foolish

Some Christians may have the impression that praying "without ceasing" is a lot of work. They think, perhaps subconsciously, that continual and earnest prayer represents an additional burden or obligation in a life that is already hectic. They find it difficult to become enthusiastic about unceasing prayer because it imposes another demand on their time, which is always in short supply. These believers may recognize the inherent *value* in ceaseless prayer, or at least have some sense of it. But they are stressed and feel that they are being pulled in too many different directions as it is. ("Busyness" as an obstacle to effective prayer will be discussed in more detail on day 29.) As is often true, wise counsel here sounds paradoxical[100]: "Let us never forget that the more the work presses on us, the more time we must spend in prayer" (Torrey 80). As a rule, the more active and engaged we are, the greater *our* need for unceasing prayer becomes.

Notwithstanding that rule of wisdom, the attitude of the kind of Christians we have described does contain a kernel of truth. On this point, consider the insights of David MacIntyre. In doing so, however, bear in mind that he was referring to regenerated believers, not to human beings in general: "Moved by a divinely-implanted instinct, our natures cry out for God, for the living God. And however this instinct may be crushed by sin, it awakes to power in the consciousness of redemption....

And yet, ...no duty is more earnestly impressed upon us in scripture than the duty of continual communion with Him. The main reason for this unceasing insistence is *the arduousness of prayer*. In its nature it is a laborious undertaking, and in our endeavor to maintain the spirit of prayer we are called to wrestle against principalities and powers of darkness" (3,4).

Prayer in general, and prayer "without ceasing" in particular, can be a taxing experience. In fact, it often is. And that is because, among other things, we must overcome confrontations with evil spiritual entities under Satan's direction. (Opposition from our adversary as an obstacle to effective prayer will be discussed in greater depth on day 25.) We also have to contend with resistance from our flesh, which "lusts against the Spirit" (Galatians 5:17). When we pray, numerous forces work against us, attempting to frustrate us and to prevent us from persevering. These factors operating together can make unceasing prayer seem arduous and "laborious." And that feeling is one reason why many otherwise well-meaning Christians do not practice it.

Despite this aspect of continual prayer, a remarkable paradox[101] arises when we *do* apply our energy and time and will toward praying "without ceasing." Such prayer is easily one of the most joyous and blessed and beautiful experiences

---

[100] paradoxical (O): like a statement that seems to contradict itself or conflict with common sense but contains a truth

[101] paradox (C): a statement that is apparently absurd or self-contradictory, but is or may be really true

we can have in this life. This sweetness was captured elegantly by Mr. Spurgeon:

> "To pray is as it were to bathe oneself in a cool stream, and so to escape from the heats of earth's summer sun. To pray is to mount on eagle's wings above the clouds and get into the clear heaven where God dwells. To pray is to enter the treasure house of God and to enrich oneself out of an inexhaustible storehouse. To pray is to grasp heaven in one's arms, to embrace the Deity within one's soul, and to feel one's body made a temple of the Holy [Spirit]. Apart from the answer, prayer is in itself a benediction[102]. To pray is to cast off your burdens, it is to tear away your rags, it is to shake off your diseases, it is to be filled with spiritual vigor, it is to reach the highest point of Christian health" ("Effective Prayer" 14-15).

What a lovely description of prayer! This is a characterization that could only be sincerely stated by a saint who has *personally* experienced the truth of it.

All Christians have an open invitation to come into the Lord's presence at any time. That is a precious privilege beyond worth, and should never be lightly esteemed. From a strictly human vantage point, unceasing prayer can seem like a daunting prospect, very difficult at best. But from a spiritual perspective, continual and earnest prayer is one of the most profound blessings we can experience in this life. To help us to persevere in praying "without ceasing," whatever the cost, consider the assurance and the outstretched hand that are found in a familiar passage of Scripture: "Come to Me, all who labor and are heavy laden, and I will give you rest. Take My yoke upon you and learn from Me, for I am gentle and lowly in heart, and you will find rest for your souls. For My yoke is easy and My burden is light" (Matthew 11:28-30). Applying Christ's words to our present topic, we can see that the *ability* to persevere in praying "without ceasing" is a gracious gift from the Lord. And He provides that capacity in response to our humble requests. Or, in other words, power to pray "without ceasing" comes through petitioning Him in prayer for power.

In effect, praying continually declares, "I believe You, Lord. Place Your yoke upon me, for I believe that Your yoke is easy and Your burden is light. I am going to turn to You again and again, 'without the omission of any occasion,' on a 'constantly recurring' basis, because my rest is in You." We should not think of unceasing prayer as a chore or another bullet-point on our to-do lists. Instead, we should acknowledge and appreciate such prayer for what it is: liberating to the mind, nourishing to the soul, invigorating to the spirit. And if those qualities do not produce sufficient motivation to practice this kind of prayer, we also know beyond doubt that it "is the will of God." We can obey Him and reap the blessings, or we can disobey and accept the consequences.

---

[102] benediction (C): a solemn invocation of divine blessing on people or things

As we develop the spiritual discipline of praying "without ceasing" over time, it will become *almost* automatic for our attention to shift to Him whenever we are not concentrating on some earthly affair. As David MacIntyre observed, "We do not know the true potency of prayer until our hearts are so steadfastly inclined to God that our thoughts turn to Him, as by a divine instinct, whenever they are set free from the consideration of earthly things" (6). And R.A. Torrey expressed a similar point when he wrote, "We should walk so habitually in His presence that even when we awake in the night it would be the most natural thing for us to speak to Him in thanksgiving or petition" (81). Cultivating this type of prayer requires belief, commitment, discipline, time, and the empowerment of the Holy Spirit. But with all of those elements present and operating, a life that includes continual and earnest prayer is indeed possible. Moreover, the fruits borne by a Christian life filled with unceasing prayer are **tremendous**.

Although we are already running long today, one final point needs to be included about praying "without ceasing" before we conclude this study. Simply stated, it is not the same as persistence in prayer, even though they might seem similar on the surface. A brief illustration should help to define more clearly the distinction between the two characteristics of prayer. And since it is our current topic, we will begin with "Prayer Without Ceasing."

Throughout the course of her daily activities, a certain woman—we will call her Hannah—comes before the Lord in prayer perhaps one hundred times (the exact number is not important). These prayers are in addition to periods, morning and evening, when she enters her prayer closet and approaches the throne of grace for an extended duration. She often passes half an hour there, and occasionally as much as an hour or more. Her quick and concise prayers throughout the day typically are not more than a few sentences. Neither are they particularly sophisticated. And in these prayers, Hannah seldom mentions the same issue repeatedly. She speaks to her Father frequently during her waking hours, acknowledging Him in all her ways.

Hannah's sister, Anna, has a similar prayer life, only somewhat expanded. She also prays throughout the day, maintaining continual communion with the Lord in brief but frequent prayers. Anna has also managed to arrange her busy schedule so that, on most days, she is able to enter her prayer closet three times—morning, early afternoon, and evening. While there, she uses a prayer list to help guide her thoughts and keep her focused. Anna has four grown children, but three of them live according to the ways of the world and are not walking with God. She prays for them several times every day, interceding on their behalf in her closet and each time she thinks of them during her daily activities. Additionally, every Saturday Anna *fasts* from television, computers, and entertainment, and eats only simple food like plain bread or crackers with water. Those days, she devotes herself to prayer and worship, reading the Bible and spending prolonged periods interceding. Her children figure prominently in her intercessions as she pours out her heart to her Father.

A case could be made that Hannah prays "without ceasing." She prays more or less "without the omission of any occasion," and undeniably her prayers are "constantly recurring." But at the same time, Hannah is not particularly persistent in her prayers. Her sister, on the other hand, prays both "without ceasing" and persistently. Concerning her children, Anna is *definitely* persistent. But she also prays persistently for her beloved husband, for government leaders in her country, for her pastor and the elders in her church, and for a handful of additional subjects. Anna's prayer practices sound a lot like Paul's description of his own habits. The apostle indicated how he prayed at the beginning of his Epistle to the Philippians: "I thank my God upon every remembrance of you, always in every prayer of mine making request for you all with joy, for your fellowship in the gospel from the first day until now" (1:3-5). Paul's approach was both persistent and unceasing. Anna's is also, and ours *should be* as well.

Both "Persistence in Prayer" and "Prayer Without Ceasing" are necessary for completeness, maturity, and potency—for Christlikeness. "Oh, the power of prayer to reach down, where hope itself seems vain, and lift men and women up into fellowship with and likeness to God! It is simply wonderful! How little we appreciate this marvelous weapon!" (Torrey 20). Unquestionably, great power is available to those who "pray without ceasing." But the motivation for cultivating this kind of prayer in our own lives is not related to what *we* receive from it, strictly speaking. Instead, our primary reason for pursuing this type of prayer is that it serves to keep us in close communion with God our Father. And when it comes to the intimacy of our relationships with the Lord, closer is always better. In other words, there is no such thing as being *too* close to God! By itself, that reason should be more than sufficient to propel us to incorporate this aspect of prayer into our own practices. But above and beyond that impetus[103] is the certain knowledge that it is *God's will* for us to "pray without ceasing."

---

[103] impetus (CO): a driving force; impulse; incentive

Day 20 — Prayer and the Presence of God

"Now it was so, when Moses came down from Mount Sinai (and the two tablets of the testimony were in Moses' hand when he came down from the mountain), that Moses did not know that the skin of his face shone while he talked with Him…. Afterward all the children of Israel came near, and he gave them as commandments all that the LORD had spoken with him on Mount Sinai. And when Moses had finished speaking with them, he put a veil on his face. But whenever Moses went in before the LORD to speak with Him, he would take the veil off until he came out; and he would come out and speak to the children of Israel whatever he had been commanded" (Exodus 34:29,32-34).

Moses *literally* spent time in the presence of the Lord's glory. His proximity to the radiance of God actually altered his physical appearance, causing his face to emit a light that terrified the people of Israel. Apparently, something supernatural had occurred. And frail human beings are often fearful when confronted with the supernatural. People tend to prefer the commonplace and the familiar, the predictable and the routine—in a word, the natural. That being so, the **supernatural** comes along like a sumo wrestler and forces them outside of their "comfort zones." Ordinary experience in the world does not equip people with the tools needed to understand or to respond to supernatural phenomena[104]. That is why people typically attempt, sometimes desperately, to explain away legitimately *supernatural* occurrences using *natural* terms. And that tendency does not apply only to people in the world. We all do this at times, to varying extents. Regrettably, even within the community of God's people, the church, there is little ability or even desire to engage with the genuinely supernatural.

Consider the response of the Israelites to the "glowing" face of Moses. Here was a visible and undeniable indication that Moses had experienced a personal encounter with the Creator God. Their reactions could have taken any of several different forms: curiosity, excitement, humility, rejoicing, reverence, thrill. But of all the possibilities, they responded in *fear*, reluctant even "to come near him" (verse 30). They recognized that it was Moses, so the change to his appearance evidently was not so extensive that it obscured his features. This was the same Moses they knew, yet they were afraid of him. They kept their distance, as we would from a person who emerged unharmed from the mushroom cloud of a nuclear blast. We would have no framework of experience or understanding within which to process what we were seeing. Consequently, we would be forced to conclude that we were in the presence of the supernatural. (For an interesting thought exercise, contrast the response of the Israelites with that of the heathen King Nebuchadnezzar in Daniel 3:19-29.

---

[104] phenomena (O): facts or occurrences or changes perceived by any of the senses or by the mind

The light that emanated from the face of Moses was *reflected* light. It was not internally produced. God did not give Moses the ability to generate light himself (bioluminescence) and to project it from his face. If that were so, then he could have simply "turned it off" instead of covering his face with a veil. Also, as the Apostle Paul instructed in 2 Corinthians, the glory reflected by Moses "was passing away" (3:7). The light was not steady and enduring, such as we could expect if Moses created the light himself. Instead, it faded with time. The light of God's glory that Moses encountered when he remained in the Lord's presence impacted his countenance[105] in such a way, and to such an extent, that his face continued to shine for some time after he departed from God's presence. But the intensity of that light diminished with the passage of time.

We might be inclined to dismiss these observations as mere curiosities or interesting bits of Old Testament trivia. But they have much larger and more lasting implications. In fact, their significance is eternal, as we will see. Throughout the Bible, Moses is used as a representative of the Old Covenant under the law. That covenant had a glory all its own, as Paul explained in a powerful contrast:

> "But if the ministry of death, written and engraved on stones, was glorious, so that the children of Israel could not look steadily at the face of Moses because of the glory of his countenance, which glory was passing away, how will the ministry of the Spirit not be more glorious? For if the ministry of condemnation had glory, the ministry of righteousness exceeds much more in glory.... For if what was passing away was glorious, what remains is much more glorious" (2 Corinthians 3:7-9,11).

The Old Covenant through the law, delivered by Moses the man of God, had a distinctive glory, to be sure. But that glory faded with time because the terms of the Old Covenant could not produce life in those who were bound by it (see verse 6). By contrast, the glory of the New Covenant in the Spirit does not diminish; it "excels" (verse 10).

The glory of God that Moses witnessed on Mount Sinai acted on his face **externally**. In other words, glory proceeded from God's presence and contacted the face of Moses, causing it to shine with reflected light. And in a comparable manner, the **law** governs and influences human behavior through an elaborate system of prohibitions and restrictions applied from the outside—externally. The hearts, sinful natures, and corrupted minds of people are not *transformed* by the law, only *restrained* (see Jeremiah 17:9; remember Romans 7). Under the law, people still desire to sin, though they might strive to obey the law because they recognize that it is an expression of God's will. This capacity of

---

[105] countenance (O): the expression of the face; appearance

the law to impose boundaries on the human propensity[106] toward evil exhibits the law's specific glory. But it also reveals the limitations of that glory.

Unlike the external action of the law, the Holy Spirit transforms us **internally**. He gives us a new heart and a new nature, and He renews our minds (see Ezekiel 11:19-20; 36:26-27; Romans 8:9-17; 12:2). This transfiguration is not in *opposition* to the law, but in *fulfillment* of it (Matthew 5:17). The Spirit continuously works within us to conform us to the image of Christ, producing Christlikeness in our inward selves and in our outward lives. This is the lifelong process of sanctification that we have studied previously. Whereas the Old Covenant under the law yielded death, the New Covenant in the Spirit gives life (2 Corinthians 3:6). As Jesus taught, "I have come that they may have life, and that they may have it more abundantly" (John 10:10). Growth in Christlikeness results in *more* life—a fuller life. That life contrasts sharply with the gradual decline of our physical bodies, which ultimately culminates in death (read 2 Corinthians 4:16-18).

Under the New Covenant, we receive the gift of God's indwelling Spirit. And once He comes to live within us, the Spirit immediately begins transforming us to become just like Jesus. "But we all, with unveiled face, beholding as in a mirror the glory of the Lord, are being transformed into the same image from glory to glory, just as by the Spirit of the Lord" (3:18). From the initial glory of regeneration, the Spirit directs us unto ever greater glory as we continue to grow in Christlikeness "from glory to glory." And just as the New Covenant is superior to the Old, so also is the glory that radiates from God's people under the New Covenant proportionately greater than the light that shone from Moses's face. In fact, Paul indicated in verse 10 that the glory of the New Covenant so far "excels" that of the Old that the Old Covenant has no glory *in the same way* that the new one does. Imagine, then, how much more we Christians will reflect the Lord's glory after we spend time in His presence than did Moses.

On day 14, we discussed "the throne of grace" and the unhindered access that we have to it through Jesus Christ, our High Priest. That throne is where *we* encounter God's presence. To put it another way, the glorious presence of our Lord, the One True God, is as near as a prayer. Recall from Hebrews that we are exhorted to come "boldly" before His throne, trusting that we *will* be received into His presence because **Jesus** deserves to be there, and we belong to Him (4:14-16). Whereas Moses climbed a mountain to enter God's presence, all we have to do is pray.

Although Moses encountered and interacted with God while still in his physical body, our approach to His presence in the Spirit is no less **real**:

---

[106] propensity (O): a tendency or inclination

"It is most fitting for us to feel that we are now doing something that is real; that we are about to address ourselves to God, whom we cannot see, but who is really present: whom we can neither touch nor hear, nor by our senses can apprehend, but who, nevertheless, is as truly with us as though we were speaking to a friend of flesh and blood like ourselves. Feeling the reality of God's presence, our mind will be led by divine grace into a humble state..." ("Effective Prayer" 9-10).

Mr. Spurgeon included an important observation here that we need to heed. Coming boldly into God's presence does not mean approaching Him without proper humility and reverence. He is God—**the** God. Even though He has barred open a door to provide us with unrestricted access to His throne, we should never lose sight of **whose** throne it is (consider John 10:7-9). We cannot come on our own merits, but only on those of Jesus. Humility is in order.

The presence of God when we come to Him in prayer is real. It is not figurative or imaginary; it is **real**. We kneel before His presence in a way that is just as real as what Moses experienced. Though we cannot see Him, He is just as definitely present as He was atop Mount Sinai. We need to hold this truth always in our minds because it is critical for effective and fervent prayer. As David MacIntyre wrote, "The realization of the divine presence is the inflexible condition of a right engagement of spirit in the exercise of private prayer" (15). Translating his statement into English, for our spirits to be properly engaged when we pray, we *must* realize that we are actually entering into God's presence. But how many of us do this? How many of us approach and speak to God the way we would address Him if we were *literally* kneeling at the foot of His throne, in person?

What we must grasp, and the point that Mr. MacIntyre emphasized, is that we are literally coming before His throne when we pray—not in body but in spirit. For many saints, it is difficult to appreciate just how meaningful that truth is. "But, when we really come into God's presence, really meet Him face to face in the place of prayer, really seek the things that we desire *from Him,* then there is power" (Torrey 24). Effective and fervent prayer is prayer that "avails much" (James 5:16). Another way of stating the same truth is to declare that effective and fervent prayer is powerful prayer. And *powerful* prayer requires an enduring and penetrating consciousness that we genuinely enter the Lord's presence when we pray.

The glory of God that proceeds from His presence has a tremendous effect on us when we encounter it. Like Moses on Sinai, we do not and should not leave the same way we came. "As I meet with God in prayer and gaze into His face, I am changed into His image from glory to glory (2 Corinthians 3:18). Each day of true prayer life finds me more like my glorious Lord" (Torrey 18). Paul explained in the verse that Mr. Torrey referred to what is meant by the idea of gazing into God's face, practically speaking. Hopefully, it will be obvious that we do not *see* the face of God with our physical eyes when we come into His presence in the Spirit. "But we all, with unveiled face, beholding as in a mirror the glory of the Lord...." We "gaze into His face" and behold "the glory of the Lord" as though we are seeing it in a mirror. We do not witness His glory directly. Instead, we see the *reflected* image of His glory.

The "mirror" that reflects "the glory of the Lord" back to us is the Bible. The Word of God is His special revelation of Himself and His purposes for Creation. In another of Paul's epistles (to the same church), he observed, "For now we see in a mirror, dimly, but then face to face. Now I know in part, but then I shall know just as I also am known" (1 Corinthians 13:12). In this life we can only behold God's glory "dimly," as if we are glimpsing it reflected in a mirror. But once we shed these corruptible and mortal bodies, we will see Him "face to face" (see 1 Corinthians 15:53). We will finally behold the full majesty of the image into which the Spirit has spent our lives transforming us. We will *reside* in God's glorious presence, not for a few fleeting moments as we do now, through prayer, but for all eternity.

Since the Bible is the "mirror" that reflects "the glory of the Lord" to us, it would be wise for us to pray with God's Word open in front of us. Granted, this is not always possible. But as often as it is, we should do it. Hopefully, it goes without saying that regularly reading and studying the Scriptures is a critical component of practical Christian living. (Suffice it to say, moreover, that our prayers will *never* become effective and fervent if we neglect the Bible.) As we abide in His Word and meditate on what we read there, the Spirit transforms us by the renewing of our minds into Christlikeness—Christ's likeness— "into the same image from glory to glory" (Romans 12:2; 2 Corinthians 3:18). With the truth of Scripture in our minds and love for Him in our hearts, we enter His presence in prayer. There we encounter His glory as we "gaze into His face" in the Spirit. And the glory we behold impacts us in ways both beautiful and powerful. The more time we spend in His presence, the more His light will emanate from our lives, as it did from the face of Moses.

In order to experience victory on the spiritual battlefield, our prayers must be powerful. They need to avail much, which means they must be effective and fervent. We have to engage in combat with discipline and focus, with knowledge of our enemies and their devices, and with the power of the Holy Spirit acting on and through us. We cannot fight "as one who beats the air," or our efforts will be spent in vain (1 Corinthians 9:26). By reflecting "the glory of the Lord," our lives shine forth His light, dispelling the darkness of the world and pointing people to the source of that light (see Matthew 5:14-16; John 1:3-5). But for our lights to shine brightly, we need to spend as much time as possible in God's glorious presence. Like Peter, James, and John on the Mount of Transfiguration, we should desire to reside with the Lord in the place where His glory is revealed (Matthew 17:1-4). For Christians in our day, that means coming before His presence at "the throne of grace," abiding in Him through prayer and the study of His Word. Let us come into His presence, saints, and be transformed.

Day 21 — Prayer and Incense

In our studies yesterday of "Prayer and the Presence of God," we saw how the experience of Moses on Mount Sinai translated to the practices of Spirit-filled Christians. That was one among numerous instances that could be cited of elements in the Old Covenant reappearing in a more complete or mature form in the New Covenant. To illustrate what we mean, take the example of the temple. In the Old Covenant, the temple was a physical building made of stone, wood, and metal. It was constructed with specific dimensions and occupied by a small number of specially chosen furnishings. There the Lord made His presence to reside within the Most Holy Place, or Holy of Holies, to which only a very limited group of people was ever granted access. Under the New Covenant, by contrast, the temple became both individual saints and the body of Christ as a whole (1 Corinthians 3:16-17; 6:19). God's Spirit dwells *within* us, not in a building or a single location, so *we* are His temple. Ultimately, however, there is no temple in the New Jerusalem, "for the Lord God Almighty and the Lamb are its temple" (Revelation 21:22). Thus, we can follow the progression of the temple from a structure in Jerusalem to the body of Christ globally to the very being of God.

This paradigm[107] is not uncommon in Scripture, and it applies to the topic of our current study, "Prayer and Incense." In the Bible, incense is frequently associated with prayer. It even *represents* prayer in some places, such as Revelation 5:8: "Now when He had taken the scroll, the four living creatures and the twenty-four elders fell down before the Lamb, each having a harp, and golden bowls full of incense, which are the prayers of the saints." In his vision, John saw bowls of incense being presented to the Lamb, Jesus, and identified that incense as "the prayers of the saints." This is significant for multiple reasons.

The ceremonial structure of worship in the Old Covenant was modeled on heavenly realities, being but "copies of the things in the heavens" (Hebrews 9:23; if time permits, consider reading all of chapter 9 for clarity). To put it another way, a bridge connects the distinctive form of worship that God prescribed for the Israelites to "the true" realities in heaven (verse 24). And worship for saints under the New Covenant is an integral part of that bridge, not independent of it. (What exactly this means will become clearer in a moment.) God instructed the Israelites in remarkable detail concerning how they were to worship Him, including how to manufacture the particular incense that must be used. Nothing was to be done half-heartedly or haphazardly[108], and everything was required to be completed in precise conformity to the Lord's direction. He even warned the people against offering "strange incense" to Him and against personal use of the incense recipe that He specified for worshiping

---

[107] paradigm (O): something serving as an example or model of how things should be
[108] haphazardly (C): randomly or accidentally

Him (Exodus 30:8-9,34-38). And the consequences for violating God's design were severe: **death**. Evidently, the Lord considered this to be a very serious matter. From all of these passages and others we have visited, we arrive at the following conclusion: *That* the Israelites worshiped God and only God was mandatory, but *how* they worshiped Him was also critical.

Returning to the scene in Revelation 5, what do we see? Do we witness confusion and disorder, with angels scrambling to and fro, enough varieties of incense to fill a Turkish bazaar, and a cacophony[109] of music as different groups present their "worship" to the Almighty? No, the picture is one of perfect order, complete reverence, and total adoration. More than one-hundred million angels praise the Lord in unison, exalting the Lamb with one voice, in flawless harmony (verses 11-12). Countless other creatures—celestial, terrestrial, and marine—magnify their Creator on His throne, blessing and honoring and glorifying Him (verse 13). Not a discordant note sounds. No one pursues selfish pleasures or personal agendas. And none of the angels or creatures decide for themselves how they are going to worship. Everything is conducted in an orderly manner, and the focus throughout is fixed exclusively on the Lord God, as it should be.

Between the ceremonial structure of the Old Covenant and the worship that John witnessed in heaven lies an unbroken continuum[110], which we have represented with a bridge. Saints who are joined to Christ under the terms of the New Covenant walk through life on that bridge, in a manner of speaking. In other words, our worship is not entirely independent of the Old Covenant mode, nor is it altogether separate from "the true" realities that exist in heaven. Whether we are examining the temple, sacrifices, priests, or in today's lesson, incense, we can observe and marvel at God's awesome design as it is revealed to us in His Word. In all these aspects, and a variety of others, we witness the unfolding of God's comprehensive plan for His Creation through the pages of Scripture, and we praise Him for it. What a testament the outworking of His design in history is to His absolute sovereignty, His limitless love, and His infinite wisdom!

With these points in mind, let us consider more closely the subject of "Prayer and Incense." Though many saints may not realize it, incense remains relevant to Christian prayer. Granted, we do not manufacture incense according to a specific recipe revealed by God. And we do not burn incense on an altar that was constructed using detailed plans and precise dimensions. Simply stated, our involvement with incense is not what it was for the Israelites under the Old Covenant. Instead, the relationship of incense to *Christian* prayer concerns the

---

[109] cacophony (O): a discordant sound
[110] continuum (C): that which must be regarded as continuous and the same

quality or the **acceptability** of our prayers. These words might sound a bit off-putting or even erroneous[111] at first, but the meaning will soon become clear.

When the Lord delivered His instructions on how to produce the incense that He would accept, He made it perfectly plain that *no* other kinds of incense would be permitted. Do we suppose that God is extremely petty and obsessed with unimportant trivia? Or is there some larger issue at work here? For answer, consider what the Prophet Samuel said to Saul:

> "Has the LORD as great delight in burnt offerings and sacrifices,
> As in obeying the voice of the LORD?
> Behold, to obey is better than sacrifice,
> And to heed than the fat of rams" (1 Samuel 15:22).

Another prophet, Hosea, echoed this truth, in this instance speaking for God in the first person:

> "For I desire mercy [or faithfulness or loyalty] and not sacrifice,
> And the knowledge of God more than burnt offerings" (6:6).

God repeatedly impressed upon His people that what He really cared about was their hearts. He was concerned with whether or not they would demonstrate loyalty to Him by obeying His commands (see Psalm 51:17; Joel 2:13).

In *all* of His dealings with people, God has shown Himself to be **perfectly** faithful. And since He is always faithful in upholding His part of a covenant relationship, He expects His people to be loyal to Him in return. They demonstrate their faithfulness by obeying His will. Conversely, by *disobeying* the Lord, they exhibit *disloyalty* and violate the covenant that they have with Him. And such infractions must have consequences to discourage people from repeating them. Nadab and Abihu "offered profane fire before the LORD, which He had not commanded them. So fire went out from the LORD and devoured them, and they died before the LORD" (Leviticus 10:1-2). Instead of mourning for the two men, his nephews, Moses said to Aaron, "This is what the LORD spoke, saying:

> 'By those who come near Me
> I must be regarded as holy;
> And before all the people
> I must be glorified'" (verse 3).

God established beyond all question that we cannot approach Him in any way we please. Instead, when we come to Him in prayer and in worship, we must do so in the manner and by the means that He has specified.

---

[111] erroneous (O): mistaken, incorrect

Supposing that we can come to the Lord on our own terms is both presumptuous[112] and prideful. We have seen what the consequences of presumption were for Nadab and Abihu. Additional examples exist in Scripture of presumption meeting with disastrous and often fatal results. We must draw near to God in the way—and *only* in the way—that He stipulates. And this truth applies to *all* of humanity throughout time, whether they were residents of the ancient nation of Israel or they are Christians in the present day. **God** decides the forms of worship that He will accept. *God* determines what does and does not please Him. And God specifies what avenues or means of approach He will permit—or, in the case of Jesus, **provide**.

We have hammered on this point, possibly to an unnecessary extent, because it has extraordinary importance in every believer's life. Generally speaking, we cannot adopt the customs of pagans or of other religions, cover them with a "Christian" veneer, and suppose that they will please our Lord. Regrettably, many traditions have been introduced to Christian practice over the centuries that do not belong there. As a guide for us to avoid such errors, here is a rule of thumb to which we can all adhere: If any custom or observance or rite was not found among God's people in the first-century church that Jesus established, as recorded in the Bible, then it should not be included in our practices. A little imagination, observation, and reflection will reveal how far-reaching this prohibition is. Think about some of the unbiblical things that are regularly engaged in by professing Christians and supposedly Christian churches in our day! The simple fact is that our faith, and the practical outworking of it, are **exclusively** founded on the Word of God. Consequently, anything *contrary* to what is written there should be immediately eliminated. Moreover, anything that was purportedly[113] "sanctioned" by the church in subsequent centuries should definitely be questioned and almost certainly removed.

Our focus in this book is on effective and fervent prayer, so let us narrow our gaze to concentrate on how the general principles we have just reviewed relate to prayer. This is the point where we intersect with the relevance of incense to Christian prayer. As a springboard for our analysis, consider the wisdom of the following proverb:

> "One who turns away his ear from hearing the law,
> Even his prayer is an abomination" (Proverbs 28:9).

The instruction communicated here is relatively easy to grasp: the prayers of anyone who refuses to heed God's law are *abominations* to the Lord. God's **law** is a concrete expression of His **will**. And His will, in turn, proceeds from His **character**—who He is. Thus, a person who does not "hear" God's law turns a

---

[112] presumptuous (O): behaving with impudent boldness; acting without authority
[113] purportedly (O): intended to seem; supposedly

deaf ear to His will. And such rebellious refusal to hear translates to an indirect rejection of God Himself. Refusing to hear God's law and then praying to Him is prideful, presumptuous, and insulting. No wonder He views such prayer as "an abomination!" The Hebrew word for "abomination" conveys the most intense hatred of God that is contained in the Bible (read Proverbs 6:16-19). It indicates something that is abhorrent[114], idolatrous, or morally disgusting.

"One who turns away his ear from hearing the law" describes a person who is not completely committed to living according to God's will. The unregenerate certainly fall into that category. But we are concerned here with a professing Christian who is disobeying the Lord. This is a person who is not fully *surrendered* to serving God as Lord, and who is still trying to live to some extent for self. Such a deluded individual lives as though it is possible to obey God's will part of the time and indulge the desires of the flesh the rest of the time. When we frame the matter in these terms, the error in this attitude becomes obvious. But sadly, many people who claim to be Christians live exactly this way. Jesus mentioned these people and what would ultimately happen to them in Matthew 7:21-23 (also see Luke 6:46-49). They *call* Him Lord and earnestly expect to have a place in His kingdom, but because they refuse to do His will and "practice lawlessness," they are cast out.

Compare the abominable prayers of those who refuse to hear God's law with the "strange incense" that the Lord commanded His people not to offer (Exodus 30:9). Also relate these to the "profane fire" of Nadab and Abihu (Leviticus 10:1). What do they have in common? All three are examples of people attempting to come to God on their own terms. And in all such cases, the Lord's response is decisive and final. God repudiates[115] **all** attempts to approach Him in *any* manner or by *any* means other than those He designates (remember John 14:6).

For people who try to draw near to God or worship Him in ways of their own choosing, His definitive rejection might seem harsh. "How can God be all-loving," some people ask, "yet deny people who want to approach Him? Why is He so insistent about the means people use to come to Him?" But this assessment overlooks one crucial point: God is not *obligated* in any way to provide humanity with an avenue for approaching Him. In our natural state, we are *enemies* of God (Romans 8:7-8). Therefore, if He allowed all of us to die in our sin, never redeeming anyone and never furnishing a means of coming to Him, no one could rightly accuse Him of injustice. On the contrary, we would receive the *just* recompense or reward for our sin (Romans 6:23). Both God's justice and infinite love would remain perfectly intact. The fact that He does save us and supply us with a path to His presence is purely a demonstration of His grace (Ephesians 2:1-9; Colossians 1:21-22). And these gracious actions

---

[114] abhorrent (O): detestable
[115] repudiates (O): rejects, disowns, or denies utterly

proceed from His love, which is absolutely undeserved (Romans 5:8). As Christians, we (should) know and embrace these truths as central tenets of the gospel of salvation. But how quickly we lose sight of them when we are told that we cannot approach God in any way we please.

Thankfully, there is another side to this coin; a hopeful and joyous side that comforts and thrills all of us who sincerely belong to Him. God *welcomed* offerings, prayers, and sacrifices from the Israelites when they were presented to Him in the specified manner. Gifts of money and dead animals were not what pleased Him, though. Instead, the Lord delighted in hearts that were devoted to Him and exhibited that commitment through obedience.

> "The sacrifices of God are a broken heart,
> A broken and a contrite heart—
> These, O God, You will not despise" (Psalm 51:17).

David understood that God wants hearts that are humble, loyal, and surrendered to Him. And when those attributes genuinely describe our hearts, our lives will reflect the condition of our hearts in the form of obedience. When David pleaded, "Let my prayer be set before You as incense," he acknowledged that the prayers of a person whose heart is committed to the Lord are like a sweet-smelling aroma to Him (Psalm 141:2; also see verse 8).

These principles apply just as much to Christians of the New Covenant as they did to Israelites of the Old. We enter the Lord's presence in prayer through "the way" that He has provided (remember day 14, "Praying Before the Throne of Grace"). And we are in relationships with God that are founded on love and by means of His grace. Those things being true, He invites our prayers and welcomes them when we bring them before Him. They are a sweet-smelling aroma to Him for the same reasons that the sacrifices and offerings (and incense) under the Old Covenant were pleasing to Him. They indicate devoted hearts that desire to live according to God's will. That is why the Lord Jesus so sternly rebuked the religious leaders of His day:

> "These people draw near to Me with their mouth,
> And honor Me with their lips,
> But their heart is far from Me.
> And in vain they worship Me,
> Teaching as doctrines the commandments of men" (Matthew 15:8-9).

They went through the motions of religious observance, but their hearts were not surrendered to the Lord. They taught human customs and traditions, supposing that they could worship God in a manner of their own choosing, but their worship was "vain." It did not please God, and He rejected it.

The "golden bowls full of incense, which are the prayers of the saints" in Revelation produce a sweet aroma that delights the Lord, and He welcomes it. How do we know this? Because they "are the prayers of the **saints**" (emphasis added). By definition, these are God's children communicating with their Father in the manner and by the means that He designated. They approach His throne through Jesus, "the way," and their hearts are devoted to Him. They are committed to heeding His law and to obeying Him because they love Him (read 1 John 4:19-5:3). Prayers from *these* people, from authentic Christian saints, God always welcomes. They represent a fragrance of which He never tires.

Let us pray so frequently, so fervently, and so faithfully that the servants before God's throne will not have enough "golden bowls" to contain the incense. Let us fill all the chambers and corridors of our Father's house with the pleasant perfume of our prayers. When we draw near to the Lord, let us remain always mindful of His holiness, glorifying Him in the world through our love for Him and obedience of His will. Then our **lives** can be an acceptable sacrifice for a sweet-smelling aroma, and our prayers can be truly powerful.

Day 22 — Prayer and Waiting

Waiting in the Bible assumes many different forms. Look up the word "wait" or any of its variations in a good concordance and the listings are vast. Waiting incorporates numerous specific actions, but it also concerns an inclination of the heart while undertaking those actions. What we typically mean when we speak of waiting is only one aspect of *biblical* waiting. We tend to think of waiting as allowing time to pass until whatever we are waiting for either occurs or arrives. But that is only one part among several of waiting as it is presented in God's Word.

In its broad strokes, the *scriptural* notion of waiting includes various components that all combine to form one unifying concept. It involves earnest expectation (hope), humble dependence on the Lord, and a proper perspective on the affairs of life. Waiting entails trusting in the certainty of His promises, searching for indications of His hands at work, and submission to His timing. This kind of waiting requires belief, discipline, humility, patience, self-denial, and understanding, among other things. In fact, it would not be inaccurate to conclude that waiting on the Lord conveys the essence of godly living in an evil age. To correlate this with a concept that we encounter in the New Testament, waiting on the Lord and walking in the Spirit, while not exactly the same, are virtually synonymous in practice.

Recognizing how broad waiting is in scope, and how inclusive in content, we will try not to become mired in the details. The point is not to agonize over whether or not we are waiting correctly. Such excessive concern would generate anxiety, which in turn would rob us of peace. And that impact is the polar-opposite of one effect that biblical waiting has.

"You will keep him in perfect peace,
Whose mind is stayed on You,
Because he trusts in You" (Isaiah 26:3).

In this well-known verse, the Prophet Isaiah highlighted the peace that results from keeping our minds focused on the Lord and trusting in Him. As emphasized repeatedly throughout Scripture, God gives us peace and strength for the challenges we confront when we wait on Him. "In returning and rest you shall be saved," the Lord declared through Isaiah, "In quietness and confidence shall be your strength" (30:15).

God instructs His people to wait on Him, just as He directs us to "walk in the Spirit" (Galatians 5:16).

"Wait on the LORD;
Be of good courage,
And He shall strengthen your heart;

Wait, I say, on the LORD!" (Psalm 27:14).

David wrote numerous times in the psalms that he authored of waiting on the Lord. In addition to Psalm 27, another of his compositions is often referred to when waiting is discussed:

"I waited patiently for the LORD;
And He inclined to me,
And heard my cry" (Psalm 40:1).

Here David spotlighted the outcome of his experience. He waited on the Lord, and *only* on the Lord, with a believing heart that earnestly expected God would hear him and respond to his "cry." And what happened? Almighty God, Creator and Sustainer of the whole universe, "inclined" to him, focusing His loving attention on helping this one trusting servant.

We find the same attitude of heart evidenced among believers throughout the Bible, in both testaments. Consider another familiar passage from the Book of Isaiah that beautifully illustrates the results of waiting on Him:

"But those who wait on the LORD
Shall renew their strength;
They shall mount up with wings like eagles,
They shall run and not be weary,
They shall walk and not faint" (40:31).

The strength and fortitude[116] to complete any task that God wills us to undertake; the ability to persevere through adversity and persecution; the energy and discipline to run our race to the end; the capacity to soar above the trappings and intrigues of the world around us: these all proceed from waiting on the Lord. And in this we can see the overlap or parallel with walking in the Spirit. Strictly speaking, all of these products of waiting are given to us *by* His Spirit who dwells within us. But they are supplied *as* we wait on Him. "Be anxious for nothing," the Apostle Paul wrote, "but in everything by prayer and supplication, with thanksgiving, let your requests be made known to God; and the peace of God, which surpasses all understanding, will guard your hearts and minds through Christ Jesus" (Philippians 4:6-7). Paul's admonition here is a picture of waiting on the Lord.

To this point, we have surveyed some of the *results* of waiting on God, all of which are wonderful and greatly to be desired. Many others could be included if we had space to explore the "fruits" of waiting in more depth. (For anyone with the time and inclination, consider Psalms 37:9,34; 62:1,5; Proverbs 20:22; Isaiah 25:9.) But since our focus in this book is on effective and fervent prayer,

---

[116] fortitude (O): courage in bearing pain or trouble

the question needs to be asked, "What does waiting look like in practice?" We have seen that our typical idea of waiting is not the same as the scriptural notion. It stands to reason, then, that biblical waiting will be different in *practice* from ordinary waiting. In other words, it would be unwise to read "wait on the Lord" and assume that we already know what the verse instructs us to do.

No single verse or passage of Scripture explains comprehensively what "waiting on the Lord" entails. Instead, as with all doctrines and concepts distilled from the Bible, the whole counsel of God's Word must be assembled and allowed to shape our understanding. As a useful launching-point for this exploration, David MacIntyre recorded some helpful insights:

> "To wait is not merely to remain impassive. It is to expect—to look for with patience, and also with submission. It is to long for, but not impatiently; to look for, but not to fret at the delay; to watch for, but not restlessly; to feel that if He does not come we will acquiesce[117], and yet to refuse to let the mind acquiesce in the feeling that He will not come" (6-7).

These observations are beneficial to us because they incorporate both the attitude of heart and some of the practical dimensions of waiting.

Above and before all other factors, waiting requires **belief.** This seems almost like stating the obvious, but too many Christians and too many prayers fail at this point. As Charles Spurgeon noted, "Ye cannot pray so as to be heard in heaven and answered to your soul's satisfaction, unless you believe that God really hears and will answer you" ("True Prayer" 5). And sincere belief cannot be faked. God sees everything, so if our profession of belief is not altogether legitimate, that fact cannot be concealed from Him (see Jeremiah 17:10; Hebrews 4:13). And as we have discussed in previous lessons, failure or refusal to believe God is tantamount[118] to calling Him a liar (recall Romans 3:3-4). When we wait on the Lord, we must do so with a heart that proclaims, "I believe, Lord God, that You are perfectly true and faithful and loving. And I believe that you *will* do all that You have said You will do."

Related to belief and extending from it, we place our **hope** *solely* in the Lord when we wait for Him. As we have mentioned elsewhere, this hope is not like the wishful thinking that the word is commonly used to indicate in our day. Biblical hope signifies an earnest expectation that God will respond. It implies confidence that is founded on who God is, including His established and documented record of perfect faithfulness. We see this type of believing hope while waiting expressed throughout the Psalms. It also appears, among other places, in a declaration of the Prophet Micah:

---

[117] acquiesce (O): to agree without protest, to assent
[118] tantamount (C): equivalent to in effect or meaning

"Therefore I will look to the LORD;
I will wait for the God of my salvation;
My God will hear me" (Micah 7:7; also consider Psalm 121).

This is not a statement of resignation or apathy but of resolute confidence. To use Mr. MacIntyre's word, it is not "impassive." Instead, a sense of stout trust and expectation is conveyed. The prophet did not hope in the Lord as a last resort because there was no one else to whom he could turn. He consciously chose to hope in and wait on God because he knew that there was no greater power or person in whom to invest his hope (recall Psalm 118:8-9). Of this we can be completely certain: Hope in our heavenly Father is hope that "does not disappoint," that serves "as an anchor of the soul" (Romans 5:5; Hebrews 6:17-19). It helps to steady us amid the storms of life as we continue to wait on the Lord.

Aside from belief and hope, another essential attribute of heart that is involved in waiting is **patience**. Regrettably, this virtue has been largely lost among residents of modern society, with the possible exception of farmers and select individuals in assorted occupations. In the majority of preindustrial cultures, patience was widely developed, almost automatically, through the trials of life that most people had to endure. They did not have the comforts, luxuries, and mechanized ease that people in post-industrial, urbanized, and automated societies have today. In other words, *life* schooled them in patience. Today, especially in relatively affluent areas, life teaches self-indulgence, instant gratification, and poor impulse-control. Most people are not comfortable waiting for long periods of time, and are certainly not accustomed to waiting patiently. Generally speaking, when we want something, we want it *now*. And when we ask for something, we expect to receive it soon.

Patience is critical to waiting on the Lord, both as a matter of character and as a practical issue. With patience, we can submit ourselves to God's timing. Our sense of timing in many cases is not aligned with the Lord's, yet we know beyond question that His timing is *always* perfect. Patience helps to bridge the disparity between His timing and ours, enabling us to wait for as long as necessary while earnestly expecting that He will respond. If we know that our requests are according to God's will, then we can (and should) continue praying until He answers. To put it another way, if our desires are godly, then it is not wrong for us to long for them and to look for their fulfillment. But we must be patient as we persist in praying for them, and submissive to His will with respect to both the timing and the outcome.

As revealed by the astonishing scarcity of patience in industrialized societies, this virtue is not easily developed. It requires discipline, self-denial, and humility, none of which are encouraged or actively pursued by mainstream culture. Growing in patience forces us to subject our own impulses and preferences and tendencies to the Lordship of God. Oftentimes, this submission is not easy, and in some instances obedience can be extremely difficult. But surrendering to the Lord's direction and timing would not be characterized as a "living sacrifice" if the action came easily to us (Romans 12:1). As we can see, these attributes are all connected, inseparable from each other: sacrifice is necessary to submission; submission is essential for obedience; obedience is required for patience; and patience is mandatory for waiting on the Lord.

From beginning to end, patiently waiting on God will constrain us to make sacrifices. But we can do so with certain knowledge that no sacrifice we might make is even worthy to be compared with the inestimable sacrifice that He has already made for us (see 1 Peter 1:2). We should also note that patience is one component of "the fruit of the Spirit" described in Galatians 5:22-23. God's Spirit will teach us patience as we mature spiritually. And if we struggle with impatience, we can pray for His divine aid to help us learn to be more patient. We are not asked to confront this challenge in our own strength (nor should we).

We have examined several dimensions of the attitude of heart that we should have while we are praying and waiting on the Lord. In *practice*, waiting on God is not terribly complicated. The previous aspects of prayer that we have considered over the past three weeks are all involved in the prayer that we engage in while waiting on Him. In sum, it is fully-formed and persistent prayer without ceasing, according to God's will and before the throne of grace, in the name and through the mediation of Jesus. Added to such prayer are reading and contemplation of Scripture. As was commended previously, praying with an open Bible in front of us, whenever possible, is a wise practice. When we come before Him with hearts that desire and are prepared to hear from Him, He often "speaks" to us through His inspired Word. In the context of waiting on Him, we want His will to direct us at every step, not only regarding the outcome but all along the way. And He may use the Bible to make known His will concerning the specific issue about which we are waiting. He might impress upon us that He *is* going to grant our requests, but only in accordance with His perfect timing. In any case, His Word is our guide, so we need to abide in it as we wait on Him.

While we pray and search the Scriptures daily, we must be ready to respond and obey as He prompts us. We cannot be stiff-necked or hard-hearted or proud, as were the Pharisees who refused to hear Jesus (refer to Matthew 13:12-17). "For God resists the proud," James reminded his readers, "But gives grace to the humble" (4:6). We wait in vain if we are not prepared to follow where He leads. Instead, we must depend on Him, trust Him, lean on Him, and acknowledge Him every step of the way (remember Proverbs 3:5-6). And what is the assurance that He gives us when we do these things? He will direct our paths. But if He is directing, then we need to follow humbly and obediently where He guides us.

Apart from full-bodied Christian prayer and abiding in His Word, waiting on the Lord involves exercising discernment regarding when to act and when to refrain from acting. We might be inclined to take steps that seem reasonable to us, while God is calling us to remain quiet and leave the matter in His hands:

> "Be still, and know that I am God;
> I will be exalted among the nations,
> I will be exalted in the earth!" (Psalm 46:10).

On the other hand, He may be prompting us to act while we continue praying and waiting for guidance; either because of our inherent resistance to obedience or because we lack the spiritual discernment to recognize His direction. Here, again, we encounter the parallel with walking in the Spirit. As we walk in the Spirit, the stubborn rebellion of our flesh is crucified with Christ, enabling us to obey the Lord's leading (recall Galatians 2:20; 5:16-25). At the same time, He instructs us in wisdom and understanding, both of which are necessary for sound discernment. In other words, by consistently following His direction, our capacity to perceive His leading develops toward maturity. (Read Hebrews 5:14. Also, as time allows, consider James 1:2-8 in light of the general concepts and the specific points that we have explored today.)

"See then that you walk circumspectly, not as fools but as wise, redeeming the time, because the days are evil. Therefore do not be unwise, but understand what the will of the Lord is" (Ephesians 5:15-17). We live in an evil age. In fact, the world we live in is not "just" evil. It glories in its perversions, celebrating its abominations and vices with festivals in the streets (recall Romans 1:32).

> "The moral condition of the world is disgusting, sickening, and appalling…. We need a revival—deep, widespread, general—in the power of the Holy Spirit. It is either a general revival or the dissolution of the church, of the home, and of the state. A revival, new life from God, is the cure—the only cure. Revival will halt the awful tide of immorality and unbelief" (Torrey 92-93).

In the midst of every form and degree of wickedness, through a world *saturated* with darkness, we are called to walk "as children of light…. And have no fellowship with the unfruitful works of darkness, but rather expose [or reprove] them" (Ephesians 5:8,11). Apart from the Holy Spirit awakening God's people, goading them to greater zeal, deeper devotion, and more effective and fervent prayer, the moral situation will only continue to deteriorate.

Some might be inclined to protest that this assessment of the world is excessively gloomy, that things are not really so bad. Satan loves such deception. He wants people to carry on with their lives as though all is well, eating and drinking and making merry until, as in Noah's day, judgment arrives with devastating finality. Some national and religious leaders provide the public with honest appraisals of the conditions, supported by hard data. For their candor, they are ridiculed as pessimists or accused of distorting the facts—in other words, lying. Truth is mislabeled a self-serving lie, while perverse lies are presented as truth. But authentic Christians who study the Bible and strive to live according to God's will are not sucked in by Satan's deception. They "are not ignorant of his devices" (2 Corinthians 2:11). These saints would probably agree with Mr. Torrey's proclamation: "If facing the facts is pessimistic, I am willing to be a pessimist. If in order to be an optimist one must shut his eyes and call black white, error truth, sin righteousness, and death life, I don't want to be an optimist" (87).

The world is like a runaway train. Careening down a slope with no brakes, this train carries a cargo of combustibles, poisonous chemicals, infectious diseases, and nuclear waste. The thundering steel snake continues to accelerate as it hurtles toward a huge metropolis. The catastrophe that will occur when this behemoth eventually derails defies imagination. But no one is foolish enough to deny the train's increasing velocity or to dispute the manifest that lists its cargo. Although solutions are in short supply, everyone with sense recognizes that denying the situation does not alter the reality of it. And the first step toward addressing the impending crisis is to assess the circumstances soberly and honestly.

Even when conditions are correctly understood, we cannot reform the world any more than one person could stop a runaway train. "With men this is impossible," Jesus taught, "but with God all things are possible" (Matthew 19:26). By ourselves, even the most capable among us cannot produce any meaningful transformation in the world. But with God, nothing is too difficult. And in accordance with His good pleasure, He uses His children as instruments to carry out His will. One way in which Christians are involved in bringing about a transformation, if one is to come, is through prayer. Certainly, this prayer *must* be effective and fervent if it is to prevail on the spiritual battlefield; if it is to pull down enemy strongholds and cast down arguments (see 2 Corinthians 10:4,5). In a word, our prayer needs to be **biblical.** And that means it should—no, it must—incorporate all that the Word of God tells us biblical Christian prayer entails. Hopefully it is clear by now that waiting on the Lord is included. Waiting is an indispensable piece in the complex entity that is powerful prayer.

Although we are already running long, one final (and brief) point should be inserted. The phrase "waiting on the Lord" can have an entirely different meaning from the one that is normally stressed. As we have already discussed today, we can wait on God in the sense of waiting for Him to act, respond, provide, comfort, direct. But we can also wait on the Lord in the sense of waiting *for* Him. "We are waiting on William to finish brushing his teeth so we can leave for church." Some of the ancient Israelites waited on (or for) the coming of the promised Messiah (read Isaiah 25:9). And we who have trusted in Jesus Christ as our Lord and Savior "eagerly wait for Him" to return for us, as He has promised He will (Hebrews 9:28; also John 14:1-3). Probably more than any other kind of waiting, looking for Christ's return when we know what it signifies—and having a vague idea of what awaits us—can be extremely difficult. Being patient is not easy when we yearn so intensely for Him to come. But wait we must. And while we wait on the Lord, let us wait on the Lord.

Day 23 — Prayer and Watching

Near the end of one of his letters to the Church of Corinth, the Apostle Paul issued some closing instructions that could serve well as marching orders for every Christian soldier. "Watch, stand fast in the faith, be brave, be strong" (1 Corinthians 16:13). With these concise commands, the battle-tested Colonel of Christianity was telling recruits and junior officers to remain *vigilant*. He directed them to hold their ground with unrelenting determination, never yielding to the forces of opposition. He challenged them to summon and display maximum valor, even in the face of seemingly overwhelming foes. And He called upon them to persevere resolutely when weary or wounded. If such orders were delivered to an earthly army, the soldiers in that force would know what to do. In a similar way, for us to implement Paul's instructions, we need to understand what specific actions he wanted the saints to take.

To "stand fast in the faith" is to trust the timeless truthfulness of the biblical doctrine that we have received. This is not to suggest that all doctrines which purport to be based in Scripture actually are. Even in the earliest years of the church, the apostles were forced to confront false doctrines and outright heresies that arose to challenge the revealed truth which was given to them. In fact, straying from correct doctrine is relatively easy if we fail to consider the whole counsel of God's Word on a given subject. And as we have seen previously, such a comprehensive understanding includes the various contexts of all relevant passages. Consequently, developing sound doctrine is a tremendous undertaking. It requires, in some cases, months or years of intensive (and prayerful) study.

Most of us *receive* the doctrines of the faith through the Bible-centered teaching of others. We are not required to "reinvent the wheel" by forming and refining the doctrines ourselves. But that is one major reason that it is absolutely *critical* for us to check what we are taught against what the Scriptures record. And whenever we encounter an apparent discrepancy, we need to follow up by asking the teacher about it in a spirit of love and a desire for truth. This practice helps to ensure that we receive and believe only sound biblical doctrine, and it also holds our teachers accountable. Once we have a solid footing of scripturally-sound doctrine, we stand firmly upon it without wavering. When error asserts itself and attempts to undermine our sure foundation, we refuse to yield. We allow our enemies to crash and ruin themselves against the mighty fortress of our God, thwarted by the invincibility of His eternal truth.

Standing with such confidence against our spiritual foes requires both bravery and strength. The enemy has many tactics in his playbook, some subtle and some overt. But he will stop at nothing to defeat and destroy us, if he can. Like Joshua, we must "be strong and very courageous" if we are going to continue standing defiantly when Satan or his minions assail us (Joshua 1:7-9). We are armed with "the sword of the Spirit," but we must be able to wield that sword skillfully by knowing and understanding what the Bible says—having sound doctrine. Only then can we "stand fast in the faith" with flint-faced determination, withstanding all of our enemy's assaults.

One of the centerpieces of Christian soldiery is *watchfulness*, an essential practice that uses several different names. Whether we call it vigilance or circumspection, being alert or attentive or observant, it amounts to the same thing. "Watch" conveys the idea of paying close attention to what is happening without becoming distracted or preoccupied with other concerns. The latter parts of Paul's orders are relatively easy to grasp, but why would he tell us to watch? Recall one of the scriptures that we discussed yesterday, from Ephesians 5:15-16: "See then that you walk circumspectly, not as fools but as wise, redeeming the time, because the days are evil." We watch as we journey through life because we inhabit an *evil* age. God desires for us to become more and more like Jesus through the lifelong process of sanctification (remember 1 Thessalonians 4:3). But that transformation will be stunted if we do not watch to guard against the corrupting influences that surround us (read 1 Corinthians 15:33).

Another reason it is imperative for all Christians to remain vigilant is that there are countless hosts of menacing spiritual adversaries everywhere in the world. Lest we forget, we are at **war**. The sole ambition of our enemies, consuming all of their attention and animating everything they do, is to combat the kingdom of God. "For we do not wrestle against flesh and blood, but against principalities, against powers, against the rulers of the darkness of this age, against spiritual hosts of wickedness in the heavenly places" (Ephesians 6:12). These malevolent spiritual beings detest the citizens of God's kingdom. And they will do anything and everything necessary to prevent other people from becoming citizens of His kingdom, if possible. Just as there is great "joy in heaven over one sinner who repents," all hell wails in outrage and defiance when another person receives citizenship and eternal life from God (see Luke 15:37). As soldiers in the army of the Lord, we must be attentive to the spiritual realities operating in the world around us. We may not see them as Elisha did, but we can discern the evidence of their work and the hallmarks of their diabolical schemes. We must watch for their assaults and observe their movements so we will not be caught unaware in a surprise attack. Satan's forces are crafty and shrewd, as he is, so we need to be careful and alert—to watch diligently.

The Apostle Peter endured some daunting challenges in his service of the Lord, so he understood well what Christians confront in their warfare with Satan and his minions: "But the end of all things is at hand," he wrote; "therefore be serious and watchful in your prayers" (1 Peter 4:7). Seriousness and sobriety, self-control and self-discipline are stressed repeatedly throughout Scripture. And the emphasis on these qualities is heavy in the New Testament, as biblically-minded believers might anticipate. We are indwelt by the Holy Spirit of God, as individual saints and as a corporate body of Christ. Having His Spirit within us, we are caught up in continuous and strenuous spiritual warfare on behalf of Christ and His kingdom. Whether or not we are aware of the war, it is real, and it never stops. Far more than any earthly conflict, this war has eternal consequences. The stakes are unimaginably high. And that being the case, the corresponding need for seriousness and sobriety in those who contend with the enemy is equally great.

To this point, we have seen that watchfulness (or vigilance) is one of the characteristics of a good and faithful Christian soldier, according to God's Word. Also included are seriousness and sobriety, without which we are easily distracted and any watching we do is of little benefit. But for any soldiers of light to be effective in battle against the emissaries of evil, they must be equipped with proper weaponry. Sentries standing a post or warriors deployed to the front line will be quickly overcome if unarmed, regardless of how vigilant they might be. And just as importantly, they must be trained well in how to use their weapons. Obviously, for a spiritual war, the weapons we use must also be spiritual: "For though we walk in the flesh, we do not war according to the flesh. For the weapons of our warfare are not carnal but mighty in God for pulling down strongholds, casting down arguments and every high thing that exalts itself against the knowledge of God..." (2 Corinthians 10:3-5). Prayer is one of the most potent weapons in the Christian arsenal, as our keynote scripture testifies: "The effective, fervent prayer of a righteous man avails much" (James 5:16). But as the verse indicates, and as this book has elaborated, the kind of prayer that "avails much" has several qualifying characteristics. To put it another way, it is meaningful that James did not simply declare, "Prayer avails much."

As we have seen elsewhere, another powerful weapon in the saint's spiritual armory is "the sword of the Spirit, which is the word of God" (Ephesians 6:17). And we noted that this "sword" is most effective when we are properly instructed in how to use it. A child cannot pick up a longsword and swing it with the expertise of Lancelot. Similarly, a spiritual "child" must be *taught* how to wield "the sword of the Spirit" in combat. Included in that training program must be an acknowledgment that the power of the "sword" is not intrinsic[119]. In one sense, the Bible is simply a book of words printed on paper and protected by a cover, similar to any other book. But we know that "the word of God is living and powerful, and sharper than any two-edged sword..." (Hebrews 4:12). The life and the power come from God. He makes His Word powerful because it is *His* Word, and He is all-powerful (omnipotent). Simply stated, the power resides in *Him*; it is intrinsic to *Him*. No power is inherent in the book or the words themselves, like some sort of magic talisman or incantation. The words "Let there be light" did not bring forth light. Rather, light came into existence because *God* issued the command.

---

[119] intrinsic (O): belonging to the basic nature of a person or thing

The same principle applies to prayer. Its potency as a weapon derives *exclusively* from the One to whom we pray. Thus we notice that Paul followed his instructions about "the sword of the Spirit" with a proviso[120] that we have considered elsewhere: "...praying always with all prayer and supplication in the Spirit, being watchful to this end with all perseverance and supplication for all the saints" (Ephesians 6:18). Persistent and "watchful" prayer must figure prominently in any discussion of spiritual warfare. Moreover, the "sword of the Spirit" is wielded most lethally when the blade is dipped in prayer (in a manner of speaking). Whoever our human teachers might be, the *Lord* must enable and train us to manipulate the powerful weapon of His Word. This He does and will do when we pray and watch. If this proposition is not self-evident, just review how skillfully Jesus employed "the sword of the Lord," then note how much time He spent in prayer.

We know that watchfulness in itself does not avail much if it is not paired with an effective weapon. At the same time, vigilance by Christian soldiers is of limited benefit if they know not for what (or whom) they should be watching. Normally, a sentinel guarding a post does not sound a general alarm when a stray dog wanders near the perimeter defenses. But if enemy troops are known to be exceptionally skilled in the use of camouflage, then a rustling bush might be more than just a rustling bush. Competent sentries know what to watch for and what can be dismissed. In a comparable way, not everything disagreeable or undesirable that happens in our lives is an assault by the enemy. But those things that *are* attacks need to be responded to as such. Consequently, we want to grow and mature in our ability to tell the difference. And that kind of discernment influences how we watch.

Consider, for example, the instruction that Jesus conveyed to His disciples in the garden of Gethsemane: "Watch and pray, lest you enter into temptation. The spirit indeed is willing, but the flesh is weak" (Matthew 26:41). We need to be conscious of our fleshly weaknesses so that we can always be on the alert for anything that might tempt us to sin. As we continue to mature spiritually, the Lord supplies us with deeper understanding of our own vulnerabilities. And Paul provided sound counsel concerning how best to handle those weaknesses: "But put on the Lord Jesus Christ, and make no provision for the flesh, to fulfill its lusts" (Romans 13:14). A Christian who is highly susceptible to substance abuse should be exceptionally careful to avoid circumstances in which such substances might be available. For that believer knowingly to enter a situation in which such temptations will be present is to make "provision for the flesh, to fulfill its lusts." A saint who is extraordinarily vulnerable to sexual lust must be extremely vigilant concerning television programs, films, Web sites, magazines, and anything else in which suggestive images might be displayed. Similar principles apply to other sins and pitfalls.

---

[120] proviso (O): something that is insisted upon as a condition of an agreement

173

A helpful rule of thumb that we can use in times of uncertainty is easy to remember: Whenever there is any doubt, there is no doubt. Should we attend a friend's wedding reception, where alcohol will flow in abundance? There is no doubt. Should we watch the television program with the preview that depicts young men and women in tiny bathing suits? There is no doubt. Or how about this one: Should we visit that political Web site, knowing how the opposition candidates will be portrayed, and the anger that we are likely to experience? Again, there is no doubt. As we make these kinds of choices, we must watch and pray, taking into account our own vulnerabilities and tendencies. The command to "make no provision for the flesh" reaches into every area of our lives, making it altogether critical that we watch and pray, as Jesus instructed, so that we will not enter into temptation.

To some, it might seem like we are being excessively restrictive with ourselves. It may appear that we are denying ourselves opportunities and experiences that we would like to enjoy under the umbrella of Christian liberty. But an important phrase deliberately embedded in that statement makes a world of difference: "denying ourselves." Recall what Jesus taught in the Sermon on the Mount:

> "If your right eye causes you to sin, pluck it out and cast it from you; for it is more profitable for you that one of your members perish, than for your whole body to be cast into hell. And if your right hand causes you to sin, cut it off and cast it from you; for it is more profitable for you that one of your members perish, than for your whole body to be cast into hell" (Matthew 5:29-30).

Was Jesus advocating self-mutilation? Of course not! He was using hyperbole[121] to stress the point that we should go to great lengths to avoid temptations to sin. Admittedly, by "denying ourselves" we will forego some experiences and pleasures that might be permissible for us. But what have we really given up? Surely we must realize that **nothing** this life offers is worthy to be compared to what the Lord has prepared for us in His kingdom (consider Romans 8:18; 1 Corinthians 2:9). In that context, is it really asking a lot to pass on some fleeting, temporal satisfaction so as to avoid a situation in which we discern that we might be tempted to sin (read Matthew 16:24-26)?

Other things we need to watch for as well, in addition to the various pitfalls and snares that could result in sin. Satan, for instance, our foremost adversary, constantly schemes and contrives ways to compel people to transgress God's will. Remember the familiar admonition of Peter in his epistle: "Be sober, be vigilant; because your adversary the devil walks about like a roaring lion, seeking whom he may devour. Resist him, steadfast in the faith, knowing that the same sufferings are experienced by your brotherhood in the world" (1 Peter

---

[121] hyperbole (O): an exaggerated statement that is not meant to be taken literally

5:8-9). His exhortation is so widely quoted that many Christians overlook its emotional intensity. "**Be** sober, **be** vigilant! The devil is like a rabid, bloodthirsty predator constantly searching for another victim. Fight him! Watch out for him! Stand fast in the faith, be brave, be strong!" In Peter's words, we hear echoes of Paul's instructions with which we began today's lesson (1 Corinthians 16:13).

Some things we should be watching for are decidedly positive. In fact, one of them is the most wonderful and exciting event of all, the return of Christ. Jesus commanded, "Watch therefore, for you know neither the day nor the hour in which the Son of Man is coming" (Matthew 25:13). Like sentinels standing a post, we scan the horizon at the furthest reach of our vision, watching for any sign of our Lord's return. And like weary warriors atop the wall of a besieged city, we search for the promised arrival of our Commander, leading an awesome host that is too vast to number. All our hopes hang on Him, so we eagerly wait for Him and maintain a constant vigil, seeking for any indication of His approach. We want to be found as the five wise virgins of Jesus's parable, who already had oil for their lamps when the bridegroom arrived (verses 1-12).

Ministers, pastors, elders—all who serve by shepherding saints through their lives of faith are solemnly charged with the responsibility to watch for threats to their flocks. These dangers can arise both internally and externally. Paul affirmed this fact in his counsel to Timothy:

> "Preach the word! Be ready in season and out of season. Convince, rebuke, exhort, with all longsuffering and teaching. For the time will come when they will not endure sound doctrine, but according to their own desires, because they have itching ears, they will heap up for themselves teachers; and they will turn their ears away from the truth, and be turned aside to fables. But you be watchful in all things, endure afflictions, do the work of an evangelist, fulfill your ministry" (2 Timothy 4:2-5).

Internal schisms, disputes over doctrines, factions, divided loyalties, and numerous other problems can rise up to cause havoc in a church. Consequently, everyone in leadership, and all mature Christians in the congregation, should watch and pray to detect and counteract such issues before they establish footholds.

Additionally, **external** threats to the church are severe in opposition, many in number, and growing in both ways with each day that passes. Where they have existed at all, religious freedom laws are being aggressively eroded or even eliminated. This makes it increasingly difficult for saints to obey God's will by practicing the tenets of their faith without coming under attack by government officials. Churches are sued just for teaching what the Bible says, denounced by the media, and portrayed as havens of backwards bigots by antagonists in the public square. In the name of "tolerance" or "equality," laws are being instituted all over the United States that heavily impact the ability of Christians to worship according to the dictates of their consciences. And in other parts of the world, the dangers and threats and overt attacks that God's people face are significantly greater than in America. Through all of these perils and many others, shepherds must struggle to lead their flocks. This task has always required church and group leaders to "be watchful in all things." But in these "perilous times," teachers who instruct their congregations in the *whole* counsel of God's Word are increasingly the exception and not the rule (2 Timothy 3:1). In such days, all genuine Christians need to watch and pray. Enemy forces are gathering and their assaults are intensifying. We are living in the days about which Paul warned Timothy; the days that Jesus assured His disciples would come just prior to His return (Matthew 24:36-44). More than ever before in human history, we need to watch and pray.

No less important than vigilance by shepherds (and the sheep), parents must be equally attentive to their children. Young people growing up—particularly in highly industrialized countries—are beset on all sides by perils and pitfalls that will severely harm or even ruin them if not avoided. Most lack the wisdom and the experience to recognize all of those threats. Consequently, parents need to be constantly alert both for their own spiritual welfare and for that of their children. Needless to say, this is a tremendous responsibility. And for Christian parents to succeed, they must watch and pray.

At the same time, we all need to watch for threats to our marriages. The most fundamental unit of human society, deeper even than the family, is the one-flesh union of a man and a woman in marriage. As much care as we dedicate to vigilance for our own spiritual well-being, equal concern should be devoted to attentiveness regarding our marriages. Although this may be difficult for some people to accept, the simple truth is that we should attend even more earnestly to the welfare of our spouse than we do to the spiritual health of our children. In other words, of all people in our lives, our wives or husbands should always come *first*. Admittedly, this is not how marriage is currently understood by most people in developed countries. But the Bible clearly teaches that the bond a married man and woman have is entirely unique among all the relationships in human existence. They are "one flesh" (Genesis 2:24; Matthew 19:5-6). Therefore, each should watch and pray for the other with utmost diligence.

Like a patchwork quilt, practical Christian living is composed of numerous different pieces, all of which combine to form the whole. We all know this from personal experience, and we have discussed it throughout this book. Woven into the rich fabric of such a life is the golden thread of biblical prayer, infusing the whole assembly with beauty, resilience, and strength. Obviously, no sane soldier would ever stride into battle without a weapon in hand and some type of sturdy garment to protect the body. In the case of prayer, it is both. Prayer is like the tunic that we put on before all of the pieces of "the whole armor of God" are strapped to our bodies. Prayer is the leather thongs that secure the armor in place. Prayer coats the blade of "the sword of the Spirit," and prayer welds the grip to our hand. The necessity and the value of watchful prayer in representing Christ as His ambassadors, in an increasingly evil and hostile world, cannot be overstated. Whether we are assigned as spiritual sentries guarding stationary posts, lieutenants maintaining order and discipline in the ranks, or seasoned warriors swinging swords in frontline combat, watchfulness and prayer are *essential.*

Watch and pray, Christians, soldiers in the army of the Lord. Stand fast, be sober, be vigilant, walk circumspectly, not as fools but as wise, redeeming the time, because the days *are* evil. Watch, because we know not at what hour our Lord is coming.

Day 24 — Prayer and Readiness

"Also I heard the voice of the LORD, saying:
'Whom shall I send?
And who will go for Us?'
Then I said, 'Here am I! Send me'" (Isaiah 6:8).

This is another one of those passages of Scripture that is frequently quoted, especially in evangelical circles. We have seen numerous such verses throughout this book (most recently, 1 Peter 5:8). These scriptures are cited as often as they are, we should note, because they are particularly well-suited to the truth being communicated. When any biblical topic is mentioned, usually a handful of verses will immediately spring to mind which acutely illustrate the related doctrine. This excerpt from the Book of Isaiah pertains to several truths. But what we are most concerned with here is its relevance to readiness. Simply stated, Isaiah's response to God's question displayed the prophet's attitude of **readiness**. And that is the same heart we Christians need to have when we come before the Lord in prayer.

The word "readiness" can signify different things. And it will probably surprise no one at this point in the book that, when we mention readiness, we intend all of those meanings. First, readiness indicates a **willingness** to obey God's direction, to go where He sends us and do as He leads. This aspect of readiness is the one most prominently exhibited by Isaiah. So keen was the prophet's willingness that as soon as the Lord inquired, Isaiah replied swiftly and decisively. His response demonstrated that his heart was already oriented toward God, leaning on Him, acknowledging Him, and waiting on Him. And we have already seen in previous lessons how such an attitude of heart should describe all of us as well.

Willingness is illustrated well by a pair of verses found near the end of the Book of Joshua: "So Joshua said to the people, 'You are witnesses against yourselves that you have chosen the LORD for yourselves, to serve Him....' And the people said to Joshua, 'The LORD our God we will serve, and His voice we will obey!'" (24:22,24). By their collective statement, the people displayed their willingness—their *readiness*—to do all that the Lord commanded them. They even bore witness against themselves, entering into a covenant with Joshua that bound them to uphold their profession (verse 25). In effect, Isaiah and the Israelites both proclaimed through their impassioned responses, "Command us, Lord! We will go where You send us and do as You bid."

To highlight the value of willingness as a component of readiness, consider the contrasting reaction of the Prophet Jonah: "Now the word of the LORD came to Jonah the son of Amittai, saying, 'Arise, go to Nineveh, that great city, and cry out against it; for their wickedness has come up before Me.' But Jonah arose

178

to flee to Tarshish from the presence of the LORD..." (Jonah 1:1-3). We will overlook the foolishness of anyone trying "to flee...from the presence of the LORD" (read Psalm 139:7-10). What concerns us here is Jonah's *unwillingness* to go where the Lord told him to go and do what the Lord told him to do. Compare Jonah's response to Isaiah's. In Isaiah's case, God *asked* "who will go" and Isaiah's hand shot into the air. By contrast, God *commanded* Jonah to go and he bolted in the opposite direction.

Jonah's experience raises an important point that we need to include. From a strictly human perspective, the prophet's reaction to God's order is somewhat understandable. After all, at that time Nineveh was the capital city of the hated and vicious Assyrian Empire. "You want me to go *where*, God?" No Israelite with an ounce of sense would travel there on purpose, to say nothing of going there to denounce their wickedness and summon them to repentance. If we were put in Jonah's position, how willing would any of us be to follow the Lord's direction? Most people in the developed world know what some so-called "Islamic extremists" have done to Christians and other people they captured. The Assyrians did all those things and *worse* to the people they considered enemies. So even though the prophet's response was disobedient and therefore sinful, it was also understandable to some extent.

However we might empathize with Jonah's reluctance, his unwillingness is still shameful and condemnable. Willingness to follow the Lord's leading should never extend only to the boundaries of our preferences or our "comfort zones." Like devotion and obedience and surrender, willingness should be complete. Granted, we are not yet made perfect, so we will fall short at times. But as we have noted before, the standard does not change simply because we fail to live up to it.

A second meaning of readiness is **preparedness**, an awkward term that signifies being prepared to act as soon as He calls upon us. It describes those saints who have **pre**-pared ahead of time to participate in the kingdom-related work to which they (we) are summoned. They are ready when He calls. This dimension of readiness is depicted in both negative and positive ways by a couple of passages from the New Testament. We will look at the negative first:

"Then He [Jesus] said to another, 'Follow Me.'
But he said, 'Lord, let me first go and bury my father.'
Jesus said to him, 'Let the dead bury their own dead, but you go
and preach the kingdom of God.'

And another also said, 'Lord, I will follow You, but let me first
go and bid them farewell who are at my house.'
But Jesus said to him, 'No one, having put his hand to the plow,
and looking back, is fit for the kingdom of God'" (Luke 9:59-62).

Both of these men expressed *willingness* to follow Jesus. So in that sense, they were ready. But they were unprepared to follow Him when He called because they had other things that they wanted to attend to first. In that sense, they were not ready. True readiness requires saints to be both willing *and* prepared, never one or the other.

Preparedness as an aspect of readiness is also portrayed in a positive way in a familiar scene from Mark's Gospel: "And as He walked by the Sea of Galilee, He saw Simon and Andrew his brother casting a net into the sea; for they were fishermen. Then Jesus said to them, 'Follow Me, and I will make you become fishers of men.' They immediately left their nets and followed Him" (1:16-18). These two fellows were busily plying their chosen trade, conducting their normal daily business, trying to earn an honest living. As soon as Jesus called, they dropped what they were doing and followed Him. They did not respond that they wanted to stow their equipment first or haul in one last catch. Unlike the two men in Luke's Gospel, Simon and Andrew did not answer, "Lord, I will follow You, but first let me go and…." They did not inquire what traveling with Jesus would entail, where He intended to take them, or what might be required of them along the way. They were **ready**, both willing and prepared, so when Jesus summoned them to participate in His ministry, they left everything and followed Him.

Are we supposed to glean from this that we should abandon our careers, our families, and all of our commitments to become missionaries in some under-evangelized place? No, not necessarily, though if God is calling some of us into foreign missions, then we need to obey (remember Jonah). Yet again, we must consider the whole counsel of God's Word. The point to stress here is the *readiness* of Simon and Andrew in both dimensions. Many of us are *willing* to serve the Lord, and some are even willing to endure profound hardships and sacrifices in the process. But fewer are *prepared* to go wherever He leads, to do whatever He prompts us to do. The reasons for our lack of preparedness are as numerous as they are varied. But what they boil down to is a simple question: Is the Lord our highest priority?

From this probing question flows a host of others. And those questions can help us to identify areas of our lives in which we are not as prepared as we should be. Is following God's direction more important to us than physical comfort? Than knowing where we will obtain our next meal? Is obeying our Father more valuable to us than career advancement? Are we laboring to make a name for ourselves or to magnify His name? Would we follow the Lord's leading if it meant that every one of our family members turned against us? Would we sell everything we have and distribute to the needs of the poor if we knew it was God's will for us (see Mark 10:17-22)? Such self-examining questions could proceed for pages, but the point has been made. In all *honesty* before our Creator (who knows the truth anyway), is the Lord our highest priority (recall Jeremiah

17:10)? If we can sincerely answer "Yes" to that question, then another must closely follow it: Is anything in our lives a close second to Him?

For many of us, the second question is more difficult (because it is more convicting) than the first. Yes, God comes first in our lives, but our children are not far behind. Yes, the Lord is our foremost priority, but our spouses are a close second. Honestly, Jesus is above all else for us, but not by much. Christians, this should not be! Our devotion to the Lord God should be so complete, consuming, focused, unrivaled, and zealous that nothing else compares! Did our children love us enough to suffer horribly and die innocently for us while we were their avowed enemies? Did our spouses create us from dust? Do they graciously give us every breath and heartbeat, every morsel of food and sip of clean water?

Willingness to follow the Lord cannot be discounted; it is important. But by itself, willingness is not enough. By itself, it is not readiness. We must also be prepared to do whatever He instructs us to do, and to go wherever He directs us to go. If this seems a bit scary to some, perhaps even terrifying, it is because our human nature craves a sense of security. We gravitate toward the routine, the predictable, the comfortably familiar. And when we dare to venture outside of those boundaries, we want our adventures to be strictly within limits that we define. But when God calls us, He does not leave us the liberty to impose conditions on our obedience: "Lord, I will follow You, but...." "Father, use me for Your glory, except...." "God, show me Your will, but...." Anyone who attempts to follow the Lord conditionally is not "fit for the kingdom of God" (reread Luke 9:62). If that describes the attitude of our hearts when we approach Him in prayer, then we should not be surprised to discover that we are not plowing in straight lines. To pray with a heart of **readiness,** both *willing* and *prepared,* our vision should be so keenly fixed on Jesus that the furrow we cut points directly to Him.

By now it is probably not necessary to point out that the effective and fervent prayer we desire requires readiness. In a scene that we examined during our study of "Prayer and Watching," Jesus informed His disciples, "The spirit indeed is willing, but the flesh is weak" (Matthew 26:41). Part of the Holy Spirit's work through the process of sanctification includes developing in us a genuine love for what God loves and a corresponding hatred for what God hates—specifically, sin (see Psalm 97:10; Proverbs 8:13; Romans 12:9). As He transforms us, we become more *willing* to follow the Lord's direction. We walk more in the Spirit, not fulfilling the lusts of the flesh (as much). By *His* Spirit's action, our spirits become willing, but our flesh remains weak while we reside in these feeble bodies. It continues to hinder us, impairing our ability to be fully *ready* when we come before His throne in prayer.

Since potent prayer requires readiness, and since our flesh inhibits development of readiness, what are we supposed to do? Paul answered this question, albeit indirectly: "And those who are Christ's have crucified the flesh with its passions and desires" (Galatians 5:24). Our flesh has been crucified. Therefore, we should treat it as a dead thing, not heeding its prompting or permitting it to exercise any control over us. "Likewise you also, reckon yourselves to be dead indeed to sin, but alive to God in Christ Jesus our Lord" (Romans 6:11; also read verses 12-13). In order to pray with readiness, we should consider everything fleshly and sinful as dead to us. Our lives are bound up with His Spirit, and His Spirit has no fellowship with our flesh. "If we live in the Spirit," Paul wrote, "let us also walk in the Spirit" (Galatians 5:25). We can pray in readiness by faithfully walking in the Spirit, closely following His lead and heeding His direction. (For further reflection on the subject of readiness, if desired, consider Jesus's "Parable of the Sower" in Matthew 13:3-9. Specifically, think about how the seed that fell among thorns relates to the theme of readiness.)

To this point in today's study, we have discussed readiness in terms of its dual components, willingness and preparedness. Before we leave this subject, there is another dimension of readiness that we should investigate. It relates to a separate meaning of the word *readiness*—another way of looking at it. Recall that in our exploration of "Prayer and Waiting," we noted the different senses in which the word *waiting* can be interpreted: waiting *on* the Lord and waiting *for* the Lord. A similar quality applies to readiness. In addition to the aspects that we have already covered, we can also speak of being ready for the Lord's Second Coming.

Readiness in this context relates more to waiting and watching than to willingness and preparedness. We "eagerly wait for Him" because we believe Jesus *will* return, as He promised He would. We watch for His arrival, earnestly expecting that Christ could appear at any moment. Jesus assured His followers that we would not know the day nor the hour. And He impressed upon His disciples the need to be found ready for His return when He comes. Waiting and watching, wanting to be ready, significantly influences how we conduct ourselves in the present. Our lives are (or should be) structured around a confident belief that any second could be our last in these bodies. The Bible provides us with some indication of what will transpire when He arrives. With that knowledge in mind, we should recognize the utter futility—the complete **pointlessness**—of living how the world lives or valuing what the world values.

Peter emphasized these truths toward the end of one of his epistles. And though the passage is somewhat long, it speaks so poignantly to our present topic that it is worth quoting in its entirety:

"But the day of the Lord will come as a thief in the night, in which the heavens will pass away with a great noise, and the elements will melt with fervent heat; both the earth and the works that are in it will be burned up. Therefore, since all these things will be dissolved, what manner of persons ought you to be in holy conduct and godliness, looking for and hastening the coming of the day of God, because of which the heavens will be dissolved, being on fire, and the elements will melt with fervent heat? Nevertheless we, according to His promise, look for new heavens and a new earth in which righteousness dwells.

Therefore, beloved, looking forward to these things, be diligent to be found by Him in peace, without spot and blameless; and consider that the longsuffering of our Lord is salvation....

You therefore, beloved, since you know this beforehand, beware lest you also fall from your own steadfastness, being led away with the error of the wicked; but grow in the grace and knowledge of our Lord and Savior Jesus Christ" (2 Peter 3:10-15,17-18).

In a word, what Peter described here was **readiness**. He captured, in a compact and compelling package, what it means to live in a state of readiness for the Lord's arrival.

All of the most salient[122] points are presented there in one concise statement:

1.   The Second Coming of Christ will be sudden and unexpected (in terms of its timing).
2.   The earth in its current form will be destroyed.
3.   God will provide new heavens and a new earth.
4.   Material things will not survive, so what truly matters are "holy conduct and godliness."
5.   The Lord's delay translates to salvation for more people.
6.   Christians know in advance how things end, so we should not be caught up in the current of the world's ways.
7.   Enduring value is obtained through growth in "the grace and knowledge of" Jesus.

All of the time and resources and energy that we devote to accumulating possessions, building a name for ourselves in our careers, and establishing our personal empires will amount to **nothing** when Jesus returns. Our businesses and homes, our vehicles and clothes, our jewelry and gadgets: all of it will *burn*. The world treasures such things, but Christians should know better.

The world carries on as it always has, "eating and drinking, marrying and giving in marriage," supposing that circumstances will continue as they are (Matthew 24:38). But God's people know that the time is short. Saints understand that "the form of this world is passing away" (1 Corinthians 7:31). Sadly, too many professing Christians are drawn into living after the fashion of the world. They

---

[122] salient (CO): outstanding, projecting, prominent, striking

live as though Jesus will *not* return anytime soon. The Apostle John had strong words for anyone who attempts to blend biblical Christianity with the world's ways: "Do not love the world or the things in the world. If anyone loves the world, the love of the Father is not in him. For all that is in the world—the lust of the flesh, the lust of the eyes, and the pride of life—is not of the Father but is of the world. And the world is passing away, and the lust of it; but he who does the will of God abides forever" (1 John 2:15-17).

Children of God, the Second Coming of Christ is the single most wonderful event in all of human history! Both the number and magnitude of awesome things that will occur when He appears are beyond imagination. Let us be found ready! Disregard the honey tongues of those who "speak great swelling words of emptiness," who cater to "itching ears" and lead believers astray with assurances that are contrary to the plain teachings of Scripture (1 Peter 2:18; 2 Timothy 4:3). Saints, heed the Word of God! The world will do what it has always done. But let us remain intently focused. Let us pursue the will of our Father and orient our lives around the certain knowledge that Jesus **will** return soon. When He arrives, let us be *ready;* not caught up in living according to the world's ways, but eagerly waiting and watching for Him. "No one engaged in warfare entangles himself with the affairs of this life, that he may please him who enlisted him as a soldier" (2 Timothy 2:4).

Christians understand that we *are* at war, so let us live in a constant state of readiness. "The [saint] who spends little time in prayer, who is not steadfast and constant in prayer, will not be ready for the Lord when He comes" (Torrey 17).

Obstacles to Effective Prayer

Day 25 — Satan's Opposition

At this point in our studies, we have spent 24 days intently investigating what constitutes effective and fervent prayer. For three days, we briefly considered the *logistics* of prayer. Then we devoted five days to exploring various *components* of biblical prayer. Since then, we have committed a bit more than two weeks to delving deeper into numerous *characteristics* of Christian prayer. Where we now stand, we should have a relatively well-informed understanding of what comprises powerful prayer. We have also developed a clearer image of how such prayer is embodied in the everyday practice of God's people. Admittedly, there is a lot of information to process and absorb. And implementing everything we have covered could require some substantial or even radical modifications in our lives.

Before we proceed any further, let us pause a moment to translate what we have surveyed into the context of spiritual warfare. For us to maintain consciousness of the spiritual war in which we are continuously engaged is of utmost importance. The war is *real*. It rages on incessantly[123], though we might forget about it or desire to be excused from it for awhile. We strap on "the whole armor of God," brandish "the sword of the Spirit" and clutch "the shield of faith," and we fight on. Through prayer, the infinite power of God upholds and invigorates us, surrounds us with angelic hosts of light, and infuses both our assaults and defenses with tremendous strength. Biblical prayer is an extremely potent presence on the spiritual battlefield. When practiced according to the teachings of Scripture, Christian prayer definitely "avails much."

But as with any earthly war, one army gathered on a field does not a battle make. Arrayed against us is a colossal horde of evil entities, seething with hatred and obsessed with opposing God's kingdom. These malicious creatures lust for our destruction, certainly physical but especially spiritual. By themselves, these foes are formidable adversaries. Only through the power of our Commander can we defeat them. And even then, we persevere in combat knowing that the war will continue without interruption until the precise moment appointed by our Commander-in-chief (Matthew 24:36). In that instant, the Lord Himself will stride forward into the fray and, in a glorious display of His majesty, bring a sudden and decisive end to the war.

In the meantime, we fight and we pray. Regrettably, our spiritual enemies are not the only forces contending with us on the battlefield. We also have the

---

[123] incessantly (O): unceasing, continually repeated

"terrain" to overcome. The world around us exerts a greater influence than most of us realize. It introduces additional obstacles and hazards that make it substantially more difficult to fight effectively. Some of these barriers and pitfalls are produced by our adversaries. At other times, the battleground itself challenges us because we have not persevered with proper training, including rigorous conditioning. To put it another way, in some circumstances we are "our own worst enemies." Soldiers can grow weary of countless drills and endless routine, but they immediately become thankful for that training once they discover how much it helps them in battle.

Apart from the opposing host and the difficult terrain, we also have to conquer our own shortcomings and vulnerabilities. These impact how effectively we fight and how earnestly we pray. None of us is an ideal soldier. We all have flaws that adversely affect how well we fight. But Jesus did not recruit us because He deemed us to be perfect warriors. In fact, He uses us in part because *our* weakness magnifies *His* strength (see 2 Corinthians 4:7). He displays additional glory by achieving victory with a ragtag army of misfits like us (12:9). At the same time, He empowers us to overcome our wayward tendencies and He compensates for our deficiencies. Our Commander is very gracious and loving toward us, and He protects us even more than we know. But whatever role He allows (and enables) us to occupy in the war, the battle definitely belongs to Him, as does the glory of victory.

We see, then, that we encounter opposition from Satan and his minions, from the world, and from within (our flesh). These all inhibit our ability to fight, and they also undermine the effectiveness and fervency of our prayers. In his writing, David MacIntyre described some of the forces that counteract powerful prayer, all of which fit into the three general categories that we have identified: the enemy, the world, the flesh.

> "Sometimes we are conscious of a satanic impulse directed immediately against the life of prayer in our souls. Sometimes we are led into 'dry' and wilderness-experiences, and the face of God grows dark above us. Sometimes, when we strive most earnestly to bring every thought and imagination under obedience to Christ, we seem to be given over to disorder and unrest. Sometimes the inbred slothfulness of our nature lends itself to the evil one as an instrument by which he may turn our minds back from the exercise of prayer. Because of all these things, therefore, we must be diligent and resolved, watching as a sentry who remembers that the lives of men are lying at the hazard of his wakefulness, resourcefulness, and courage" (5).

Many obstacles interfere with potent prayer. Moreover, those obstructions impact how well we are able to serve as soldiers in the army of the Lord.

In our final week of study, we will explore seven of the most prominent and damaging handicaps to genuinely powerful prayer. Although these seven are prevalent and experienced by most Christians to different extents, they are certainly not an exhaustive survey of the possibilities. Satan is exquisitely shrewd and crafty. He constantly devises new ways to thwart us, modifying his tactics or repurposing old devices and deploying them in novel ways. He may engage us directly in a frontal assault, either attacking us himself or sending one of his lieutenants. He might use some aspect of the world system in an attempt to frustrate our efforts or to make it exceedingly difficult to combat him—a kind of spiritual sabotage. Or he may exploit our flesh, using detailed knowledge of our tendencies and vulnerabilities, the spiritual equivalent of psychological warfare. At times he uses our flesh to lure us away from the battle. He prompts us to focus on other things instead of fighting him—"fiddling while Rome burns." Or he appeals to the appetites of our flesh, tempting us to sin so that we lay down our arms and wander aimlessly about the battlefield. His schemes are endlessly inventive and he has more cunning than any earthly adversary. Granted, we must be careful not to give the devil too much credit, understanding that he is a fallen angel and by no means God's equal. But at the same time, wise counsel applies here just as well as it does to earthly wars: "Know your enemy."

A familiar passage of Scripture that we considered two days ago serves as a good launching point from which to analyze our foe: "Be sober, be vigilant; your adversary the devil walks about like a roaring lion, seeking whom he may devour. Resist him, steadfast in the faith, knowing that the same sufferings are experienced by your brotherhood in the world" (1 Peter 5:8-9). Our focus here is different from what it was in "Prayer and Watching." First, Peter referred to the devil as "your adversary." The Greek word he employed has a significance which immediately becomes apparent when we see it written with English letters: *satanas*. This term, in turn, was derived from an Aramaic word which appeared in the Hebrew scriptures: *satan*. To state these details in a simpler form, the name associated with our archenemy, Satan, literally means "adversary." In other words, the fallen angel whom we know as Satan received his *name* from his *function* (or occupation).

Satan is the adversary of all humanity. And even more than human beings in general, he vehemently[124] opposes God's people. He viciously antagonized the people of God under the Old Covenant, and has only intensified his opposition (if that is possible) to Christians under the New Covenant. His singular goal, animating everything he does, is to frustrate and attempt to defeat all movements of human beings toward God. This ambition applies to those who are already citizens of Christ's kingdom and to those who are being drawn in by the Lord. Satan strives to sow seeds of evil everywhere, in everyone, at all

---

[124] vehemently (C): passionately, urgently, violently, furiously, very eagerly

times. He despises God, and his hatred for God fuels his antipathy[125] for everything that the Lord has created. This is especially true of humans because they alone of all creation were made in God's image. By assaulting humans, Satan attacks God's image.

One of Satan's methods for propagating[126] evil in the world is the source of his other common name, the Devil. The Greek term translated "devil" is *diabolos*, which means "an accuser" or "a slanderer." For instance, Satan the Devil is referred to as "the accuser of the brethren" in Revelation 12:10. Some older versions of the Bible mistakenly translate the Greek word for "demon" as "devil." In reality, however, there is only one Devil. Under him is a numberless horde of subordinate demons who participate in the black work that he orchestrates (see Revelation 12:9). Although he is indeed powerful, Satan is, after all, "only" an angel. Therefore, he cannot *force* people to do evil except by direct possession. And since the Holy Spirit of God dwells inside all genuine Christians, Satan and his demons *cannot* possess them. Again, for emphasis, authentic Christians **cannot** be demonically possessed. Because the Devil is incapable of *forcing* us to do his bidding, he must resort to using suggestion, accusation, and temptation to goad and entice us into transgressing God's will. Although with saints Satan must rely on persuasion, he is a master at employing deception and intimation to manipulate the unwary.

Jesus referred to the Devil's cunning use of falsehood in a challenge to the Jewish religious leaders of His day. At the same time, He revealed some disturbing attributes of this utterly evil being: "He was a murderer from the beginning, and does not stand in the truth, because there is no truth in him. When he speaks a lie, he speaks from his own resources, for he is a liar and the father of it" (John 8:44). Satan is a murderer, a liar, and a deceiver. He is an accuser, a slanderer, and a tempter. He is our adversary. Such a devious enemy should never be underestimated, and we ignore him at our own peril.

Peter's comparison of Satan to a "roaring lion" proves to be a very appropriate analogy on closer examination. Lions are ambush predators. They use stealth and concealment to approach their prey without detection, moving slowly and almost imperceptibly until they are within range to strike. If their prey is not vigilant, its attention too occupied with feeding or mating, then the lion can launch a surprise attack. That is why we observe prey animals constantly surveilling their surroundings, watching not only for their own survival but also for the other animals around them. The analogy here to Peter's warning is fairly obvious. His admonition to be "sober" and "vigilant" was intended to safeguard not only ourselves, but other Christians as well. (Think of the numerous comparisons in Scripture between saints and sheep.) As Paul wrote, "Let each of you look out not only for his own interests, but also for the interests of others"

---

[125] antipathy (CO): strong, settled, deeply-rooted dislike
[126] propagating (O): spreading, transmitting, breeding, reproducing

(Philippians 2:4). Like soldiers on a battlefield, we must watch for threats to ourselves and for dangers to the saints around us. Their welfare should be just as important to us as our own.

For prey animals to detect the approach of a stalking lion, their senses need to be as alert as possible. They must pay close attention to everything happening around them: movements, sounds, smells, signals from other animals. In a comparable way, we need to maintain clear minds and sharp senses—to "have our wits about us." This certainly requires sobriety in the literal sense, as well as self-control and mindfulness of the perils that threaten us. The world denies Satan's very existence, but we know that he and his minions are real. If we are not careful, the world can lull us into letting down our guards and living as if there is no Devil. Satan loves this and readily uses it to his advantage. At the precise moment when we are most complacent and least alert, he pounces. Hence Peter's exhortation to be "sober" *and* "vigilant"—to be self-controlled and watchful. We must keep our guards up, spiritually speaking. And when we detect a threat to ourselves or other Christians, we give the signal to indicate danger. Or, to continue the battlefield analogy, when we observe the enemy approaching, we sound the alarm and summon our comrades to arms.

Like many ambush predators, lions frequently target prey animals that appear to be weak, diseased, injured, or isolated. These properties make those animals more vulnerable to attack and (generally) easier to kill. In a similar way, Christians can be physically *or* spiritually weak, diseased, injured, or isolated. We might be weak because of immaturity or through neglect of God's Word. Our hearts could be infected with the disease of anger or bitterness, lust or envy. We might be injured through a betrayal of trust or through another saint's grievous sin; adultery, for example, or even murder. And the Book of Proverbs specifically addresses isolation:

> "A man who isolates himself seeks his own desire;
> He rages against all wise judgment" (18:1).

Christians are not armies of one. We are soldiers in the army of the Lord, individual "units" that are all parts of a greater whole. "Now you are the body of Christ," Paul wrote, "and members individually" (1 Corinthians 12:27). When any of our number are attacked, we assemble ourselves and form a defensive perimeter around them. We "circle the wagons" and protect our own, encouraging and strengthening and supporting them as needed. And when they are isolated for any reason, we send a squad to retrieve them and escort them back to our company.

Oftentimes when powerful ambush predators encounter fierce and sustained resistance, they forfeit and retreat to await a better opportunity. They prefer to attack using the element of surprise, trying to incapacitate their prey before it can mount a forceful counterattack. In many cases, once the predator is detected and surprise lost, the assault is abandoned. For example, a lion stalking toward a herd of water buffalo through tall grass, realizing that it has been spotted, might simply stand up and walk casually toward the massive beasts. Occasionally it will attack anyway, but usually without success. In a similar manner, Satan and his demons typically operate using stealth and surprise. They prefer to maneuver covertly instead of engaging people directly. Although they might still strike when we are aware of their movements, the intensity of their assaults diminishes when they meet with concentrated resistance. Additionally, our ability to defend against spiritual attacks increases substantially when we perceive the enemy's approach.

This brings us to an important consideration concerning what the appropriate response is when Satan or one of his foot soldiers attacks. On this issue, we find the same instruction provided by Peter, Paul, and James. Referring to the Devil, Peter counseled, "Resist him, steadfast in the faith" (1 Peter 5:9). We are called to stand our ground firmly without yielding, and to use "the shield of faith" to "quench all the fiery darts of the wicked one" (Ephesians 6:16). In the same passage of Ephesians, Paul admonished, "Put on the whole armor of God, that you may be able to stand against the wiles [or schemings] of the devil" (verse 11). Here again, we are told to "stand against" Satan and all of his diabolical tactics, protected by the "armor of God." James recorded a similar mandate that sheds further light on the subject: "Therefore submit to God. Resist the devil and he will flee from you. Draw near to God and He will draw near to you" (4:7-8). Appropriately, James situated our resistance of the enemy in context with submitting and drawing near to God.

Satan understands the potency of prayer better than we do. He knows all too well that the "effective, fervent prayer of a righteous man avails much" (5:16). Such prayer has been employed as a weapon against him and his hordes for thousands of years. He has watched in seething fury as strongholds were splintered, arguments were cast down, and idols that he schemed to exalt "against the knowledge of God" were laid waste (recall 2 Corinthians 10:4-5; also 1 Kings 18:20-39). Most of what passes for prayer in our day does not trouble him at all, for he knows that it possesses no real power. He laughs derisively[127] at "carnal Christians" who suppose their petitions and intercessions threaten his dominion. But when obedient and sincere saints devote themselves to diligently cultivating the practice of earnest and biblical prayer, Satan rages. He knows what results from such prayer and he hates it. Thus, he will stop at *nothing* to prevent or discourage the children of God from praying in a fully-formed and scripturally-sound manner. He will deploy every tactic, device, and scheme he can contrive to stop saints from praying in that way.

---

[127] derisively (O): scornfully; showing ridicule

The Devil strives zealously to thwart Christian prayer, for a particular reason. And that reason relates to his prime objective. In order for the prayers of God's people to wield legitimate power, those believers must be submitted to the Lord. They also have to draw near to God, a spiritual movement which involves numerous elements that we have discussed over the past 24 days. To Satan's horror and outrage, when God's children draw near to their Father, *He* draws near to *them!* Human beings entering into closer relationship with the Lord, whose image they bear and whom the Devil utterly despises, is infuriating to him. He yearns for nothing more than to separate them from God. He longs to ensure that as many as possible will be damned along with him. And those elect saints whom the Lord redeems, Satan vehemently opposes, striving to render them ineffective on the spiritual battlefield. In fact, it would be difficult to *overstate* how desperately and furiously the Devil lusts to keep people away from God and to stop Christians from praying.

All praise and thanks be to God, however, that none of this need cause us a moment's fear. Although the Devil *is* horrible and evil beyond imagining, the Lord Almighty is perfectly sovereign. Moreover, the Holy Spirit of the omnipotent Creator dwells *inside* each of us. We serve a God whose power is measureless, whose love is infinite, and whose promises are absolutely certain. His Word of truth assures us that when we resist the Devil, "he will flee." Satan is not granted authority to harm us at will, and he can do nothing to threaten our eternal life (remember John 10:27-30). All he can really impact is how effective we are as soldiers in the army of the Lord. He can influence us in many different ways, so that our prayers become powerless, our minds polluted, our hearts unloving, and our spirits despondent. The Holy Spirit will address all of these issues (and any others that exist) through His work of sanctification, *when* we submit to God. He will transform us into the likeness of Christ as we draw near to Him; as we present our bodies a living sacrifice (refer to Romans 12:1-2; 2 Corinthians 3:18). He will also empower and equip us to stand against the Devil's assaults until, as he will, our adversary flees.

One important caveat[128] must be inserted before we leave this topic. Because many Christians have never understood, much less practiced, genuinely effective and fervent prayer, they have never encountered the ferocity of Satan's opposition. But anyone who commits to implementing everything in this book needs to know that his attacks *will* come. Prepare for them, but do not fear. "You are of God, little children, and have overcome them, because He who is in you is greater than he who is in the world" (1 John 4:4). Then again, anyone putting the lessons of this book into practice *as we go* has probably already experienced some of the adversary's assaults.

*   *   *   *   *   *

---

[128] caveat (C): a notice or warning

[Anyone who desires to learn more about how the Devil operates should read *The Strategy of Satan*, by Warren Wiersbe. Although his accessible book was not consulted in the composition of this work, it will undoubtedly help any reader to "know your enemy" better.]

Day 26 — Unconfessed Sin

Unconfessed sin usually falls into one of two categories: first are *transgressions* of God's will that we are unaware of, but which we have not honestly acknowledged and repented of before the Lord; second are *trespasses* against other people that we know should be addressed, but which we have not disclosed to them in a sincere commitment to doing what God desires. Both types of unconfessed sin interfere with our ability to pray effectively and fervently. They deprive us of intimacy with our heavenly Father and with our brethren in the body of Christ. Some of the material we explore today might sound somewhat familiar, as it was referred to on day 5, "Confession." But here we will concentrate on the repercussions of failing or refusing to confess our transgressions and trespasses. And since our primary subject is powerful prayer, we will also consider how those consequences hinder such prayer.

The author of Hebrews included a clear and direct admonition: "Pursue peace with all people, and holiness, without which no one will see the Lord: looking carefully lest anyone fall short of the grace of God" (12:14-15). Much could be written about this brief yet substantial directive. But in the interest of space, we will focus on one portion of it: without holiness, "no one will see the Lord." Immediately we recognize that seeing the Lord could signify several different things. We are not referring here to seeing Him when He returns in glory at His Second Coming. Nor do we mean seeing the Lord as His wisdom, power, and love are revealed through Creation. And we are certainly not speaking of seeing the Lord in a vision such as the Apostle John had in Revelation. Narrowing our scope a bit further, our emphasis here is on seeing the Lord's power operating in and through our lives; seeing Him respond marvelously to our prayers. Without holiness, no one will enjoy the awesome blessing and privilege of seeing the glory of God displayed through His answers to prayer. And since that is the express aim of this book, the importance of holiness in that regard is readily apparent.

We already know that sin separates people from God, who is perfectly holy. We understand this because the Bible plainly teaches it, and many of us have repeatedly learned this painful truth through personal experience.

Sin is like a massive wedge driven between God and humanity, and we are the ones swinging sledge hammers. Under the terms of the Old Covenant, priests were required to perform elaborate cleansing rituals before they were permitted to enter the Lord's presence in the temple. But the sacrifices and washings those priests completed did not actually rinse away their sins, as though the contamination of sin resided on the skin. "For it is not possible that the blood of bulls and goats could take away sins" (Hebrews 10:4). Instead, those prescribed rituals served a dual purpose: 1) representing or foreshadowing the ultimate purifying sacrifice of Christ which truly cleanses us from sin; 2) impressing upon the priests (and the people of Israel) the *gravity* of sin as an offense against the holiness of God. The Lord allowed the high priest to enter His presence only once a year. Even then, the priest might have to be dragged out because he had approached God's presence in an unworthy manner.

"By those who come near Me
I must be regarded as holy;
And before all the people
I must be glorified" (Leviticus 10:3).

Absolutely no taint of sin can reside in the Lord's perfectly holy presence. Consequently, anyone who attempted to draw near to God in a sinful state would instantly and necessarily perish (read Exodus 19:21-22).

A risk arises here of belaboring a point that we have already grasped. But at the same time, the holiness of God is not appropriately honored and revered in our day. Christians are called to holiness with just as much emphasis as were the priests of ancient Israel. The Apostle Peter affirmed this truth in one of his epistles: "But as He who called you is holy, you also be holy in all your conduct, because it is written, 'Be holy, for I am holy'" (1 Peter 1:15-16). The commandment that Peter quoted was from Leviticus 11:44-45. In other words, Peter appealed to an Old Testament mandate as the authority for his command to New Testament saints to "be holy." The moral law of God, as we have discussed elsewhere, still applies to us. We see then that the atonement for sin of Jesus in *no way* nullified[129] the requirement that the people of God conduct themselves in a holy manner. Under the Old Covenant, the Israelites were God's chosen people, and they were commanded to be holy. Christians under the New Covenant are held to the same standard.

We needed to revisit the holiness of God so that we can properly appreciate (as well as possible) how offensive our sins are to Him. And we must establish that frame of mind so we can understand why *unconfessed* sin presents such a formidable barrier to effective prayer. When we approach the throne of grace in prayer, if we are harboring sin that we neglect or refuse to confess, then how can we expect Him to welcome us into His presence? To be clear, our *access* to His throne is eternally secure because of Jesus, as we covered on day 14. But the idea that we would come before Him with known sin and *not* confess it is unthinkable. If we are unaware of a sin, then that is another matter. The Holy Spirit will reveal our sins to us (and convict us of them) as He continues to transform us through the process of sanctification. But when we know about some transgression of God's will that we are guilty of, we *must* confess it. "When, in the course of the day's engagements, our conscience witnesses against us that we have sinned, we should at once confess our guilt, claim by faith the cleansing of the blood of Christ, and so wash our hands in innocence" (MacIntyre 26).

---

[129] nullified (C): made of no value or efficacy; invalidated

What possible benefit could result from not confessing our sin, anyway? Do we suppose that our transgressions are concealed from Him? On the contrary, "there is no creature hidden from His sight, but all things are naked and open to the eyes of Him to whom we must give account" (Hebrews 4:13; also Jeremiah 17:10). Or do we love our sins so much that we are committed to holding onto them, even at the expense of intimacy with the Lord? Paul wrote, "Abhor what is evil. Cling to what is good" (Romans 12:9). As we grow in Christlikeness, we will come to love what God loves and hate what He hates. Instead of loving our sin and clinging to it, we will be ashamed of it, sorrowful over it, and eager to be rid of it. We will run to the Lord, cast ourselves at the foot of His throne of grace, and ask Him to cleanse us of our iniquity. Like David, we will avail ourselves of God's lovingkindness and tender mercies, acknowledging our sins to Him and seeking His forgiveness (read Psalm 51:1-4). *Only* good comes from confessing our transgressions to the Lord, and only evil results from failing or refusing to confess.

We know that all genuine Christians are indwelled by the Holy Spirit. To put that another way, we have *God's Spirit* living inside each of us. By itself, that is an amazing fact, and it should not be lightly esteemed. One of the works of the Spirit within all of God's children is to convict of sin, laying upon our hearts the gravity of our offenses against the supreme holiness of our Father. In the hearts of sincere saints, that conviction leads to godly sorrow which produces repentance (read 2 Corinthians 7:9-10). When we then ignore or repel the influence of the Holy Spirit within, Scripture informs us that He is *grieved* (see, for example, Ephesians 4:30). Here is how David MacIntyre expressed this truth: "Conviction of sin will naturally prompt to confession. When such promptings are disregarded, the Spirit who has wrought in us that conviction is grieved" (27). His statement reiterates what we have seen in the Word. In the lives of all whose hearts belong to the Lord, confession follows conviction as if by a natural progression. And that being the case, it is critical that we appreciate just how terrible it is when we grieve the Holy Spirit.

With that truth in mind, consider this: When we cause grief to the Spirit of God by dismissing His promptings to confess, we *sin.* In other words, failing or refusing to confess our sin is itself sin. Reflect on this insight from the Epistle of James: "Therefore, to him who knows to do good and does not do it, to him it is sin" (4:17). The Spirit *within* us impresses *upon* us that we have transgressed our Father's will, indicating *to* us that the Lord desires *for* us to acknowledge our sin to Him. At that point, we know to do good, since everything God wills is good. If we then choose not to do that good, we sin again. This horrible cycle could continue indefinitely, unless the godly sorrow that we experience finally drives us to confess and repent of our iniquity before the Lord.

At this point in our studies, we know that the Holy Spirit is instrumental in powerful prayer. When we pray to God Almighty while at the same time grieving His Spirit, we effectively attempt to do two entirely incompatible things at once. With one hand we push Him away, separating ourselves from Him through our failure to confess. With the other hand we reach out to Him, pleading for Him to answer us when we call and to grant our petitions. Such duplicity[130] is clearly denounced throughout the Bible. And since we are already in the Epistle of James, let us turn a few chapters to the left to read an example of how this type of behavior is condemned: "But let him ask in faith, with no doubting, for he who doubts is like a wave of the sea driven and tossed by the wind. For let not that man suppose that he will receive anything from the Lord; he is a double-minded man, unstable in all his ways" (1:6-7). The word translated "double-minded" here literally means "two souls." It describes a person who is divided between allegiance to God and attachment to the world. Such a duplicitous individual tries to "serve two masters," to use Jesus's illustration (see Matthew 6:24).

The prospect of grieving the Holy Spirit is not something that any sincere Christian should take lightly. Instead, it is a very serious matter, both on its own and as it impacts the effectiveness and the fervency of our prayers. The obvious remedy to this problem is to confess our sins honestly to the Lord. But to correct the harm inflicted by our unconfessed sin, we need to go a bit further than confession alone. In the second half of the verse that we examined yesterday, James recorded what we must do through a stirring series of commands: "Draw near to God and He will draw near to you. Cleanse your hands, you sinners; and purify your hearts, you double-minded.... Humble yourselves in the sight of the Lord, and He will lift you up" (4:8,10).

Instead of pushing ourselves away from God through failure to confess, we need to "draw near" to Him. We must turn from (repent of) the habitual sins that we continue to commit and acknowledge those transgressions to the Lord (remember David). Beyond that, we need to *surrender* ourselves completely to Him. With hearts that are pure in devotion to Him, we will no longer have "two souls," in a manner of speaking. And since refusal to confess almost always stems in some way from foolish pride, we must humble ourselves in His sight. Pride is an **abomination** in the eyes of the Lord (verse 6; also Proverbs 6:16-17). We must forsake it and should avoid it at all costs.

It should now be apparent that failure to confess, double-mindedness, pride, and powerlessness in prayer are all bound up together. To state the matter very simply, if we desire prayer that "avails much," then we *must* acknowledge our transgressions of God's will as soon as the Spirit brings them to our awareness. By contrast, our prayer *cannot* avail much—it *will not* contain any real power if we harbor unconfessed sin (read Psalm 66:18). But what about our trespasses

---

[130] duplicity (O): double-dealing, deceitfulness

against other people? Is it equally destructive to the effectiveness and fervency of our prayer if we neglect to confess those? Before we transition to that topic, consider the truth of this statement from R.A. Torrey: "Sin is an awful thing.... It severs the connection between us and the source of all grace and power and blessing. Anyone who desires power in prayer must be merciless in dealing with his own sins" (67).

We have noted elsewhere that the law is a concrete expression of the will of our Creator. One consequence of that fact is that everything contrary to the Moral Law of God is also against His will. And anything that violates the Lord's will is **sin**. "Whoever commits sin also commits lawlessness," the Apostle John observed, "and sin is lawlessness" (1 John 3:4). Another way of looking at this would be to state that only transgressions of God's law constitute *sin*, in the strictest sense of that word. In Romans 5:13, the Apostle Paul recognized this important distinction: "For until the law sin was in the world, but sin is not imputed when there is no law." Over in chapter 7, he expanded on that observation and personalized it: "I would not have known sin except through the law.... For apart from the law sin was dead" (verses 7,8). This might seem a bit confusing, but we need to grasp it. God's will is **perfect**, we can all affirm, so *His* will is *the* will that we must obey (Romans 12:2). His supreme will is communicated definitively through His law, which He delivered (7:12). Therefore, all violations of His law are sins against Him. In other words, sin in the narrow sense is against God and only against God. "Against You, You only, have I sinned," David confessed, "And done this evil in Your sight" (Psalm 51:4).

These statements might raise a few objections or questions, so let us clarify. In our everyday conversations with other Christians, we are accustomed to speaking of "sinning against" our neighbors or "sinning against" our spouses. We talk about "sinning against" people when we mean that we have wronged them, treated them unjustly, or wounded them. In some way, we have done or said something to another person that we should not have done or said, and we call it sin. An argument could be made that using the label "sin" for that purpose is permissible, as long as it is understood that the term is being defined loosely. Strictly speaking, however, according to the *biblical* significance of the word, sin is specifically an offense against God. That might seem like splitting hairs or like a purely semantic matter, but the distinction is actually quite important, as we will discover.

We know that unconfessed sin tremendously impacts the effectiveness and fervency of our prayer. But trespasses against other people technically cannot qualify as sin. Therefore, failing or refusing to acknowledge the wrongs we have done to those people cannot impact the power of our prayer in the same way, or to the same degree, that unconfessed *sin* does. This is not to suggest that offenses against other people are not important, nor that we should experience no sense of urgency in addressing them. Of course they are, and of course we should! Our purpose here is only to establish that transgressions against God and trespasses against other people differ not only in degree of impact but also in kind. This might be confusing, so let us continue and hopefully it will become clearer.

In His Sermon on the Mount, Jesus delivered some instruction that will help to illuminate this issue: "Therefore if you bring your gift to the altar, and there remember that your brother has something against you, leave your gift there before the altar, and go your way. First be reconciled to your brother, and then come and offer your gift" (Matthew 5:23-24). In this scenario, I have wronged my brother in some way. As I am bringing a freewill offering to the Lord to be presented on the altar, I suddenly remember that my brother has something against me. Obviously, Christians in our day no longer practice the freewill offering ceremony that was prescribed to the nation of Israel under the Old Covenant. So what we want to concentrate on here are two things: the importance Jesus assigned to reconciliation; and the urgency He stressed concerning the actions that we take to make peace with a brother whom we have wronged.

As we studied on day 13, unity within the body of Christ should earnestly be pursued in its own right. Our Lord wants us to be of one mind, of one accord, striving together in our service unto Him. But beyond seeking unity for the sake of unity, it is instrumental to effective and fervent prayer. When we trespass against another Christian, we disrupt that unity. We cause a fracture or an infection within Christ's body, figuratively speaking, that needs to be healed. And since we are responsible for the offense, we must prioritize whatever action would be appropriate to reconcile with the saint whom we have wronged. In truth, this precept applies generally to all of our relations with other people. But it is especially important when the injured person is another child of God. Recall that the verse from Hebrews at the beginning of today's lesson commanded, "Pursue peace with all people..." (12:14). And over in Romans, Paul wrote, "If it is possible, as much as depends on you, live peaceably with all men" (12:18). But in his Epistle to the Galatians he exhorted, "Therefore, as we have opportunity, let us do good to all, especially to those who are of the household of faith" (6:10).

Christians are not merely one category of people among many in society. We are more than just another wedge on a demographic pie chart. In other words, authentic Christians are not simply a separate *group* of people; we are a different *type* of people. We are **regenerated**. We have God's own Spirit dwelling inside each of us. Consequently, we should not interact with each other in the same manner that we engage with people in the world. Moreover, that distinction applies to how we handle our offenses against those people. When we trespass against a brother or sister in Christ, the Lord views it as being done to Him (see, for example, Matthew 25:40). What we do or say to God's people, we do or say to Him. That is a sobering thought. And it puts in perspective the importance of reconciling with other saints when we wrong them in some way.

Jesus expressed the urgency of the need to make peace through His command to leave our "gift there before the altar" (5:24). To aid understanding, this principle can be rephrased in familiar, modern terms: When we are busily pursuing the affairs of life and suddenly remember that we wronged someone and have not made peace, we should "drop what we are doing" and seek reconciliation immediately. Again, for emphasis, this communicates *urgency*; it is not a prescription for action. We are not suggesting that people should walk away from their jobs or anything so drastic. The point, rather, is that we need to prioritize reconciliation very highly. We can write ourselves a brief reminder note if there is a possibility that we will forget before an opportunity arises to take action. But we must make an attempt at peace a top priority. If doing so requires us to humble ourselves, then so be it. (We know how God views pride.) Whatever we are compelled to do in order to seek peace with someone we have wronged, that we must do.

The keynote verse on potent prayer that is woven throughout this book is actually the second half of James 5:16. The first half pertains directly to our current topic: "Confess your trespasses to one another, and pray for one another, that you may be healed." The mandate here is so straightforward that it requires no elaboration. When we trespass, we need to confess. Additionally, we should "pray for one another," both regarding the specific issue of trespass and in general. Confession and prayer bring healing—of *relationships*, certainly, and sometimes of bodily sickness as well.

Unconfessed *sin* inhibits powerful prayer. Unconfessed *trespasses* hinder unity and fruitfulness, and can also interfere with effective and fervent prayer. But we need not become preoccupied with determining whether a particular act is a sin or a trespass. Such concerns "miss the forest for the trees." They prompt us to become so focused on nonessential details that we lose sight of the bigger picture. In this instance, the "forest" is confession. When we do wrong, we **must** confess—period. As we walk consistently in the Spirit, He will impress upon us when we have done or said anything that needs to be acknowledged. And when He does bring remembrance and conviction, we should humble ourselves, purify our hearts, and confess—either to Him or to the other person, as the circumstances warrant.

Day 27 — Unforgiveness

"And whenever you stand praying, if you have anything against anyone, forgive him, that your Father in heaven may also forgive you your trespasses. But if you do not forgive, neither will your Father in heaven forgive your trespasses" (Mark 11:25-26). If we view unconfessed sin as one side of a coin, then unforgiveness is the other side. Both have no place in any sincere Christian's life. And both are terribly obstructive to effective and fervent prayer, in different but related ways. We explored yesterday how sin against God and trespasses against other people interfere with our ability to pray in a way that "avails much." But as Jesus clearly proclaimed in this excerpt from Mark's Gospel, unforgiveness exerts a similarly harmful impact on our prayer. In effect, we arrive at the same destination (or dead end) by an alternate course.

More than once in his epistles, the Apostle Paul stated that Christians "were bought at a price" (see 1 Corinthians 6:20 and 7:23, where that wording appears; the idea is repeated elsewhere). For us to appreciate what that phrase signifies, we need to understand two distinct concepts: first, what it means for a person to be "bought"; second, what "price" was paid to buy us. And this information is critical to grasping the gravity of unforgiveness, so we will examine each concept in turn.

Before the Lord purchased us, we were all *slaves* to sin (Romans 6 discusses this at length). Sin was a cruel and sadistic taskmaster, whipping us mercilessly and driving us ever onward unto more wickedness. Worse yet, the more we obeyed sin, the more hopelessly enslaved we became. Each act of service tightened the shackles that bound us to our demented overlord. No possibility existed that we could free ourselves from captivity through personal effort or with the assistance of other people (John 1:12-13). And for all of that, the only compensation we received was misery and death (Romans 6:23). Knowing our plight, and loving us in spite of our extreme unloveliness, *God* paid to liberate us from our slavery to sin.

> "For when we were still without strength, in due time Christ died for the ungodly. For scarcely for a righteous man will one die; yet perhaps for a good man someone would even dare to die. But God demonstrates His own love toward us, in that while we were still sinners, Christ died for us" (Romans 5:6-8).

When we were His *enemies*, God purchased us from our slavery to sin; not because He was obligated in any way, but solely because of His love.

Once the Lord paid to release us from our bondage, we became His in a different way from before. Strictly speaking, all things belong to Him because He is the Creator and Sustainer of the universe. But when He purchased us, He sealed us with His Holy Spirit, marking us as His precious possession. As Paul questioned, "Or do you not know that your body is the temple of the Holy Spirit who is in you, whom you have from God, and you are not your own? For you were bought at a price; therefore glorify God in your body and in your spirit, which are God's" (1 Corinthians 6:19-20).

Saints, we are not our own. Our bodies and our spirits *belong* to God, not to ourselves. To speak of people as "property" is not really appropriate since human beings are so much more than mere objects. But in a sense, nonetheless, we are "God's property." And just as we are normally free to do as we please with our *own* property, God alone decides what He will do with *His*. In fact, our autonomy is subject to certain boundaries; His is limitless. Thankfully, our Father is loving, merciful, and generous. Everything He wills to do with us is both for His glory and our greatest good. He does not abuse or destroy or discard His property on a whim, as we might.

Unlike the gods (idols) of Greek, Roman, Egyptian, and Norse mythologies (among others), the Eternal Creator God is not capricious[131]. Consequently, knowing what we do about the One True God, we can *embrace* the fact that we do not belong to ourselves. Profound joy and comfort and freedom are found in belonging to Him. That is what it means for us to be "bought." We are not transferred from one detestable owner to another, like slaves at auction. Instead, we are introduced to the most amazing and unimaginable liberty that exists. Redemption is truly a wonderful doctrine, and a thrilling reality for all who are genuinely saved. But at what "price" did the Lord purchase us?

The Apostle Peter answered that question memorably in one of his epistles. While exhorting the saints to holiness, he recognized "that you were not redeemed with corruptible [or perishable] things, like silver or gold, from your aimless conduct received by tradition from your fathers, but with the precious blood of Christ, as of a lamb without blemish and without spot" (1 Peter 1:18-19; also read Acts 20:28). The only currency valuable enough to secure our freedom from slavery to sin was the blood of God's only begotten Son. Consider for a moment what that means. Think about what it reveals. So strong were the spiritual shackles by which sin held us captive that only the blood of God incarnate would suffice to remove them! And yet, so immeasurable is the love of Almighty God that He willingly paid that price to liberate His *enemies* from their bondage. "Behold what manner of love the Father has bestowed on us, that we should be called children of God!" (1 John 3:1). No wonder Paul seemed to be at a loss for words to describe the magnitude of God's love (Ephesians 3:18-19). The man who thought of himself as the chief of sinners would surely appreciate what was required to save him, and the love that animated that sacrifice (1 Timothy 1:15).

---

[131] capricious (C): having a disposition or mood inclined to changes of humor or opinion without reason

None of this is new information for sincere Christians who have believed the gospel of salvation and received Jesus as Lord and Savior. In fact, these truths are essential components of the gospel. But in order to comprehend as fully as possible the barrier that unforgiveness presents to powerful prayer, we need to consider the practical ramifications of the fact that we were "bought at a price." And that understanding operates along two parallel lines. First, since we were bought and we are not our own, when God commands us, we must obey.

> "In this the love of God was manifested toward us, that God has sent
> His only begotten Son into the world, that we might live through Him.
> In this is love, not that we loved God, but that He loved us and sent
> His Son to be the propitiation[132] for our sins....
>
> ...For this is the love of God, that we keep His commandments"
> (1 John 4:9-10; 5:3).

God displayed *His* love for us, among other ways, by sacrificing His Son to redeem us. Now we are called upon to demonstrate *our* love for Him by obeying His commandments. And, incidentally, "His commandments are not burdensome" (5:3). Our Lord commands us, His purchased possession, to forgive others when they trespass against us (read Ephesians 1:14). We encountered one such mandate in the passage from Mark's Gospel that opened today's lesson. And comparable orders are located elsewhere in Scripture. For example, Jesus taught, "Judge not and you shall not be judged. Condemn not, and you shall not be condemned. Forgive, and you will be forgiven" (Luke 6:37). Then there is Paul's well-known admonition that was directed specifically to saints in the body of Christ: "And be kind to one another, tenderhearted, forgiving one another, even as God in Christ Jesus forgave you" (Ephesians 4:32). Since we are not our own, we belong to God, and He *commands* us to forgive others, does that mean we sin when we do not forgive? Indeed, it does. Unforgiveness is sin.

Take a moment to read and contemplate the recital of human moral failure that Paul recorded in Romans 1:28-32. That series is one of the most comprehensive listings of our inborn capacity for evil and perversion in the whole Bible. And included there is the entry "unforgiving," sandwiched between "unloving" and "unmerciful" (verse 31). All three of those qualities are polar opposites of the heart that God demonstrates toward undeserving sinners by offering His Son. (Some versions of the Bible omit "unforgiving" from this passage. But the point that unforgiveness is sin remains indisputable. Failure to forgive violates the Lord's commandment and is therefore contrary to His will.) Knowing that unforgiveness is sin, we should be able at this point to anticipate how it functions as an obstacle to effective prayer. We have stressed repeatedly how sin interferes with prayer that "avails much."

---

[132] propitiation (C): something that attains favor or appeases; atonement

Now that we have seen how being "bought" relates to effective and fervent prayer, we can shift our attention to the second line of instruction generated by that phrase: the "price." When we ponder the magnitude of Christ's sacrifice, meditating on all that He endured and the agony that He experienced, we can develop a sense of the "price" that was paid to liberate us. And such reflection should inform our actions, prompting us to obedience, which in this instance means forgiveness. Paul expounded on these concepts at length in his letters, particularly his Epistle to the Romans:

> "For there is no difference; for all have sinned and fall short of the glory of God, being justified freely by His grace through the redemption that is in Christ Jesus, whom God set forth as a propitiation by His blood, through faith, to demonstrate His righteousness, because in His forbearance God had passed over the sins that were previously committed, to demonstrate at the present time His righteousness, that He might be just and the justifier of the one who has faith in Jesus" (3:22-26).

God is just. But if He justified sinners without punishing their sin, He would compromise His justice. He would no longer be just. However, the Almighty **cannot** act contrary to His own character. Consequently, to preserve His justness while justifying sinful human beings, He punished the sins of His chosen ones in the person of Jesus, His own Son (see Romans 5:18-19). That is the "price" God paid to make forgiveness possible.

Considering what it cost the Lord to enable our forgiveness, *nothing* that we might have to sacrifice in order to forgive other people of their trespasses is worthy of comparison. The magnitude of His sacrifice cannot even be comprehended, let alone appreciated for its value. By contrast, our greatest sacrifices are never asking too much. Keeping everything in proper perspective, we can and we must forgive all offenses and trespasses against us by other people. God's Word never promises that forgiveness will always be easy. In fact, even with correct understanding and an appropriate attitude toward forgiveness, there are occasions in life in which it might appear impossible. A mother whose daughter was brutally murdered; a young man whose perverted father sexually abused his brother; a man whose wife was violently raped; the countless people whose loved ones were savagely murdered by terrorists: all of these and many others may feel that they are incapable of forgiving the offender(s). But as difficult as the truth may be to accept, forgiveness is not optional; it is mandatory.

For all who are not Spirit-filled Christians, there are indeed some things that are impossible to forgive. But for the saints of God, anything *can* be forgiven, and everything **must** be forgiven. We trust the Lord with all our hearts, knowing that He is sovereign. Nothing occurs in our lives that He has not ordained or allowed, and everything that He does permit always happens for a reason. When evil intersects our paths, as it will, we choose to trust Him, leaning not on our own understanding. When the question cycling continually through our minds is "Why, Lord?", we take ourselves firmly in hand and remind ourselves of who God is, what He has done, and what He has promised to do. We trust that anywhere vengeance is warranted, He will execute it according to His own immutable designs and in His own perfect timing. And we rest in the knowledge that wherever injustice appears to prevail, He will ensure justice is satisfied in the end. Ultimately, we are forced to confront the fact that harboring unforgiveness, like hatred and bitterness, only exerts a harmful impact on ourselves. It has no effect on the person or people whom we refuse to forgive.

When a person wrongs us in some way and we find forgiveness especially difficult, we are not completely without recourse. Nor are we expected to grit our teeth and knuckle through professing forgiveness so that we appear to comply with God's will. That would be futile, anyway, since the Lord desires our forgiveness to be sincere. As a rule, all insincere statements of forgiveness are pointless. Recall what Jesus taught about the unforgiving servant in Matthew 18:21-35. After contrasting the king's mercy with the hardness of his unforgiving servant, Jesus concluded His object lesson with a stern warning: "So My heavenly Father also will do to you if each of you, from his heart, does not forgive his brother his trespasses" (verse 35). God wants—no, **commands**—forgiveness that proceeds from our hearts. And besides, how can we withhold our forgiveness from others in light of all that He has forgiven us?

We know that forgiving other people from the heart is undoubtedly the Lord's will for us. We also know "that if we ask anything according to His will, He hears us. And if we know that He hears us, whatever we ask, we know that we have the petitions that we have asked of Him" (1 John 5:14-15). Therefore, when we find it difficult to forgive someone for a particular offense, we should pray and ask God to provide us with the ability to forgive sincerely. And we can present this petition to our Father with complete confidence that He *will* hear and He *will* grant what we have asked. For specially challenging trespasses that seem nearly impossible to forgive, we may find it necessary to be persistent in our prayers. We might (and probably will) have to humble ourselves; to remind ourselves of our own sinfulness and how undeserving *we* are of *God's* forgiveness. But when we pray continually and diligently for the ability to forgive from the heart, He *will* supply it.

A paradox arises here that warrants mentioning: unforgiveness inhibits us from praying effectively and fervently, yet to overcome an unforgiving spirit, we should pray. As we continue to pray for the Lord to transform our hearts and enable us to forgive, our capacity to pray powerfully will increase. Then as we persist in praying earnestly, forgiveness will come more easily to us and the inclination toward unforgiveness within us will gradually diminish. How marvelous and humbling it is to witness the Holy Spirit of God working in our lives! We "were bought at a price," Christians, and the cost of *our* forgiveness was immeasurably high. Let us, therefore, readily forgive others from the heart for their trespasses against us, whatever those offenses might be. In its own right, this is important and necessary to do, as a matter of obedience and faith demonstrated through works. But it also ensures the removal from our lives of one major obstacle to effective and fervent prayer.

Day 28 — Anxiety

Some obstacles to effective prayer function almost exclusively on the spiritual level. They *incapacitate* us, in a manner of speaking, by rendering us incapable of praying powerfully (for example, unconfessed sin). Other barriers operate primarily in the physical or material dimension by interfering with our *ability* to pray. They might consume an inordinate amount of our time or attention or both (for example, busyness). And a third type of hindrance works in *both* ways, impacting us spiritually and physically. Anxiety is an obstruction of the third kind, and those Christians who wrestle with this adversary know how formidable it is. Anxiety can suck the effectiveness and the fervency out of our prayer with alarming efficiency. We will investigate the physical aspects of anxiety first, since they are relatively common and easier to address than the others.

Everyone experiences anxiety in life at different times, to various degrees. Anxiety is part of the so-called human condition, an unavoidable aspect of living in a fallen world. Although anxiety exists everywhere in the world, it tends to be particularly prevalent in highly-developed, industrialized societies. Consequently, the issue for us is not *if* we will confront anxiety, but *how* we deal with it when we do. In terms of its physical effects, anxiety can cause increased heart-rate, sweating, nervous agitation (irritability), and an assortment of additional issues, including inability to remain still (restlessness). From all that we have explored throughout this book, it must be obvious that such conditions are not conducive to concentrated prayer. To address these symptoms, some sources advocate deep breathing and other exercises aimed at calming the body and focusing the mind on something serene. It is interesting to note, however, that the best remedy for the *physical* components of anxiety is *spiritual* in nature, as we will see.

Anxiety can overwhelm the mind with disjointed thoughts and distracting cares. Our attention fixates on the specifics of a possible future occurrence; on present circumstances; on concerns for our families or our jobs or our communities or an approaching election or.... Our minds can latch onto almost anything when we are anxious, and our thoughts begin to pile on top of each other. In fact, one of the most insidious[133] and maddening attributes of anxiety is that it self-propagates[134]. The more our minds focus on whatever is causing our anxiety, the more anxious we become. And the more anxious we become, the more our minds focus on whatever is causing our anxiety. Thus it grows, feeding itself, like a mental tumor that stifles the positive functions of the mind in its greedy quest for total domination. Obviously, not everyone experiences anxiety to this extreme degree. But those who are prone to it know all too well how suffocating

---

[133] insidious (O): spreading or developing or acting inconspicuously but with harmful effect
[134] self-propagate (O): breeding or reproducing or spreading without assistance

and imprisoning it can be. (In fact, the English word "anxious" comes from a Latin term meaning "to press tightly.")

Imagine how difficult it would be to pray in a concentrated manner when our minds are troubled by anxious thoughts and our bodies are oppressed by symptoms of anxiety. Such focused prayer—such effective and fervent prayer—borders on impossible. But the impacts of anxiety do not stop there. The affliction also affects us spiritually:

"Anxiety in the heart of man causes depression,
But a good word makes it glad" (Proverbs 12:25).

Regrettably, "depression" is one of those terms that can mean several different things, so in order to use it, we need first to define it. In other words, not all depression is depression.

Many people experience some degree of what is commonly thought of as depression at different stages in life. This condition is characterized by a barrage of common symptoms:

- a feeling of low spirits
- a lack of zest for life
- diminished interest in activities that are normally enjoyed
- some withdrawal from social engagement
- altered appetite and sleep patterns
- (possibly) a sense of hopelessness

As anxiety increases, it can intensify this kind of depression and magnify the symptoms. On the other hand, such depression can be *significantly* improved by addressing the underlying anxieties. These treatments have different forms, some secular and some Christian, as we will explore. (For anyone interested, David Martyn Lloyd-Jones penned an excellent book, *Spiritual Depression*, that examines this type of depression and how to confront it from a Christian perspective.)

Another kind of depression is considerably more severe than the common variety. In many cases, perhaps most, it is caused by a chemical imbalance in the body that disrupts the normal operations of nerve impulses and hormones. The worst instances of this kind of depression are categorized as "Major Depressive Disorder" by professionals who study and treat it. And the symptoms of this type are often dramatically more severe than their counterparts:

- feelings of abject misery and despair
- persistent thoughts of suicide (called "suicidal ideations")

- extremely disrupted or even nonexistent appetite and sleep
- near-complete isolation from social interaction
- anger that is frequently intense and diffuse
- pronounced irritability

Additionally, people with this affliction may experience generalized body pain or acute soreness in the neck and spine areas—or both. Just living with Major Depressive Disorder is terribly difficult, to say nothing of functioning well enough to pray with any regularity.

Anxiety typically does accompany clinical (as opposed to spiritual) depression, but it is more of a corollary[135] than a cause. Consequently, treating the anxiety is like administering dialysis to a person with kidney disease. It might enable the person to live a fuller and more fruitful life, but it will not cure the underlying problem. The same is true if the chemical imbalance that is causing the depression is addressed with medication, while the anxiety is left untreated. Continuing our simile, that is like providing a kidney transplant to a person who survives on nothing but fast food. Since anxiety and major depression tend to occur together, exacerbating[136] but not strictly *causing* each other, both issues must be confronted simultaneously in order to achieve genuine improvement.

Why does this matter? And what connection does it have to potent prayer? We need to understand the differences between spiritual depression and clinical depression for two important reasons: one, spiritual depression in Christians can be largely rectified by resolving the anxiety that causes it, applying the truth of God's living and powerful Word; two, none of the scriptural remedies for anxiety will eliminate the chemical cause of Major Depressive Disorder. Simply stated, anyone who is *clinically* depressed should seek counsel from a competent (and ideally Christian) professional. With those distinctions in place, let us return our attention to anxiety, the focus of today's lesson.

At the conclusion of Psalm 139, David recorded a few lines that are more revealing than they might appear at first reading:

"Search me, O God, and know my heart;
Try me, and know my anxieties;
And see if there is any wicked way in me,
And lead me in the way everlasting" (verses 23-24).

Despite his well-known failures, David was a man after God's heart (1 Samuel 16:7,12). He loved the Lord sincerely and desired to walk according to His will. He recognized and confessed that he was far from perfect. But he understood that growth in godliness proceeds from studying Scripture, prayer, and

---

[135] corollary (O): a natural consequence or result
[136] exacerbating (C): rendering more violent or severe

faithfully following the Lord's direction. These truths are abundantly evidenced in the many psalms that he composed. Yet here David acknowledged that he experienced "anxieties" just like everyone else. This man of admirable faith, who singlehandedly slayed a giant through strident trust in God, became anxious as we all do at times.

The important point to observe in this instance is not that David experienced anxiety. He was not superhuman, so the fact that he endured anxiety is not exactly headline news. What we want to highlight here is how David *dealt* with his anxieties; how he addressed them. He brought them to the Lord in prayer. He invited God to examine his heart, to assess what wickedness resided there, and to eliminate it. His closing request summarized his desire to be conformed to the Father's will: "And lead me in the way everlasting." Such a transformation would necessarily include removing his anxiety. David's statements in these verses are instructive to us along several different avenues: first, anxiety focuses our attention on temporal issues, robbing us of eternal perspective; second, anxiety left unchecked quickly changes shape and becomes unbelief, a deficiency of trust in the Lord; and third, the correct approach for saints to confront anxiety always begins with prayer. We will briefly consider each of these in order.

When we contemplate the world and our places in it from a biblical perspective, we quickly recognize that a human lifespan is actually quite brief. David acknowledged as much, among other places, in Psalm 39:

> "LORD, make me to know my end,
> And what is the measure of my days,
> That I may know how frail I am.
> Indeed, You have made my days as handbreadths,
> And my age is as nothing before You;
> Certainly every man at his best state is but vapor.
> Surely every man walks about like a shadow" (verses 4-6).

"For what is your life?" James questioned. "It is even a vapor that appears for a little time and then vanishes away" (4:14). Realizing how limited our time is on this earth, we are admonished to use the days that are given to us as fruitfully as possible. We pursue an eternal perspective because that is God's viewpoint. We want—as far as we are able—to interpret and respond to the circumstances of life with *His* understanding (remember Proverbs 3:5). "So teach us to number our days," Moses wrote, "that we may gain a heart of wisdom" (Psalm 90:12). For biblically-minded Christians, appreciation of the brevity of life should impress upon us the importance of occupying each day in service of the Lord (read Proverbs 9:10).

Anxiety displaces eternal perspective. It compels us to turn our attention to temporal or worldly concerns, which is exactly the opposite of what Paul admonished: "If then you were raised with Christ, seek those things which are above, where Christ is, sitting at the right hand of God. Set your mind on things above, not on things on the earth" (Colossians 3:1-2). When we become anxious, our minds focus "on things on the earth." We become inordinately concerned by circumstances, situations, and events, to the point that we remove our eyes from the Lord. To put it another way, we set our gaze on the pitfalls and snares, the forks and bottlenecks along the road of life. We lose sight of our destination. Consider that Peter actually *walked on water* for a moment, looking unto Jesus. "But when he saw that the wind was boisterous," his faith faltered and he began to sink (Matthew 14:28-31). Anxiety has a comparable effect on us. It prompts us to divert our eyes from the Lord and to become preoccupied by the conditions we face.

The example of Peter's experience illustrates well the second line of instruction from David's statements in Psalm 139. Anxiety can swiftly develop into unbelief if not quickly addressed. Unbelief is an insidious evil with numerous components or facets, one of which is *worry*. As anxiety deepens and continues to reproduce itself, eventually it matures to a point at which it becomes outright worry. And though we may not realize it, worry is a form of unbelief. When we worry, we tacitly[137] question if God *can* do everything that He has promised; if He loves us enough *to* do it all; if His will truly *is* the perfect course; if His timing is not somehow flawed. Of course, we pose these questions subconsciously in most instances. But they are, nonetheless, what our worry represents to God. We demonstrate doubt that our Father was telling the truth when He proclaimed His many assurances.

From the Lord's perspective, the fact that He, Almighty God, declares anything to be true *should* be the final word on the matter. As the Eternal Creator, He is the Author and Source of truth (Psalm 119:142; John 14:6; 17:17; Romans 3:4). But we are weak creatures who think too highly and too frequently of ourselves. The inherent selfishness of our sinful human nature propels us to focus on ourselves, expressing doubt concerning what God has revealed to humanity in His Word. And as soon as we display doubt (or unbelief) regarding the total truthfulness and trustworthiness of God, the *evidence* of His power disappears from our lives (see Matthew 13:58; James 1:6-7).

In His Word, our Father has supplied us with abundant assurances and proofs of His love, His faithfulness, His protection, His providence, His sovereignty. Despite all of that, we worry, we doubt, and we fret. We turn inward, indulging our native selfishness instead of trusting Him. "When one thinks of the selfishness of the professing church today, it is no wonder that the Church has so little power in prayer" (Torrey 70). To summarize for clarity: anxiety matures into worry, like a child into an adult; worry displays doubt, a type of unbelief; and unbelief demolishes the effectiveness and the fervency of our

---

[137] tacitly (C): implied, not expressed by words; in effect

prayer. Or, more simply still: unbelieving prayer is powerless prayer, and anxiety functions as a precursor[138] to unbelief.

The third avenue of instruction from David's statements in Psalm 139 specifically relates to how we confront anxiety when it emerges. Here we encounter a familiar paradox[139]. Anxiety is one of the major obstacles to effective prayer, yet the first thing we must do to overcome anxiety is pray about it. In these situations, "we walk by faith, not by sight" (2 Corinthians 5:7). We continue doing what we know we are supposed to do, whatever our senses or even our reason may contend. We trust in the Lord with all our hearts, and we lean not on our own understanding. In that position and with stalwart faith, we pray. We honestly acknowledge to our Father that we are experiencing anxiety, and we ask Him to intervene. We consciously choose to direct our eyes off of ourselves and our circumstances and fix them instead on the Lord. Then we petition Him in faith to replace our anxiety with His marvelous peace.

One beautiful and edifying quality of such prayer is the *complete* confidence we can have that we are asking according to His will. Although anxiety impedes powerful prayer, when we ask anything according to His will, "we know that we have the petitions that we have asked of Him" (1 John 5:15). God's desire for us is most emphatically *not* to be anxious. On the contrary, His will is for us to have strident faith, unwavering belief, and the penetrating peace of His Spirit (see Galatians 5:22). Here we intersect with Paul's well-known counsel to the Philippians: "Be anxious for nothing, but in everything by prayer and supplication, with thanksgiving, let your requests be made known to God; and the peace of God, which surpasses all understanding, will guard your hearts and minds through Christ Jesus" (4:6-7).

As the apostle indicated here, prayer is both the first line of attack to *overcome* anxiety and one of the principal modes of *defense* against it. When our lives are filled with diligent prayer in conformity to all that we understand of biblical instruction, our sovereign Lord protects us from experiencing the crippling effects of anxiety by supplying us with His peace. That peace, we have seen, is part of the fruit of the Spirit. And anywhere the peace of God resides, anxiety cannot coexist.

Although earnest prayer is our primary means of combating anxiety, and our foremost defense against it, prayer is not the only weapon or shield that we possess. (The parallel here to Ephesians 6 is probably obvious). But we are not referring in this instance to "the shield of faith," as important as that is. We are speaking instead of "the sword of the Spirit, which is the word of God" (verse 17). As the children of God, we should continually fill our minds with the

---

[138] precursor (O): a thing that precedes a later and more developed form
[139] paradox (C): a statement that is apparently absurd or self-contradictory, but is or may be real or true

"living and powerful" truth of Scripture (remember Hebrews 4:12). We should not only read it consistently but also meditate on what it teaches. Thus we see that Paul followed his admonition in Philippians 4 with an exhortation that relates directly to studying the Bible: "Finally, brethren, whatever things are true, whatever things are noble, whatever things are just, whatever things are pure, whatever things are lovely, whatever things are of good report, if there is any virtue and if there is anything praiseworthy—meditate on these things" (verse 8). When our thoughts are focused on Scripture, and we *believe* what we read there, we will not easily become anxious. Our attention will not be readily diverted to ourselves, our circumstances, or what is happening in the world. Additionally, when we do begin to feel anxious, consciously concentrating on the kinds of subjects that Paul mentioned serves as an effective countermeasure to anxiety.

The Bible includes ample material for fruitful reflection, but it is not the only source for such content. We might read about the faith and the prayer life of devoted Christians like George Mueller. We could survey the heroic deeds, the self-sacrifice, and the dedication to biblical principles of many who founded the United States of America. We can gaze in humble amazement at the arresting grandeur of a scene from God's Creation. Many options are available from which we can receive edification and mental reinforcement, and with which we can challenge any tendencies toward anxiety that arise. But before and beyond anything we feed our minds and hearts, the Scriptures are a vast repository[140] of unimaginable riches in truth, nobility, purity, virtue, and all the rest. These are "things above" on which we should set our minds. They are instruments that the Holy Spirit uses to transform us by the renewing of our minds, protecting us from being "conformed to this world" (see Romans 12:2).

These Christlike qualities are guideposts along "the way everlasting" of which David wrote. Meditating on such things is a potent antidote to the spiritual poison of anxiety. And in order for us to pray effectively and fervently, the toxic impact of anxiety must be counteracted. (For further reflection, if desired, contemplate Psalms 37 and 73 in the light of what we have studied today.)

Author's Note

I am not a psychiatrist or a psychologist. I have no professional training in treating mental illness. But I have battled a propensity toward anxiety as well as Major Depressive Disorder for about 27 years, as of this writing. What I wrote for today's lesson about anxiety and depression was drawn from everything that I have learned in that time about those afflictions—mostly from doctors and books. It also reflects my own experience with combating anxiety and enduring severe depression. In all candor, I am fully convinced that I have weathered some of the worst anxiety and the most extreme depression of which

---

[140] repository (C): a place or receptacle in which anything is stored

human beings are capable, while still emerging on the other side both alive and (relatively) sane. Here I am compelled to add swiftly another belief of which I am equally certain: I survived these horrendous episodes entirely because of the Lord's gracious intervention.

I have two reasons for including this note, neither of which involves calling attention to myself: first, I have personal knowledge of how powerfully anxiety (and worry and depression) can interfere with effective prayer. I have also witnessed firsthand the marvelous counteraction of honest prayer and abiding in God's Word. Whenever I begin to feel anxious or sense a bout of depression approaching, I spend as much time as possible in prayer and I "camp out" in the Word. Abundant experience has impressed upon me that the Book of Psalms is particularly helpful at such times. The Lord is always faithful to guide and deliver me through the dark valleys, usually not unscathed but perhaps a little wiser. As I trust in Him, lean on Him, and acknowledge Him, He directs my paths. What an awesome and loving God we serve, Christians!

Second, since I have endured the blackest horrors of anxiety and depression, I would spare others from such afflictions, if possible. Consequently, I cannot urge you emphatically enough: Seek assistance from a professional if there is any chance that what you are experiencing is more severe than the common anxiety or spiritual depression that all people weather periodically.

I stubbornly refused to accept help for years, and countless people have suffered terribly for my stiff-necked pride. Having said that, if at all possible, try to locate a mental-health professional who is also a *devout* Christian. That might be more difficult than finding a leprechaun riding a unicorn, but there are some competent Christian psychiatrists and psychologists whose faith is founded on sound doctrine. I include this caveat[141] because I have spoken to a lot of these doctors in my life, and to state that most of them are secular humanists is like saying that Sir Isaac Newton was smart. Without question, anxiety can deplete the power from our prayer, but depression can be spiritually *devastating*. Please do not repeat my folly, and seek help if there is any possibility that it might be needed.

---

[141] caveat (O): a notice or warning

Day 29 — Busyness

To state the obvious, everyone reading this book is alive in the twenty-first century. And that being the case, *no one* reading this book needs to be taught what it means to be busy. Anyone who has so much leisure time that busyness is not an issue almost certainly is not concerned about developing powerful prayer. Therefore, we will assume that everyone reading these words is already well-acquainted with *busyness*. And since both the word and the condition that it describes require no definition, we will approach our investigation of busyness from a different perspective. In so doing, we will discover why busyness poses such a formidable obstacle to earnest prayer.

Many people, including some sincere Christians, attend to the assorted affairs of life assuming that a frenzied pace is just a normal aspect of existence in the modern world. In particular, this observation holds true in highly-developed, consumerist societies such as those in the United States, much of Europe, and East Asia. But how many of these people realize that busyness which interferes with our ability to devote quality time to prayer is a form of **idolatry**? Even many secular people would not wish to be thought of as idol-worshipers. Certainly all genuine Christians would (and should) shudder at the prospect. But however objectionable it may be, the fact remains: Busyness in a saint's life that significantly hinders spending time each day in concentrated prayer represents a fundamental problem in that person's priorities. As a rule, *anything* that we give precedence over the Lord becomes an idol. And when we continually "manufacture" idols through the way we live, we are guilty of idolatry.

Our idols assume many different forms. For a tremendous number of people, work is an idol. They spend countless hours laboring away each week, striving to earn more money or to advance their careers or to ensure that they will be able to retire at a given age. For others, hobbies or recreational pursuits, exercise or outdoor activities can become idols. In fact, *most* of the things we convert to idols are not wrong in themselves. Moreover, they do not ascend to the role of an idol because of *how much* time we allocate to them. The critical issue, rather, is one of **priority**.

The *Oxford American Dictionary* defines priority as "something that is more important than other items or considerations." For example, in an emergency situation, we normally give highest priority to our children, then our animals. Only after we have ensured their safety do we attempt to rescue our most treasured possessions. And how often are those cherished possessions objects of little *intrinsic* value? Oftentimes, the material things that we are most eager to save from destruction or loss are old family photographs; a blanket that grandma crocheted; the Bible carried by an ancestor on the voyage that transported the family to America from its native land. "Natural" disasters, wars, and similarly dire circumstances have a peculiar way of forcefully streamlining our priorities. Suddenly we are confronted with a need to determine what we deem to be the truly important things in life. In an instant, we recognize what should be given precedence, and what is expendable.

If we can sort our priorities almost immediately when the need arises, then why are so many of us seemingly unable to live with our priorities correctly aligned? Why do we live in endless pursuit of various idols, only to cast them away readily in a time of crisis? If we know in our hearts what are the genuinely important things in life, then should we not also *live* each day giving precedence to those things that warrant it? Should we not dismiss or at least minimize those things that we understand have no enduring value? This seems like a straightforward proposition, and one with which all authentic Christians would heartily agree. But remarkably few of us actually live this way. Many of us who identify as Christian—perhaps most—openly declare that our hearts are committed to the Lord. We *want* to think that God is our highest priority. But the ways we live demonstrate that our hearts are divided. The various ways that we allocate our time reveal our efforts to serve two different masters.

Most of us know what Jesus taught with regard to serving multiple masters: "No servant can serve two masters; for either he will hate the one and love the other, or else he will be loyal to the one and despise the other. You cannot serve God and mammon" (Luke 16:13). The word "mammon" in the Greek means "*wealth*, personified" or "*avarice*[142] (deified)" (*Strong's* 3126). Understanding what the term signifies, we can see how the pursuit (or service) of wealth for its own sake swiftly becomes an idol. The desire for gain impacts our hearts in such a way that it displaces some of our devotion to the Lord God. And the outward manifestation or form of that divided allegiance is evident in how we manage our time. But the split condition of the heart is the more pressing problem. Quoting from Deuteronomy, Jesus commanded, "You shall love the Lord your God with all your heart, with all your soul, and with all your mind" (Matthew 22:37). But we cannot love Him with *all* of ourselves when part of us is bent on chasing the things of the world. By His own admission, our God— *the* God—is "a jealous God," and He will not share our allegiance with anything or anyone (Exodus 20:5).

Jesus specifically addressed what our attitude should be toward worldly concerns in His Sermon on the Mount: "Do not lay up for yourselves treasures on earth, where moth and rust destroy and where thieves break in and steal; but lay up for yourselves treasures in heaven, where neither moth nor rust destroys and where thieves do not break in and steal. For where your treasure is, there your heart will be also" (Matthew 6:19-21). These words are so familiar to many of us that often we do not allow their significance to penetrate deeply into our hearts and minds. Consider first what Jesus was *not* saying. He was not teaching that it is morally wrong to purchase insurance policies, to buy a larger

---

[142] avarice (C): eager desire for gain; covetousness

home as our families grow, or to lay aside funds in a savings account. To be clear, none of these actions is inherently sinful. In fact, wisdom dictates that we take *reasonable* precautions to ensure that we are prepared for unexpected expenses, and that we will be able to support ourselves financially as we age. Note that the operative word in that statement is "reasonable." And the extent to which our precautionary measures are reasonable reflects how devoted our hearts are to the Lord. Do we love Him with *all* of ourselves, or do we privately trust to some extent in our accumulated wealth? Do we serve God wholeheartedly, or do we strive to build a large retirement account so that we can take our ease in the last quarter of our lives? (Consider the "Parable of the Rich Fool" in Luke 12:13-21.)

These questions point to a truth that Jesus highlighted when He spoke of laying up treasure. He was instructing His followers concerning to which things they (we) should and should not give priority. "Do not make that a priority; your heart should not be focused there. Make this a priority; your heart should be committed here." The reason that Jesus gave for prioritizing one thing over another centered on the allegiance of our hearts. And according to the greatest commandment, that devotion should be our preeminent motivation for giving priority to a particular course or thing. Simply stated, we make it a priority because it is the object of our love. But there are at least three other reasons why we should give precedence to some things while dismissing or minimizing others: First, any time spent doing other things is time not spent in prayer or studying God's Word. Second, our lives are easily filled with distractions, so as a matter of prudence we need to identify which ones we can eliminate. And third, *none* of the material things that we amass during our lives will survive the purifying fire that the Lord will bring upon the earth. We will briefly consider each of these in turn.

In a familiar passage from Luke's Gospel, "a certain woman named Martha welcomed Him [Jesus] into her house.

> "And she had a sister called Mary, who also sat at Jesus' feet and heard His word. But Martha was distracted with much serving, and she approached Him and said, 'Lord, do You not care that my sister has left me to serve alone? Therefore tell her to help me.'
>
> And Jesus answered and said to her, 'Martha, Martha, you are worried and troubled about many things. But one thing is needed, and Mary has chosen that good part, which will not be taken away from her'" (10:38-42).

Martha's service was not inherently wrong. Most people with decent manners try to ensure that guests in their homes are well-attended and as comfortable as possible. Martha should not be reproached for being a good hostess. The problem was that she made too high a priority of her service, when only "one thing is needed." We might say that Martha was *busy* preparing finger sandwiches and spiced tea while the Son of God reclined in the next room. "What was she thinking?" we ask critically. But we need to recognize that we all do essentially the same thing, at times, in different ways.

Each day has only 24 hours; each week 168. Assuming (however unrealistically) that 56 of those hours are spent sleeping, that leaves only 112 hours per week. We fill that time with work, church attendance, ministry involvement, meals, bathing, household chores, children's activities, recreation, traveling from place to place. Oftentimes, it can seem like 112 hours is less than half the number that we need to satisfy all of the demands on our time. But what is missing from that series? Prayer and studying the Bible. We tend to fill every available hour in each day (and then some) with so many activities that sometimes prayer and time in the Word are treated as afterthoughts. Like Martha, we become so *busy* with other, less important things that we neglect what should be our *highest* priority. By doing so, giving precedence to other matters in place of the Lord, we effectively convert those things to idols. To combat this tendency, we should learn from the example of Mary. Unlike her sister, Mary had her priorities straight. She sat at Christ's feet, abiding in His presence and listening to what He said (verse 39). Even if her choice meant that lesser concerns went unattended, so be it. Being with Jesus was her foremost priority, and it should be ours as well.

Digital technology and an array of electronic distractions saturate much of the modern world. "Smart" phones, social media, and the Internet have become almost universal in human society. And in most places where they are still unavailable or uncommon, they are eagerly desired. Many people celebrate the ubiquity[143] of these things, viewing them as platforms for social interaction and as avenues for exchanging information. Such instruments they can be, and they do facilitate some level of communication, as their supporters argue. But serious and thoughtful Christians need to recognize the *threat* that some technological innovations present. Many of these devices and the functions they enable are like black holes, consuming massive amounts of time as well as the attention and energy of their users. As much as some people may appreciate the capabilities that these gadgets provide, it is virtually impossible to develop spiritual maturity or to cultivate an intimate relationship with God when our eyes are cemented to the screens of our "smart" phones. (Some material related to these devices and applications will be discussed tomorrow in our exploration of "Entertainment or Amusement.")

Paul's counsel in the "marriage chapter" of First Corinthians offers some helpful insights pertaining to our current topic. In the context, he was specifically addressing the potential problems in our priorities that being married can produce. But his remarks certainly apply to the subject of our present investigation:

---

[143] ubiquity (C): existence everywhere at the same time

"But this I say, brethren, the time is short, so that from now on even those who have wives should be as though they had none, those who weep as though they did not weep, those who rejoice as though they did not rejoice, those who buy as though they did not possess, and those who use this world as not misusing it. For the form of this world is passing away.

...And this I say for your own profit, not that I may put a leash on you, but for what is proper, and that you may serve the Lord without distraction" (7:29-31,35).

We want to highlight three segments of this passage in particular: "the form of this world is passing away"; "what is proper"; and "serve the Lord without distraction."

Knowing that "the form of this world is passing away" should heavily influence how we live, including how we allocate our time. In the final analysis, how many "followers" or "friends" or "hits" we have will not matter *one bit* (no pun intended). The brands of cars we drive, the designer labels on our clothing, the sizes of our televisions, the types of "toys" in our driveways: while this fact may be difficult for some people to accept, these things are all utterly **meaningless**. The world values such things. But as Christians, we should recognize these concerns for what they are: distractions. So instead of pursuing these empty and fleeting vanities, our focus should be on "what is proper." That phrase indicates priorities that are correctly aligned with unchanging truth. And that means living the way God wants us to live (according to His will), praying the way His Word teaches us to pray, valuing what He values, loving what He loves, and hating what He hates. It also includes looking expectantly for His return, believing His promise that He *will* come again, and acknowledging that His appearance could occur at any moment ("the time is short"). Understanding what the Bible foretells will happen in "the day of the Lord," we should make a conscious effort to eliminate distractions from our lives, as much as possible. To put this another way, the sincerity of our belief that Jesus is going to return will be evidenced in the steps we take to "serve the Lord without distraction."

If these instructions sound familiar, it is probably because we have encountered them before. They relate to the eternal perspective that all saints should seek to develop. We understand from what the Bible teaches that the days of this world are numbered, in both senses of that term: 1) God knows *precisely* how many days this world will exist in its present "form"; 2) the days remaining to this world are few (as in "Your days are numbered, Satan!").

We live in "the last days" (2 Peter 3:3). When the appointed day and hour arrive, "the heavens will pass away with a great noise, and the elements will melt with fervent heat; both the earth and the works that are in it will be burned up.

"Therefore, since all these things will be dissolved, what manner of persons ought you to be in holy conduct and godliness, looking for and hastening the coming of the day of God, because of which the heavens will be dissolved, being on fire, and the elements will melt with fervent heat? Nevertheless we, according to His promise, look for new heavens and a new earth in which righteousness dwells.... You therefore, beloved, since you know this beforehand, beware lest you also fall from your own steadfastness, being led away with the error of the wicked; but grow in the grace and knowledge of our Lord and Savior Jesus Christ" (2 Peter 3:10-13,17-18).

Consider carefully what Peter wrote in these verses. Meditate on the truths presented here. His statements were not just some uplifting words of inspiration at the conclusion of his letter. They were (and are) inspired directions for how all authentic Christians should live while awaiting the Second Coming of Christ.

The fire associated with "the day of the Lord" will be so intense that "the heavens will be dissolved" and "the elements will melt." The earth and everything on it "will be burned up [or laid bare]." Our homes will burn. Our vehicles will melt. Our clothes and tools and jewelry and gadgets, as well as every penny we have acquired, will be incinerated and *utterly* destroyed. Every material thing we have in this life will burn until it is no more. Why, then, do we dedicate so much of our time and energy and resources to building our little empires? Why do we allow ourselves to become so busy, neglecting time spent in earnest prayer and studying God's Word? Is it because we have been "led away with the error of the wicked"? We of all people cannot plead the excuse of ignorance, since we have been forewarned of what will happen when Christ returns. We know—or we *should* know—that the legitimately valuable things in life are those that endure beyond "the day of the Lord": holiness, godliness, blamelessness, kindness, steadfastness—growing "in the grace and knowledge of our Lord and Savior Jesus Christ." (We could also include everything listed as "the fruit of the Spirit" in Galatians 5:22-23, as well as the character of the new man described in Colossians 3:12-17.) Unlike many of the activities that contribute to our busyness, prayer has *eternal* value. Sincere and biblical prayer from a devoted Christian heart will survive the fire that "will test each one's work, of what sort it is" (1 Corinthians 3:13; read verses 11-15).

Remember what James wrote: "Do you not know that friendship with the world is enmity with God? Whoever therefore wants to be a friend of the world makes himself an enemy of God. Or do you think that the Scripture says in vain, 'The Spirit who dwells in us yearns jealously'?" (4:4-5). Our God is a jealous God. And we cannot serve two masters. We cannot profess allegiance to the Lord and live how the world lives, pursuing what the world values. If we genuinely love Him with all of ourselves, then our lives should display that love through our priorities. We will not be "led away with the error of the wicked," turned aside to idols by prioritizing anything more highly than God. Instead, we will demonstrate our love for Him by eliminating distractions and doing "what is proper."

"Each day is a vessel to be freighted with holy deeds and earnest endeavors before it weighs anchor and sets sail for the eternal shores. How many hours we misspend! How many occasions we lose! How many precious gifts of God we squander! And the world passes away, and the fashion of it fadeth" (MacIntyre 28-29); If "holy deeds and earnest endeavors" are the cargo of each day, then prayer must be the ballast that balances the ship to keep it upright. Every day should be loaded with prayer. But *effective* and *fervent* prayer requires time. It involves focus and persistence, waiting and watching, and everything else that we have studied. But almost every aspect and characteristic of powerful prayer will be virtually impossible—or at the very least extremely difficult—if we are weighed down by busyness.

Day 30 — Entertainment (or Amusement)

On the surface, the obstacle that entertainment presents to effective and fervent prayer might seem like it should have been included in yesterday's lesson on busyness. Amusement is not inherently wrong, that is, but when given precedence over time with the Lord, then it becomes a problem. In reality, however, entertainment in its many forms poses a potent and insidious[144] threat to powerful prayer. And the hazards that it represents will be realized if Christians are not both vigilant and conscientious. The dangers from our different amusements typically operate along two distinct channels (no pun intended): one, how we allocate our time, which incorporates the important issues of priority and stewardship; and two, the impacts that some entertaining activities have upon our minds and hearts.

Before we examine these two avenues in greater detail, note the wording that was used above: "entertainment in its many forms poses." The tense of the verb was deliberate. We did not write "can pose" because all entertainment *does* constitute a threat if we are not discerning and self-controlled in how we avail ourselves of it. Even amusements that are harmless in themselves can impair the effectiveness and fervency of our prayers under certain circumstances. This will become more apparent as we investigate today's topic further, but it is important to note here at the beginning. *Any* kind of entertainment can negatively impact the power of our prayer. And *all* types of amusement will interfere with prayer that "avails much" in the right conditions.

As our guide for the subsequent exploration, we will use a familiar passage from the Apostle Paul's Epistle to the Ephesians. It will function as a helpful hub because it incorporates both of the channels by which entertainment threatens potent prayer:

> "For you were once darkness, but now you are light in the Lord. Walk as children of light (for the fruit of the Spirit is in all goodness, righteousness, and truth), finding out what is acceptable to the Lord. And have no fellowship with the unfruitful works of darkness, but rather expose [or reprove] them. For it is shameful even to speak of those things which are done by them in secret....
>
> See then that you walk circumspectly [or carefully], not as fools but as wise, redeeming the time, because the days are evil.
>
> Therefore do not be unwise, but understand what the will of the Lord is" (5:8-12,15-17).

---

[144] insidious (O): spreading or developing or acting inconspicuously but with harmful effect

The phrase "children of light" is observational, not aspirational. It does not describe who we *aspire* to be, but who we *are*. "Behold what manner of love the Father has bestowed on us, that we should be called children of God! Therefore the world does not know us, because it did not know Him. Beloved, now we are children of God..." (1 John 3:1-2). The "children of light" are the "children of God." And we are the "children of light."

As God's children, "finding out what is acceptable to the Lord" is our solemn responsibility. We are charged with an obligation to learn our Father's will. And since "the days are evil," we are exhorted to exercise wisdom in the way that we live. So that we will "not be unwise," we need to "understand what the will of the Lord is." The implications of these instructions permeate[145] our lives. To begin with, we do not live for ourselves. We are not the lords of our own existences. If we were, then we would not be authentic Christians. Genuine saints live for God—for His glory, His kingdom, His purposes, and His pleasure (read, for example, 1 Corinthians 6:19-20; Galatians 2:20; Ephesians 2:10). Therefore, the time that He supplies to us on this earth does not belong to us. It is not our personal possession, to dispose of as *we* please. As strange as it may sound, our time belongs to Him. The Lord has placed it under our stewardship, charging us to allocate it with wisdom and understanding according to His direction. And in order to discharge the duties of our stewardship in a way that will please our Father, we need to know "what is acceptable to the Lord"— "what the will of the Lord is." This conforms to the supreme example established by Jesus: "For I have come down from heaven, not to do My own will, but the will of Him who sent Me" (John 6:38).

In His earthly life, Jesus was a perfectly obedient steward of the resources entrusted to His custody, including His time. He dedicated His time to accomplishing what His Father wanted Him to do; what was "acceptable" to Him. And since we are "servants of Christ and stewards of the mysteries of God," our task is to emulate our Lord Jesus in the way we manage what God has placed under our stewardship (1 Corinthians 4:1). Everything we have in life—even life itself—is provided to us by Almighty God the Creator (Acts 17:25; James 1:17). That being the case, we are accountable to Him for what we do with His things: time, possessions, money, abilities, opportunities, everything (remember Hebrews 4:13). These things are all furnished by Him and are intended to be used for His glory, in the service of His immutable[146] purposes. Stewards are required to answer to their masters for how well they fulfill their masters' bidding in the execution of their duties. In a comparable way, we will have to provide an account to our Master, God, for how we handle the gifts that He entrusts to our keeping. "For everyone to whom much is given, from him much will be required; and to whom much has been committed, of him they will ask the more" (Luke 13:48).

---

[145] permeate (O): to pass or flow or spread into every part of
[146] immutable (O): unchangeable

Recall what we discussed yesterday about busyness, priority, idols, and the ultimate destiny of all material things on this earth. If we occupy a significant portion of our God-given time in pursuit of entertainment, then obviously we will have less time available for prayer. We will have fewer hours for studying God's Word, for "finding out what is acceptable to the Lord," for "redeeming the time" by using it for His glory. When our time is spent on numerous forms of amusement, prayer of the type that "avails much" becomes an afterthought. Most of us know the truth of this from personal experience. When we engage in some activity that we find particularly entertaining, how inclined are we to set it aside so that we can come before the throne of grace in prayer? How easy is it to pull ourselves away from our favored diversions in order to meditate on Scripture? Usually it is quite difficult, and that is the point. When our priorities are correctly ordered, the Lord comes first—period. If entertainment has to be sacrificed to free up some time, then so be it. But when our amusements repeatedly displace time with the Lord, entertainment has become an idol.

By its very nature, amusement is pleasurable. In other words, we experience feelings of enjoyment and satisfaction from the forms of entertainment that appeal to us. Films, television, video games, sports, social media, smart-phone applications, outdoor activities: we all receive positive feedback by sensing pleasure when we participate in certain kinds of amusement. Consequently, to forego the powerful allure of such feelings in order to pray and study God's Word, our priorities must be in order. We have to be fully convinced of the importance and the efficacy[147] of biblical prayer. We also must be willing to exercise self-discipline and to sacrifice, as necessary, to pursue one priority while neglecting others. Such sacrifices can be particularly difficult to make in view of the depth of enjoyment that we encounter in entertainment. But without sacrifice and self-discipline, we will never develop effective and fervent prayer.

Our amusements can certainly inhibit powerful prayer through the demands that they place upon our time, as we have seen. But they can also douse the flame of prayer through the spiritually-damaging influences that many of our diversions have upon our minds and hearts. To put it another way, in some of the *content* of the entertainment media we use, we have "fellowship with the unfruitful works of darkness." Instead of exposing or reproving the evil that is present in these things, we partake of it. In many cases, the evil is so cleverly disguised that we are not even aware of it. Sexual immorality and the most depraved forms of perversion are packaged as comedy, as though God's design for the family would change to make it more *modern*. Sorcery, witchcraft, and many other nakedly satanic practices are featured in such a way that even young children embrace them. More than a few entertainers and so-called artists presume to tell us what we should and should not value. Many times they cite the fact that we live in the twenty-first century as the reason why we should

---

[147] efficacy (O): ability to produce a desired result

forsake our "traditional values." (By traditional, they usually mean antiquated and therefore obsolete.) But for those who have eyes to see, who "walk circumspectly, not as fools but as wise," the evidence of Satan's deception of the whole world is everywhere abundant (refer to Revelation 12:9).

We know that the world has been full of evil from its very beginning, as demonstrated by Cain's brutal murder of his brother. But as terrible as it is to recognize, the days have only grown *more* evil with the passage of time. Less than two millennia after Adam and Eve were formed, evil was so prevalent that God was actually *sorry* He had created man. "Then the LORD saw that the wickedness of man was great in the earth, and that every intent of the thoughts of his heart was only evil continually" (Genesis 6:5; also read verse 6). Although God destroyed all but eight human beings from the earth, evil remained. And in all the years since Noah and his family departed the ark, evil has metastasized[148]. It has filled the earth like a virus overtaking its host, infecting every cell with its destructive influence. As 2 Timothy 3 clearly foretold, the presence of evil has exploded in the world in "the last days," the very times in which we live. Notice one portion in particular: "For men will be...lovers of pleasure rather than lovers of God, having a form of godliness but denying its power" (verses 2,4-5).

According to outward appearances, some people *seem* to have a relationship with God, or at least a measure of reverence for Him. But beneath the surface, they love their pleasures more than they love God. They will not sacrifice their pursuit of pleasure, in whatever form they favor, in order to cultivate a proper and intimate relationship with the Lord. Thus, their apparent godliness is powerless. Although many profess love for God, their lives reveal the truth. In reality, they love themselves, money, pleasure, entertainment, and we could also include power and fame. We know this to be true, though we may not like to acknowledge it. Consider honestly for a moment: How many authentic, Bible-believing, prayerful, uncompromising Christians serve in the halls of government? How many are professional athletes, successful entertainers, or executives of large corporations? We did not ask how many *claim* they are devout Christians, but how many *show* they are by how they live? Those who have eyes to see will recognize that the number in all cases is woefully small. And that is because "the days are evil."

When the people in general walk in darkness, they will not choose for themselves leaders and role models who "walk in the light." "For everyone practicing evil hates the light and does not come to the light, lest his deeds should be exposed" (John 3:20). In these dark and wicked times, most of the people who ascend to positions of prominence in the world are not "children of light." Some genuine Christians there are, to be sure, but not many. That is understandable and should be expected, since the light of truth that such people

---

[148] metastasized (O): passed from one part or organ of the body to another

represent is hated and shunned by those around them. They face ridicule and intense opposition. Or, in some ways worse than active adversity, they are encouraged to compromise biblical principles for the sake of career advancement. Certainly, God has elevated some people to positions of influence while enabling them to remain faithful to Him, but their number is exceedingly few.

As "children of light" who seek to "walk circumspectly, not as fools but as wise," we should know enough to anticipate that these conditions will prevail in an increasingly wicked world. "Yes, and all who desire to live godly in Christ Jesus will suffer persecution. But evil men and impostors will grow worse and worse, deceiving and being deceived" (2 Timothy 3:12-13). Seeing this, it would be all too easy to become cynical or dejected about the state of the world. Instead, we need to understand the times we inhabit so that we can navigate through the perils and pitfalls of "the last days" (verse 1). We must "have no fellowship with the unfruitful works of darkness, but rather expose them.... But all things that are exposed are made manifest by the light, for whatever makes manifest is light" (Ephesians 5:11,13).

As we journey through life on the narrow road, the light of Christ illuminates the darkness around us. Snares and traps and detours are revealed, and we are responsible to identify them for what they are. When a squad of soldiers on patrol winds its way through a minefield, the keen-eyed trailblazer in front marks the locations of mines as they are detected. Troops coming behind know to avoid these areas, and trust that their leader is committed to ensuring their safety, as much as possible. We are called upon to supply a similar service to our fellow soldiers in the army of the Lord. "Let each of you look out not only for his own interests, but also for the interests of others" (Philippians 2:4). Out of love for the "children of God," our brothers and sisters, we should warn them humbly of threats to their spiritual welfare when the Lord makes us aware of them. And that includes the content of the various types of entertainment media we use.

King David was one man whom God raised to a place of prominence, elevating him from a lowly shepherd to rule all of Israel. In one of his many psalms, he proclaimed:

> "I will behave wisely in a perfect [or blameless] way,
> Oh, when will You come to me?
> I will walk within my house with a perfect heart.
> I will set nothing wicked before my eyes. . . .
> A perverse heart shall depart from me;
> I will not know wickedness.
> Whoever... has a haughty look and a proud heart,
> Him I will not endure.
> My eyes shall be on the faithful of the land....

He who works deceit shall not dwell within my house;
He who tells lies shall not continue in my presence" (101:2-3,4,5-6,7).

David was determined to shield his mind and his heart against the corruption of evil influences, as wisdom demands. In fact, in the Book of Proverbs, Wisdom personified commands, "Keep your heart with all diligence" (4:23). David's statements emphatically declared his resolve to guard his heart against any inputs that would interfere with his relationship with the Lord. And the reason provided for keeping our hearts so attentively is equally instructive: "For out of it spring the issues of life."

Many of us are familiar with the pithy[149] expression, "Garbage in, garbage out." Whatever enters our minds through our senses, if allowed to remain there, settles into our hearts. When darkness penetrates our hearts, it works corruption there, and eventually reemerges as wickedness. "For out of the heart proceed evil thoughts, murders, adulteries, fornications, thefts, false witness, blasphemies" (Matthew 15:19). Hence the need to shield our hearts from the effects of such pollution. Most of what comes into our minds uses the senses of sight and hearing. The other three senses are involved as well, but those two usually dominate. As Jesus taught in His Sermon on the Mount, "The lamp of the body is the eye. If therefore your eye is good, your whole body will be full of light. But if your eye is bad, your whole body will be full of darkness. If therefore the light that is in you is darkness, how great is that darkness!" (Matthew 6:22-23). "Walk as children of light," Paul exhorted (Ephesians 5:8). But in order to walk that way, our eyes need to be "good" so that our bodies "will be full of light." And that means what we see (or watch) must not impart darkness to our minds. It should go without saying that the same condition applies to what we perceive with our other senses.

Living in a world as saturated with evil as this one is, how do we guard our hearts against darkness and defilement? The biblical way involves a two-pronged approach. First, we emulate David's tactic by committing ourselves to allowing nothing wicked before our eyes (or ears, etc.). We engage in our amusements—and everything else, for that matter—with stern and uncompromising resolve that we "will not know wickedness." We determine to "behave wisely in a perfect way," even when it means that we must forego certain kinds of entertainment that many people freely indulge. "All things are lawful for me," Paul wrote, "but not all things are helpful; all things are lawful for me, but not all things edify" (1 Corinthians 10:23). We may *perceive* no harm in listening to a certain genre of music or in viewing a popular program on television. We might not see anything wrong with watching a specific film or with playing a particular game. But we need to realize first that our failure or inability to recognize the threat does not necessarily mean that it is not there.

---

[149] pithy (O): brief and full of meaning

And second, the *absence* of discernible harm is in no way equivalent to the *presence* of spiritually-edifying content.

David's statements in Psalm 101 sound the appropriate note for all believers: How much better it is to err on the side of caution, foregoing fleeting pleasures and momentary amusements in the interest of preserving and protecting our relationships with the Lord! Here we recall a helpful rule of thumb from a previous lesson: Whenever there is any doubt, there is no doubt.

The second prong of keeping our hearts was mentioned by the psalmist who composed Psalm 119:

"Your word I have hidden in my heart,
That I might not sin against You" (verse 11).

By reading, studying, and meditating on the truths of God's Word, our hearts are filled with the light of godly instruction and wise counsel. When our eyes are good and our whole bodies are therefore "full of light," we are better equipped to walk as "children of light," "finding out [and then doing] what is acceptable to the Lord" Instead of having "fellowship with the unfruitful works of darkness," we will "expose them" to the light of God's eternal truth. We will also bear "the fruit of the Spirit...in all goodness, righteousness, and truth." (Some versions of the Bible have "light" in place of "Spirit" here, but the thrust of Paul's statement is essentially the same.) Additionally, by knowing the Bible intimately, we will be better able to bring "every thought into captivity to the obedience of Christ" (2 Corinthians 10:5). When we know "the mind of Christ" as revealed in Scripture, we can discern what is *not* in accordance with His mind and reject those thoughts, taking them captive (refer to 1 Corinthians 2:10-16).

Effective and fervent prayer requires a commitment of time, to be sure. For that reason, correctly-ordered priorities and faithful stewardship are necessary if we are going to develop powerful prayer. But even more critical than time are the conditions of our hearts and our relationships with the Lord. As James plainly stated in our keynote verse, "The effective, fervent prayer of a righteous man avails much" (5:16). What kind of man? A *righteous* man. In the adjective "righteous," we have a behavioral qualification for potent prayer. This righteousness is not referring to our standing before God. We are "declared righteous" (justified) through the atonement of Jesus Christ. The context in James clearly indicates that the righteousness he meant was a description of how those people live who experience great power in their prayer. David captured that manner of living beautifully in Psalm 101.

To live righteously with respect to entertainment, we must be extremely selective about the films and television shows we watch (which, incidentally, is becoming increasingly more challenging as the days grow darker). We need to be very careful about the music that we listen to and the books and magazines that we read. Moreover, we should purposefully weigh our use of social media (if any) as well as our involvement with sports or other activities. And if we or our children play video games, we must be exceptionally conscientious about which games we permit and for how long. We need to keep our hearts "with all diligence" and to "walk circumspectly, not as fools but as wise, redeeming the time, because the days are evil."

Whatever type of amusement we favor, we should try in every instance to assess both its content and its impacts as soberly and objectively as possible. If there is any indication, or even a suggestion, that the entertainment is exerting a negative influence on us, we should just skip it. That is not to say that foregoing such enjoyments will be easy. Pleasures that are easily forsaken are probably not all that pleasurable. But when any of our amusements harm us spiritually (actually or potentially), we need to eliminate the cause of the harm if we hope to cultivate a prayer practice that "avails much." (For additional reflection, if desired, consider 1 Corinthians 15:33 and Ephesians 5:1-4.)

Day 31 — Lack of Discipline

Discipline is absolutely necessary in the lives of all sincere Christians. But for many people, discipline is almost equivalent to a "four-letter word." The term has only negative connotations[150] to them. In their minds, it is associated with punishment, harshness, restrictions on individual liberty, and other undesired experiences. Naturally, when people view discipline in that way, they will not be inclined to invest their time and energy in developing it. For those who are not saints, the repercussions of lacking discipline are largely weighed on worldly, temporal scales. In other words, they are condemned anyway, so if their lives on earth are undisciplined, then that is really the least of their problems (John 3:18). For Christians, however, a shortage of discipline impacts this life *and* eternity. It affects how fruitful we are during our time in these bodies, and it also has serious ripple effects in the spiritual realm.

As children of God, we desire to serve Him. We are (or should be) committed to living how our Father wants us to live. At this point in the book, that fact needs no scriptural proofs. We read in Colossians where the Apostle Paul admonished his readers to "walk worthy of the Lord, fully pleasing Him, being fruitful in every good work and increasing in the knowledge of God" (1:10). This exhortation repeats a theme that echoes throughout the Bible; one that resonates with our hearts as His devoted children. Anyone who has made it to day 31 will almost certainly agree.

Most of us understand with equal clarity that the life to which our Lord calls us is not easy. Some might be compelled to protest that life is never easy, and there is a kernel of truth in that objection. Sin pollutes the world we inhabit, so we are forced daily to deal with the consequences of that corruption. Nonetheless, when we became Christians, we were adopted into God's family and enlisted in the army of the Lord, with all that entails. Now we earnestly desire to live in a way that glorifies God and honors the name of Jesus. But as we go about the business of life, we are constantly opposed by the devil and his minions, by the world, and by our own flesh. These challenges *amplify* the difficulty of life for those who have been regenerated.

For that reason and others, the Christian life is compared more than once in the Bible to running a race or to serving in the military. One particularly memorable passage appears in 1 Corinthians:

"Do you not know that those who run in a race all run, but one receives the prize? Run in such a way that you may obtain it. And everyone who competes for the prize is temperate in all things. Now they do it to obtain a perishable crown, but we for an imperishable crown. Therefore I run thus: not with uncertainty. Thus I fight: not as one who beats the air. But I

---

[150] connotations (O): implied meanings in addition to the primary meanings

discipline my body and bring it into subjection, lest, when I have preached to others, I myself should become disqualified" (9:24-27).

Paul was commenting on the significance of *how* competitors run in a race. In a literal race, runners pursue earthly glory and the ego boost that comes from defeating all of the other participants. And this raises several interesting points that should not be overlooked.

At its core, competition is fueled by pride. Sinful human beings are inherently prideful, so they desire the satisfaction that they derive from knowing that they have outperformed someone else. Victory or success in any kind of competition either provides or reinforces a person's sense of superiority. Someone may argue that an athlete can compete against the clock, striving for a new personal best or a comparable milestone. A corporation might seek to exceed its sales figures from the same time period in the previous year. These metrics can be used to demonstrate **improvement**, but they do not display **excellence**. Only by reference to another person's (or company's) achievements is one competitor's performance shown to be superior. A distance runner may reduce her marathon time from seven hours to five, which is a tremendous improvement. But when another runner completes her 26.2-mile course in two hours, both times are revealed for what they are. A similar principle applies in all types of competition.

Paul would *never* encourage pride. On the contrary, his epistles are peppered with admonitions to pursue humility (for example, Colossians 3:12). Paul did not employ the racing analogy because he wanted Christians to consider themselves in competition with other saints. Instead, he selected that imagery for two reasons: first, his readers would readily understand, accustomed as people of that era were to watching athletic contests. It was like someone in our day talking about "throwing a strike" or "splitting the uprights." Second, he was making a point about *how* he ran the race of life and *how* he fought. "If the Christian life *were* a competition," he implied, "then run so that you would win." And that point he established in the service of another truth that he sought to emphasize: the need for **temperance**. Here we return to the central topic of our final lesson, discipline, and how a lack of it obstructs the potency of our prayer.

So what is discipline, exactly? Before we proceed any further, we should ensure that we know what the word actually means. The *Oxford* definition for "discipline" is clear: "training that produces obedience, self-control, or a particular skill; controlled behavior produced by such training." The Greek word that is translated "discipline" in the NKJV can also be rendered "buffet" or "keep under." It refers to striking the cheekbone just below the eye, a picture of forcing the body into compliance. According to *Vine's*, the term signifies "to beat the face black and blue (to give a black eye), is used metaphorically...of Paul's suppressive treatment of his body, in order to keep himself spiritually fit" (*Vine's:* "buffet" 2). From the meaning of the Greek, we see that our English word "discipline" communicates well the substance of what Paul intended.

Discipline is not attained overnight, but must be developed over time. That fact is evident both from personal experience and in the definition of the word. Consider experience first: If discipline were easily acquired, then almost everyone would exhibit it. But even a brief survey of society is sufficient to reveal that disciplined people are by far the exception, not the rule. The definition also contains a suggestion of the time involved in cultivating discipline, which we can see by analyzing the *Oxford* definition in a bit more detail. The *object* of discipline, according to the first part, is "obedience, self-control, or a particular skill." And "training" is the *method* or the *means* through which that object is obtained. So we have a goal or a destination and the route that we must follow to arrive there. Taken together, the two things imply the passage of time. But all of this is really just a painstaking statement of what most of us already know: Developing discipline takes time.

For people to remain committed to developing discipline long enough to attain it, they need to recognize its importance. They must have an accurate appreciation of its value and understand the role of discipline in living how they desire to live. This is true in general, but it is altogether imperative for Christians. Read the definition of discipline again and note a few of the terms recorded there: "obedience, self-control," "controlled behavior." The Bible is perfectly clear in summoning all of God's children to exhibit these attributes. If they are acquired through the application of discipline, then we need to pursue that virtue as well.

Here we cross paths with an interesting distinction that we should note in passing. In the first part of the definition, we see that discipline is a *means* to an end. And since the end has considerable importance for saints, the means to that end must also be highly valuable. But the second half of the definition highlights that discipline is an *end* in itself, underscoring its value. Combining these two pieces into a single instruction produces the following conclusion: We should seek to develop discipline both for *what we attain through it* and for *its own sake*. Again, for emphasis: Discipline is absolutely necessary in the lives of all sincere Christians.

In 1 Corinthians 9:27, Paul compared how he lived to both a race and a fight. And in one of his letters to Timothy, he employed similar references. "You therefore must endure hardship as a good soldier of Jesus Christ. No one engaged in warfare entangles himself with the affairs of this life, that he may please him who enlisted him as a soldier. And also if anyone competes in athletics, he is not crowned unless he competes according to the rules" (2 Timothy 2:3-5). Both soldiers and athletes require tremendous discipline (training *and* controlled behavior) in order to fight and compete successfully.

Soldiers are not recruited one day and deployed to battle the next. If that were the case, they would be completely unprepared for the gruesome realities of war. Instead, they must first undergo training through forced obedience, conditioning, deprivation, and repetition of skills, all of which are essential in actual combat situations. Similarly, athletes aspiring to compete at a professional level must endure rigorous training for years. They relentlessly condition their bodies to withstand the punishment imposed by competition. They carefully hone their abilities in pursuit of total mastery, refining and adjusting movements to achieve precision and efficiency. They practice diligently and persistently, making whatever sacrifices are necessary along the way.

Prowess is never accomplished overnight. *Whatever* field we consider, excellence grows through substantial practice according to sound instruction for a prolonged period of time. The Christian life is no different. Continuing Paul's comparison of our journey of faith to an athletic contest, we can readily see that the Christian "race" is like an ultra-marathon, not a sprint. "If anyone desires to come after Me," Jesus said, "let him deny himself, and take up his cross, and follow Me" (Matthew 16:24). But following Jesus does not involve a series of short bursts of intense activity with long intervals of rest between them. Instead, it is usually a lengthy and steady march along a path that He unfolds before us (remember Proverbs 3:5-6). He guides us over mountains and through valleys, in fresh air and foul, marching in company with our brothers and sisters or completely surrounded by foes. He leads; we follow. He directs; we obey. He supplies light and strength and wisdom; we act. "A man's steps are of the LORD," the proverb states; "How then can a man understand his own way?" (20:24).

The type of trek represented by the Christian life is not for the faint-hearted, for the sluggard[151], or for those who are more concerned with personal comfort than with the will of God. Jesus taught that anyone coming after Him must "deny himself." And Paul proclaimed, "I discipline my body and bring it into subjection." He also stated, "You therefore must endure hardship as a good soldier of Jesus Christ." Soldiers who are timid, lazy, or preoccupied with comfort are typically **dead** soldiers. But the ability to deny ourselves, to bring our bodies into subjection, and to endure hardship must be learned. It does not come naturally to us. Prior to regeneration, we are self-centered by nature. We desire comfort and pleasure and the path of least resistance. But we learn through discipline how to make the sacrifices that are necessary as we follow Jesus.

Paul wrote that "everyone who competes for the prize is temperate in all things." This statement could also be phrased "exercises self-control in all things." We have already seen that self-control is a product of discipline.

---

[151] sluggard (C): one habitually idle or inactive

Moreover, it is included among the various aspects of "the fruit of the Spirit" in Galatians 5:22-23. On the association of temperance and self-control, the entry in *Vine's* is instructive: "'self-control' is the preferable rendering, as 'temperance' is now limited to one form of self-control; the various powers bestowed by God upon man are capable of abuse; the right use demands the controlling power of the will under the operation of the Spirit of God" (*Vine's:* "temperance, temperate"; A).

Connect the information from *Vine's* with what we learned from the dictionary definition of "discipline": the "controlling power of the will" that is demanded by "the right use" of God's gifts is developed through "training that produces obedience, self-control, or a particular skill." Is the relationship clear? "Walk in the Spirit," Paul admonished, "and you shall not fulfill the lust of the flesh.... And those who are Christ's have crucified the flesh with its passions and desires. If we live in the Spirit, let us also walk in the Spirit" (Galatians 5:16,24-25). We could rephrase the truth communicated here to incorporate the language of today's lesson: "Walk in the Spirit and you will be empowered to deny yourself. Walk in the Spirit and you will be enabled to discipline your body and bring it into subjection. Walk in the Spirit and you can endure hardship."

When Paul recorded, "I discipline my body and bring it into subjection," to what or to whom was he subjecting it? Consider this question another way: Paul committed himself to the difficult work of disciplining his body so that *he* would be in control and not enslaved by his impulses; but to what end? By subordinating[152] all of his desires and feelings and inclinations to the governance of his will, *he* would not be controlled by *them*. When he then submitted his will to the direction of the Holy Spirit, all of his fleshly passions would be brought under the Spirit's control. This might be a bit challenging for some readers to understand. Perhaps it will become clearer if we phrase it in personal terms: our wills superintend[153] our bodies through discipline. And our wills, in turn, are subjected to the Lordship of Jesus Christ, which He exercises through His Spirit.

Before we proceed, it is very important for us to have a firm grasp of this relationship. We may ask ourselves, "Do I give any weight to that feeling? Will I indulge that passion? Should I gratify that desire?" When we then tell the Lord, "Not my will but Yours be done," all of our questions are answered. If anything associated with our lives does not align with His will, then we subject ourselves to His Lordship and obey *His* will instead of our own. That is the essence of Paul's statement about disciplining his body to bring it into subjection.

---

[152] subordinating (O): treating as of lesser importance than something else
[153] superintend (C): to have oversight or charge of; control; manage; supervise

A similar idea is conveyed by another familiar verse from Paul's writing: "I beseech you therefore, brethren, by the mercies of God, that you present your bodies a living sacrifice, holy, acceptable to God, which is your reasonable service" (Romans 12:1). This exhortation is pregnant with meaning. But in the interest of space, we will not delve too deeply into its treasures. The image displayed by offering our bodies as living sacrifices is created with some of the same broad strokes as what we have discussed. We acknowledge that our bodies are *His*, to do with as *He* pleases (read 11:36). We view and treat them as set apart (holy) unto Him. We commit ourselves to using our bodies only in ways that are "acceptable to God." And why? Because that is the rational thing to do.

Sacrifice and self-control are like two sides of the same coin. Sacrifice requires self-control, and self-control involves sacrifice. The two are indivisible. And since self-control proceeds *from* discipline, we can conclude that discipline is also necessary for sacrifice. Beyond its interest as an exercise in logic, why is this important? Because here we intersect with the connection between discipline and powerful prayer. In so doing, we can understand better how a lack of discipline functions as an obstacle to effective prayer.

In our studies over the past 30 days, we have emphasized repeatedly how sacrifice is necessary if we sincerely desire to cultivate a potent prayer practice. The demands on our time are numerous and insistent, and they stem from many different sources. Some of these demands we must deny. Otherwise, "the cares of this world" will cause us to become "unfruitful" (Matthew 13:22 and the "Parable of the Soils"). Otherwise we will become entangled with "the affairs of this life" (recall 2 Timothy 2:4). In many cases, denying those impositions involves sacrifices of various magnitudes. And we make those sacrifices willingly because we have developed a proper (biblical) appreciation of the value of unceasing, earnest prayer. At the same time, however, sacrifice requires self-control, which we acquire through discipline. Now flip this sequence around and view it from the other end: A lack of discipline affects self-control, which impairs sacrifice. That impacts how we manage our (God-given) time and, ultimately, the effectiveness of our prayers. In a predictable way, insufficient discipline leeches power from our prayer lives.

What we have accomplished to this point in today's lesson might be little more than a longwinded statement of what many of us already know: **we need discipline**. But more remains to be said about the matter. For instance, discipline can be imposed by ourselves, by another person, or by God Himself. When Paul wrote, "I discipline my body and bring it into subjection," he referred to imposing discipline on himself. An exceptional passage that discusses both of the other avenues of discipline is found in Hebrews 12:7-11:

> "If you endure chastening [discipline], God deals with you as with sons; for what son is there whom a father does not chasten? But if you are without chastening, of which all have become partakers, then you are

illegitimate and not sons. Furthermore, we have had human fathers who corrected us, and we paid them respect. Shall we not much more readily be in subjection to the Father of spirits and live? [Connect this to 2 Corinthians 9:27.] For they indeed for a few days chastened us as seemed best to them, but He for our profit, that we may be partakers of His holiness. Now no chastening seems to be joyful for the present, but painful; nevertheless, afterward it yields the peaceable fruit of righteousness to those who have been trained by it."

God disciplines us *because* we are His children, just as our human parents disciplined us *because* we are their children. And the object or aim of His discipline is that we would become holy and righteous in our conduct—"obedience, self-control," "controlled behavior."

As we walk in the Spirit, He enables us to sacrifice as needed to develop a vibrant and potent prayer life. And as we have seen, among the many facets of "the fruit of the Spirit" in Galatians 5 is "self-control" (verse 23). Think about that for a moment: self-control is a product of discipline, and self-control is one part of "the fruit of the Spirit." Is it reasonable to conclude that the Holy Spirit *uses* discipline to teach us self-control? Looking at it another way, can we infer that self-control is one of the character traits that our Father develops in us through His "chastening"? Clearly, the correct answer in both cases is "yes."

By definition, competitors in a race always strive to complete the course as swiftly as possible. Consequently, they try to minimize everything that could slow them down such as excess weight or anything that causes drag. In addition, they must remain focused on their goal so they will not be distracted and so they can force themselves to persevere when their bodies want to quit. In our ultra-marathon races of faith, we must do likewise. "Therefore...let us lay aside every weight, and the sin which so easily ensnares us, and let us run with endurance the race that is set before us, looking unto Jesus, the author [originator] and finisher [perfecter] of our faith" (Hebrews 12:1-2).

As devoted followers of Christ, we are all running in this punishing race called life. And that being so, we should always run in such a way that we would receive the victor's crown if it *were* a competition. At the same time, we are soldiers in the army of the Lord. And prayer is one of the principal means by which we engage in combat with opposition forces. If we want to fight victoriously, then we must pray earnestly and persistently—biblically. Whatever metaphor we use to analyze our lives of faith, one truth emerges in every instance: discipline is critical. An undisciplined runner will never win. An undisciplined soldier will certainly fight ineffectively and will likely be overcome by the enemy. Proficiency, potency, and perseverance in running, fighting, and praying all require discipline.

Some years ago, a film was released to popular acclaim that centered on the story of a conquering Roman general who served under the emperor, Marcus Aurelius. Betrayed by the emperor's murderous son, Commodus, the general was enslaved and forced to fight as a gladiator. In one scene, the general, Maximus Decimus Meridius, is in his tent while on his final campaign in the region of Germania. Speaking to his trusted and loyal servant, the general asks, "Do you ever get tired of serving?"

"Sometimes I do what I want to do," his servant responds. "The rest of the time, I do what I have to."

The servant's reply is about as perfect a description of a disciplined life as we are likely to encounter. Sometimes we are blessed with opportunities to do what we want to do. At other times, we must do what needs to be done, regardless of whether or not we feel like doing it. Athletes who compete at the highest levels know this. Battle-seasoned soldiers know this. And as Christians, if we genuinely desire to pray effectively and fervently, then we need to know it, too.

"Let us ask for a fresh gift of the Holy Spirit to quicken our sluggish hearts, a new disclosure of the *charity of God*. The Spirit will help our infirmities, and the very compassion of the Son of God will fall upon us, clothing us with zeal as with a garment, stirring our affections into a most vehement flame, and filling our souls with heaven" (MacIntyre 6).

Epilogue

All genuine Christians are sons and daughters of God. Think about that for a moment. Let the weight of it sink into the mind and marinate in the heart. There is only One True God (John 17:3). **Everything** else that is called a god is an imposter and a counterfeit (1 Corinthians 8:4-6). The One True God created all that exists or has ever existed. And by the continuous exercise of His will, He constantly holds together every particle of every atom of every molecule of every cell and element and substance in the entire universe. By itself, that truth is staggering and beyond comprehension. And it does not even begin to glimpse the "edges of His ways" (Job 26:14). Human language lacks the ability to exclaim how awesome the One True God is.

At one time, we were God's **enemies**. We were adversaries of the God who "gives to all life, breath, and all things" (Acts 17:25). But because of His love, not because we deserved His favor in any way, God *reconciled* us to Himself (Romans 5:8-11). He eliminated the enmity that existed between us. But He went much further than "just" removing that hostility. In His marvelous grace, He was not content to dispel the enmity and leave us in a sort of neutral state— if that were possible. He *adopted* us into His own family! He sent His Spirit to dwell within each of us, and we became His sons and daughters (Romans 8:14-15; Galatians 4:4-7). "Behold what manner of love the Father has bestowed on us, that we should be called children of God!" (1 John 3:1). Do not pass lightly over this truth, saints! Stand in awe of the amazing fact that we are God's children (Ephesians 1:3-6)!

Human children are expected to obey their parents. That is the *natural order* of things. That is how families were *designed* to function by their Creator. When children disobey their parents, they are (or should be) chastened. But the object of that chastening is always to guide them toward morally upright living. In other words, it is to make them better people. Grasp the picture that is presented here because it is important. A standard of conduct is held up alongside the behavior of children by their fathers and mothers. Whenever those children fall short of the standard, they are corrected. Where necessary, they are disciplined to impress upon them the truth that actions have consequences. And illegal or immoral actions have consequences that are proportionate to the seriousness of the offense. But the *purpose* of the correction is always to bring children into closer alignment with the standard.

When children live in close conformity to the standard of moral propriety[154], they are blessed. They are living a close approximation of how they were *designed* to live. And living that way comes with blessing (read Psalm 1). The opposite is also true (refer to Luke 6:20-38.) These precepts apply to the

---

[154] propriety (O): being proper or suitable; correctness of behavior or morals

physical children of human parents and to the spiritual children of our heavenly Father. When we live how He wants us to live—according to His will—He blesses us. When we fall short or miss the mark (sin), He chastens us. He disciplines us because He loves us, because He desires to bring us into alignment with His will, and because He wants us to be holy (recall Hebrews 12:7-11).

All of these truths beg an important question: How does God our Father want us to live? Or, to phrase the question as Francis Schaeffer did in the title of one of his books, *How Shall We Then Live?* The standard held up alongside our conduct is the will of God. To live in a blessed way, we need to know how the Lord wants us to live. To know how God designed us to live, we need to know His will. And to **be** blessed, we must **do** His will. In that way, we conform to the standard that is used to assess our conduct.

Now translate this reasoning to the primary subject of this book, effective and fervent prayer—powerful prayer—prayer that "avails much." Our studies *concentrated* on prayer, but we did not examine prayer *exclusively*. And that is because everything the Bible teaches about prayer is only one part of the life that God designed for us. We cannot live as the world lives, follow a few pointers about prayer, and expect our prayers to evidence any power. God's will regarding prayer is one component of His will for our lives in general. They cannot be separated. Consequently, in order to *pray* according to God's design, we must also *live* that way.

As a foundational principle, the Lord wants us to read, to study, and to meditate on the profound riches in truth of His Word (Psalm 119:14-16; Philippians 4:8). Additionally, He calls us to be active participants in a local congregation of believers (Acts 2:42; Hebrews 10:24-25). And not just any church that professes to be Christian will do. It must be one in which the Bible is taught in its entirety, without apology or compromise or personal agenda (see Ephesians 4:11-16; compare to 2 Timothy 4:2-4). Our Father desires for us to pursue peace and unity, to deny ourselves, and to bear each other's burdens (Hebrews 12:14; Matthew 16:24; Galatians 6:2). He wants us to love each other selflessly and sincerely, as He loves us (Ephesians 5:2). That includes speaking to and treating each other with grace, honesty, and humility (Colossians 3:9-10, 12-16; 4:6).

Our Father orders all of His children, "'Put on the whole armor of God,' take up 'the sword of the Spirit' and 'the shield of faith,' and engage your spiritual adversaries in combat" (Ephesians 6:11,16,17; 1 Timothy 6:12). He summons us to pull down strongholds, cast down arguments, and obliterate "every high thing that exalts itself against the knowledge of God" (2 Corinthians 10:4-5). He bids us cooperate in fighting the forces of darkness, supporting the weary, protecting the wounded, lifting the fallen (1 Thessalonians 5:14). He directs us to confess our transgressions to Him and our trespasses to one another, and to pray for each other (Proverbs 28:13; James 5:16; 1 John 1:9).

When we became Christians and were adopted into God's family, we also enlisted in the army of the Lord. At times in our lives of faith, we may find ourselves in a position similar to David's. He gazed across a deserted battlefield at a towering and heavily-armored giant. Young and small of stature, David was armed only with a staff, a shepherd's sling, and a few smooth stones (1 Samuel 17:40, 42). But instead of shrinking from the challenge, he defied Goliath with stouthearted faith:

> "Then David said to the Philistine, 'You come to me with a sword, with a spear, and with a javelin. But I come to you in the name of the LORD of hosts, the God of the armies of Israel, whom you have defied. This day the LORD will deliver you into my hand, and I will strike you and take your head from you. And this day I will give the carcasses of the camp of the Philistines to the birds of the air and the wild beasts of the earth, that all the earth may know that there is a God in Israel. Then all this assembly shall know that the LORD does not save with sword and spear; for the battle is the LORD's, and He will give you into our hands'" (17:45-47).

David was not daunted by the menace or the size of his foe. He knew that "the battle is the LORD's," so worldly considerations like the size and strength and weapons of his adversary were irrelevant.

The steadfast trust that David exhibited against Goliath appears in some of the psalms he composed. For example,

> "The LORD is my light and my salvation;
> Whom shall I fear?
> The LORD is the strength of my life;
> Of whom shall I be afraid?
> ...Though an army may encamp against me,
> My heart shall not fear;
> Though war may rise against me,
> In this I will be confident" (Psalm 27:1, 3).

And the same type of unflinching faith is expressed poetically in Psalm 91, written by an unidentified psalmist. These men of faith understood the reality of their circumstances and trusted the Lord. "What then shall we say to these things? If God is for us, who can be against us?" (Romans 8:31; also read verses 32-39).

We should definitely aspire to the level of strident faith that David displayed. However, most of us will not face many spiritual battles comparable to the earthly contest that David fought. More often we will be like one of Gideon's three hundred, *apparently* outnumbered but trusting that God would bring victory (Judges 7). Whatever form our battles assume, we can be completely confident of several important and fortifying truths:

- The forces assembled under the Lord's banner are *vastly* superior to the opposition (remember 2 Kings 6:16; also Revelation 5:11).
- Ultimate victory is *certain*, as is the just judgment of the servants of darkness (1 Corinthians 15:57; 1 John 5:4-5; Revelation 20:11-15).
- No harm will come to us unless God permits it for His own sovereign purposes (Matthew 10:27-31).
- No matter how fierce the combat becomes, how determined our adversaries are, or how grievous the hardships we endure while the battle rages, **all** will fade in significance to the point of nonexistence when at last we behold Christ face to face (Romans 8:18; 1 Corinthians 2:9).

The outcome has already been determined, saints! Victory belongs to the Lord! But in the meantime, we are called to continue fighting.

"Therefore we do not lose heart. Even though our outward man is perishing, yet the inward man is being renewed day by day. For our light affliction, which is but for a moment, is working for us a far more exceeding and eternal weight of glory, while we do not look at the things which are seen, but at the things which are not seen. For the things which are seen are temporary, but the things which are not seen are eternal" (2 Corinthians 4:16-18). "If then you were raised with Christ, seek those things which are above, where Christ is, sitting at the right hand of God. Set your mind on things above, not on things on the earth. For you died, and your life is hidden with Christ in God. When Christ who is our life appears, then you also will appear with Him in glory" (Colossians 3:1-4).

How do we persevere in spiritual warfare without relenting or being overcome? In simplest terms, we keep our eyes fixed on the Lord. We seek and set our minds on "things above," "the things which are not seen." These things "are eternal," but because they are not seen, "we walk by faith, not by sight" (2 Corinthians 5:7). We cultivate an eternal perspective, focusing not on "things which are seen," the "temporary" things that the world values.

God has provided us with His book of truth, His holy Word (Daniel 10:21; John 17:17). He has given us His "Spirit as a guarantee" of what is to come (2 Corinthians 5:5; Ephesians 1:13-14). And He has assured us—in fact, **promised** us—that He will return. When He does, our corruptible and mortal bodies will be replaced with "incorruption" and "immortality," and "we shall see Him as He is" (1 Corinthians 15:53; 1 John 3:2).

Standing on the spiritual battlefield, shoulder to shoulder with our brothers and sisters, we have a choice to make. Will we shrink from the conflict, hoping to avoid any actual fighting but still desiring to reap the rewards of victory? Will we move ourselves to the margins of the battle, trying to give the appearance of participation because we want to avoid looking cowardly? Or will we, as truehearted and stalwart soldiers in the Lord's army, charge our foes with swords bared, armor burnished, and shields at the ready? Are we confident of our Commander's orders (His will)? And do we trust in the wisdom of His plan?

Consider what the Apostle Paul wrote in his Epistle to Titus, one of his trusted fellow laborers for the gospel:

> "For the grace of God that brings salvation has appeared to all men, teaching us that, denying ungodliness and worldly lusts, we should live soberly, righteously, and godly in the present age, looking for the blessed hope and glorious appearing of our great God and Savior Jesus Christ, who gave Himself for us, that He might redeem us from every lawless deed and purify for Himself His own special people, zealous for good works" (2:11-14; compare this to Ephesians 2:1-10).

Does this sound like a description of someone who retreats from spiritual warfare? Does "zealous for good works" characterize a person who shuffles about on the fringes of a battle?

We know that God's will is for us to participate actively and tenaciously in fighting against our spiritual adversaries. We can obey our Father and receive the bounty of His blessings. Or we can (attempt to) abstain, contrary to our Lord's desire, and accept the consequences. But if we are genuine Christians, we need to know that He will deal with us as His children. We will be chastened as He corrects our behavior and brings us into alignment with His will (the standard). So in the final analysis, the choice we face is really quite simple: "Fight the good fight of faith" or expect to be disciplined.

The world lies in darkness. New high places, idols, and strongholds constantly appear. Our Father has positioned His children of light where He wants them, where they can serve Him according to His purposes. Just as Jesus admonished His disciples not to sleep, but to "watch and pray," we are given similar commands:

> "And do this, knowing the time, that now it is high time to awake out of sleep; for now our salvation is nearer than when we first believed. The night is far spent, the day is at hand. Therefore let us cast off the works of darkness, and let us put on the armor of light. Let us walk properly, as in the day, not in revelry and drunkenness, not in lewdness and lust, not in strife and envy. But put on the Lord Jesus Christ, and make no provision for the flesh, to fulfill its lusts" (Romans 13:11-14).

> "You are all sons of light and sons of the day. We are not of the night, nor of darkness. Therefore let us not sleep, as others do, but let us watch and

be sober [or self-controlled]. For those who sleep, sleep at night, and those who get drunk are drunk at night. But let us who are of the day be sober, putting on the breastplate of faith and love, and as a helmet the hope of salvation" (1 Thessalonians 5:5-8).

We are called to be lights in this dark world, saints. And God equips us with everything we require for that task. But people do not strap on a suit of armor so they can sleep in it. Armor is worn for battle, and that is precisely why ours is given to us.

We want to close with a few concluding exhortations, deferring again to the inspired words of Paul. To begin with, "Continue earnestly in prayer, being vigilant in it with thanksgiving" (Colossians 4:2). Pray always and in everything, Christians, not only because it is God's will for all of His children, but also because our swords and shields are ineffective otherwise. We "beseech you to walk worthy of the calling with which you were called, with all lowliness and gentleness, with longsuffering, bearing with one another in love, endeavoring to keep the unity of the Spirit in the bond of peace" (Ephesians 4:1-3). In general, "whatever you do, do all to the glory of God" (1 Corinthians 10:31). "And whatever you do in word or deed, do all in the name of the Lord Jesus, giving thanks to God the Father through Him" (Colossians 3:17).

Christ is our life. He communicates with us through His Word, and we speak to Him through prayer. We can never be *too* close to Jesus, nor *too* much like Him. We can never be *too* holy. And there is no such thing as praying *too* much. Draw near to God, brothers and sisters, to our loving heavenly Father. Let go of the world, live the way He calls His children to live, and watch in awe as He displays His power through "effective, fervent prayer."

Works Cited

Ehrlich, Eugene, Stuart Berg Flexner, Gorton Carruth, Joyce M. Hawkins, eds. *Oxford American Dictionary.* New York: Avon Books, 1986. Print.

MacDonald, A.M. *Chambers Etymological English Dictionary.* New York: Pyramid, 1968. Print.

MacIntyre, David. "The Hidden Life of Prayer." Pensacola, FL: Chapel Library, 1996. Print.

Spurgeon, Charles Haddon. "Effective Prayer." Pensacola, FL: Chapel Library, 2013. Print.

— "True Prayer True Power." Pensacola, FL: Chapel Library, 1998. Print.

Strong, James. *Strong's Exhaustive Concordance of the Bible.* Peabody, MA: Hendrickson, 2007. Print.

Torrey, R.A. *How to Pray.* New Kensington, PA: Whitaker House, 1984. Print.

Vine, W.E., Merrill F. Unger, William White, Jr. *Vine's Complete Expository Dictionary of Old and New Testament Words.* Nashville, TN: Thomas Nelson, 1996. Print.

About the Author

Eric Matthew Copple became a Christian at a young age. He grew up in Southern California, attending church regularly, raised by a sincere Christian mother and professing Christian father. His belief in and love for the Word of God began in childhood. When he was a boy, his mother told him numerous times that he might be called to become an apologist or perhaps a pastor.

In his youth, however, Eric had other plans. He dreamed of joining "the long gray line" by attending the United States Military Academy at West Point. His goal was to serve as a career Army officer or to become a pediatrician—or both. But the circumstances of his life steered him in a different direction. Eric's battles with depression and anxiety began in adolescence and intensified through his teenage years. Instead of leaning on the Lord and accepting help for these issues, he strove to overcome them through discipline and strength of will.

Although Eric excelled in school, his stubborn self-reliance (read **pride**) led him down a dark road. He spent a lot of time with rebellious influences, and began abusing alcohol as an escape from his internal turmoil. When he was denied admission to West Point, his dreams were devastated and his life derailed. He "spun his wheels" for a few years in a dead-end job. At the same time, he completed courses at a local community college, seeking direction for his life and finding none.

After high school, Eric attended church intermittently, but he was not living according to God's will. His depression continued to intensify, becoming quite severe. As it increased its hold on him, he turned more and more inward, isolating himself from other people. Once he was old enough to purchase alcohol legally, his drinking escalated significantly. The self-destructive tendencies in his life worsened, but a wall was fast approaching.

Without delving into any sordid details, suffice it to say that Eric was incarcerated for murder and sentenced to life without the possibility of parole. He was going to kill himself on September 27, 2005, but God had other plans. Through a series of events orchestrated by the Lord, Eric arrived at the decision to turn himself in to the police, instead. Lying in a jail cell that night, for the first time in his life, he surrendered completely to the Lord. He devoted himself wholeheartedly to living according to God's will, nothing withheld. In the darkest hours of his life, the light of Christ illuminated that cell, and Eric's heart, and reminded him of the Lord's unfailing love (Romans 8:38-39).

Brought to the end of himself by grievous sin, Eric learned the true meaning of **grace** from personal experience. And he came to understand what Paul meant when he wrote "you were bought at a price" and "you are not your own" (1 Corinthians 6:19-20). One verse that became (and remains) especially meaningful to him was Galatians 2:20: "I have been crucified with Christ; it is no longer I who live, but Christ lives in me; and the life which I now live in the flesh I live by faith in the Son of God, who loved me and gave Himself for me." Another is Colossians 3:3: "For you died, and your life is hidden with Christ in God."

Jesus Christ is Eric's life (Philippians 1:11). Whether God gives him one more day of life or 50 years, that time belongs to the Lord (James 4:15). Eric lives each day with a commitment to "redeeming the time," to make the best possible use of every hour that is given to him (Ephesians 5:16). His overarching purposes are to glorify the Lord, to draw nearer to Him, and to become more like Him (1 Corinthians 10:31; 2 Corinthians 3:18). After years of disobedience, kicking against the goads and grieving the Holy Spirit, Eric is living with his eyes fixed on Jesus (Acts 9:5; Ephesians 4:30).

In all the years of Eric's imprisonment, the Lord has shown Himself perfectly faithful. God has graciously enabled His ambassador to bear fruit and to shine the light of Christ even in the darkness of prison. With the generous assistance of his mother, he (finally) completed two associate's degrees. He has also worked as a tutor in a voluntary education program, helping numerous inmates to obtain their G.E.D. diplomas. Additionally, he has led and taught several Bible studies, including serving as a Group Leader for Bible Study Fellowship. Now the Father has equipped His son with everything required to produce this book. Only because God has transformed Eric by the renewing of his mind has this once-prodigal son become "zealous for good works" (Romans 12:2; Titus 2:4).

Eric's life is a story of redemption. But that redemption is entirely God's doing, a product of "the exceeding riches of His grace" (Ephesians 2:7). To God alone belongs all glory! Through all of the spiritual warfare that this Christian man has faced, both before and in prison, the glory of God has been on full display. Moreover, Eric has personally witnessed the power manifested by our sovereign Lord when His children pray effectively and fervently. "Now to Him who is able to do exceedingly abundantly above all that we ask or think, according to the power that works in us, to Him be glory in the church by Christ Jesus to all generations, forever and ever…. Grace be with all those who love our Lord Jesus Christ in sincerity. Amen" (Ephesians 3:20-21; 6:24).

Made in the USA
Coppell, TX
09 December 2020